By the same author

Delius : The Paris Years
Delius : A Life in Pictures (with Robert Threlfall)
Delius : A Life in Letters, Volumes I and II

The publishers gratefully acknowledge
the kind assistance from the following
organizations towards the publication
of this book:
Royal Ministry of Foreign Affairs, Oslo
The Delius Trust, London

Lionel Carley

GRIEG AND DELIUS

A Chronicle of their Friendship in Letters

Marion Boyars
London · New York

First published in Great Britain and
the United States in 1993
by Marion Boyars Publishers

24 Lacy Road, London SW15 1NL
237 East 39th Street, New York, NY 10016

© Lionel Carley, 1993

British Library Cataloguing in Publication Data

Grieg, Edvard
    Grieg and Delius: Chronicle of Their
    Friendship in Letters
    I. Title II. Delius, Frederick
    III. Carley, Lionel
    780.92

Library of Congress Cataloging in Publication Data

Grieg, Edvard, 1843–1907.
    [Correspondence. English. Selections]
    Grieg and Delius : a chronicle of their friendship in letters /
    [compiled and translated] by Lionel Carley.
        Includes bibliographical references and index.
        1. Grieg, Edvard, 1843–1907—Correspondence. 2. Delius,
    Frederick, 1862–1934—Correspondence. 3. Composers—Norway—
    Correspondence. 4. Composers—England—Correspondence.
    5. Music—19th century—History and criticism. I. Delius,
    Frederick, 1862–1934. II. Carley, Lionel. III. Title.
    ML410.G9A4   1993
    780'.92—dc20
    [B]   93–19759

ISBN 0–7145–2961–3 Hardcover

Printed and bound in Great Britain by
Biddles Ltd, Guildford and King's Lynn

Sources of Illustrations

The illustrations in this book are largely drawn from the collection of the author or from the archive of The Delius Trust. Grateful acknowledgement is made to the following further sources: the Bergen Public Library (7, 46), the Munch Museum, Oslo (3, 21), Troldhaugen (11, 34, 45, 50), Bergen University Library (48), Oslo University Library (33), the Grainger Museum, University of Melbourne (20, 51, 55), Dr Andrew J. Boyle (1, 5, 24, 25, 35), and the Gerhardi/Steinweg Collection, Lüdenscheid (41). Photographs 8, 9 and 56 are by the author.

Introduction and Acknowledgements

This book sets out to document the friendship of Edvard Grieg and Frederick Delius: how and when it was initiated, how it developed, how it appeared to wane and how, finally, it was reaffirmed. It is in part charted by the many and varied historical and cultural landmarks through which its course was set, but the friendship is primarily documented by the letters exchanged between the two men, an exchange that gradually widens to take in the letters contributed by Nina Grieg and Jelka Delius.

It is clear that almost all of the Griegs' letters to Delius have survived. So, apparently, has the large majority of those that Delius penned to the Griegs — but in the latter case the gaps are certainly more evident. The two sides of the correspondence may have been brought together as long ago as 1935, as a result of Jelka Delius having extracted a promise from Sir Thomas Beecham that he would write a biography of her late husband. Eric Fenby, Delius's former amanuensis, wrote to Beecham on 19 January 1935: 'Mrs. D. has just written to Mrs. Grieg for D's letters to Grieg. Grieg's to Delius are very interesting, particularly when he refers to D's early works.' Just ten days later he was able to tell Beecham: 'Mrs. Grieg writes to Jelka to say that Delius's letters of that period are probably in the state library at Bergen in which all Grieg's letters and papers were deposited years ago. If they exist, for they may have been destroyed by some careless person after Grieg's death, they could be copied and sent to you. Jelka is going to write to Bergen.'

Neither of these two particular letters between Jelka and Nina remains to us, but Nina would in fact have been referring to the city (*stads*-) library, and indeed it is in the Grieg Collection of the Bergen Public Library's Music Department that Delius's letters to the Griegs reside today. Those from the Griegs to the Deliuses are housed in the Delius Trust's Archive in London. The gaps in the Grieg Collection's Delius file can probably be accounted for by any combination of the following: destruction by 'some careless person', as Nina suggests;

destruction by one or other of the Griegs themselves, probably because they felt that particular letters touching on more personal matters should not be kept; and, more haphazardly, destruction by rodents, a number of the extant letters having been exposed at some time since Grieg's death to the unwelcome attentions of house-mice. In the footnotes to the letters in this book, the editor's bland code in this latter respect is, more usually than not, 'a number of words are obliterated in the original letter.'

The translations of the letters that make up the Grieg/Delius correspondence are largely my own. Earlier working versions of the texts made for archival purposes — probably at some speed — some thirty years ago were found to be deficient, and cross-checking with them has necessitated considerable caution. Almost the entire correspondence was conducted in German. The language of the original is, therefore, only mentioned in the footnotes if the letter was written in Norwegian or English. From time to time, English, Norwegian and French words or phrases stray into the German letters. Where appropriate, these are documented and translated in the footnotes.

Of this polyglot set of friends, Jelka Delius was the most naturally gifted linguistically. Her first language was German, but she spoke and wrote English and French fluently, and was also evidently quite at home in Dano-Norwegian. Delius's German was fluent but erratic, and this is reflected in his written style. He spoke a fair French, but used it only when really necessary, and less and less willingly in later life. His Norwegian was more than adequate, but he wrote it rather rarely. Both Grieg and Nina wrote a fluent German, with only occasional errors. On the other hand, Grieg was uneasy in French, which he did not seriously study until later in his life and then without particularly conspicuous success. He seems to have been only a little more at home in English. One hopes that the translations in this book will be clear and unambiguous; as was the case with my two earlier volumes of Delius's letters, I have taken as much care as possible neither to paraphrase nor, so to speak, to manipulate the originals in order simply to offer a more stylish and free-flowing English where the German may well have been prosaic or stilted.

Two-thirds of the Grieg and Delius correspondence is here printed for the first time. The rest of the correspondence, first published in *Delius: A Life in Letters*, has been carefully rescrutinized and a few minor adjustments have been made, with fresh translations being offered for isolated words and phrases. I have not translated titles like *Herr, Frau, Fräulein* or *Fru* into English, preferring on the whole to leave them in the form found in the original letter. So, for example, if *Mr* occasionally surfaces, that is what the correspondent actually wrote. Of messages of greeting and of valedictions there is considerable variety, as is only to be expected; a variety of English expressions is duly offered for them. The commonly expressed 'thousands' of greetings sent so frequently in German is, for example, discarded in favour of the admittedly less evocative but decidedly more English 'all good wishes' or some such variant.

Words underlined in the original letter have been italicized in the text, and italics have been used to distinguish the printed or embossed elements of letter-headings. Dates are printed exactly as given in the original letter; where they are lacking, my own dating is printed in square brackets. Original punctuation — or lack of it — has been preserved as closely as possible, as have occasional spelling errors (usually place- or person-names). However, in the case of Delius's diaries of his summer tours in Norway (from which extracts are quoted), place-names are found in great profusion in varying late nineteenth-century forms, and are often misspelt into the bargain. Here, then, a general updating has been attempted and modern forms have generally been substituted, a tactic decided upon simply to avoid further confusion. In my own editorial text, the modern and most widely-accepted form of place-names is of course used, with just occasional exceptions such as Oslo, known until the end of 1924 as Christiania or Kristiania, and Stavern, known in Delius's time as Fredriksvaern.

Some years ago, when I originally transcribed Delius's closely-written tour diaries, they were only available to me in the form of poor-quality negative microfilm. Recently however, the University of Melbourne, in whose Grainger Museum the original diaries are held, has been able to supply to the Delius Trust page-copies in perfect photographic form. Some rectification of my early transcription work has in consequence become possible and minor corrections have therefore been incorporated into those extracts printed in this book.

It should perhaps be pointed out that the Norwegian language has long been in a state of flux — not just the natural flux characterized by borrowings, neologisms and slang, for example, that is common to all languages, but a flux deriving from a variety of centuries-old influences as yet unresolved: the language of Denmark, to which country Norway had until 1814 been subservient, the dialects of West and East, the speech of the peasant farmers, the speech of the clergy and the administration. Two very distinct branches of the language —

bokmål and *nynorsk* — call themselves Norwegian today, but painstaking and continuing reforms begun in the nineteenth century are haltingly pushing written usage toward a long-sought unity. The process still has a long way to go. The indecisive character of Norwegian orthography a century ago is exemplified in the Grieg/Delius correspondence by the interchangeability of the letters *ø* and *ö*, and *aa* and *å*, for example, as well as by the variety of place-name spellings already referred to.

In 1962, the centenary of Delius's birth did not pass unnoticed in Oslo. Børre Qvamme wrote of it in the pages of Norway's most venerable national daily, *Morgenbladet*, on 19 February. He wondered if some of the capital's older inhabitants remembered the fuss that had surrounded Delius's incidental music to *Folkeraadet* when it was performed in the Christiania Theatre in the autumn of 1897; and he reminded the paper's readers of just how close Delius had been to Scandinavia in general and to Norway in particular: 'You only have to read through letters and accounts of Norwegian artists from around the turn of the century and you will every now and then come across the name of Delius. He visits Troldhaugen and Aulestad, takes walking tours with Christian Sinding on the Hardangervidda, gets together with Norwegian painters, musicians and writers in Paris and Grez-sur-Loing. He writes to Norwegian friends in German, so cannot be a Scandinavian himself, but if you knew nothing else about Delius you would be hard put to it to guess that he was an Englishman.' Qvamme pointed out to his readers that it was a letter of recommendation from Grieg that finally convinced Delius's father actually to let him take up the profession of musician: 'We Norwegians ought to remember him,' he continued, 'for he had strong ties to Norway. He loved the high Norwegian fells and was called the "viddeman" by his Norwegian friends. Strindberg, Edvard Munch and Christian Sinding were among his regular companions, and he wrote music to poems by Bjørnson, Welhaven,* Vinje, J.P. Jacobsen and Drachmann.'

In fact, the following pages will show that Delius's range of acquaintanceships and his sense of identification with Norway and all things Norwegian were even more profound than Børre Qvamme

---

* Although all the early editions of Delius's *Five Songs from the Norwegian* attributed 'The Nightingale' to Welhaven, the original poem was in fact by Theodor Kjerulf. Delius himself never set Welhaven.

could have guessed. Neither Grieg, Sinding nor Edvard Munch ever had a closer English friend, nor one who would so readily and selflessly put himself out for them. One might go so far as to say that in the case of Sinding, shy, reserved, introverted and only able to open his heart to his very nearest, Delius's friendship was a revelatory experience. Munch, too, when down on his luck in Paris in the mid-nineties, found in Delius a pillar of strength, one of the very few men whom he trusted completely. And Grieg could say, after a winter in Leipzig, that his friendship with the 'admirable' Delius was one of the foremost reasons for the success of his stay and for the pleasure he had taken in it.

The same was true for Delius in respect of Grieg at this early stage of their friendship. Towards the end of his life, he told Eric Fenby: 'Had it not been that there were great opportunities for hearing music and talking music, and that I met Grieg, my studies at Leipzig were a complete waste of time' [*Delius as I knew him*, p. 168]. Fenby thought it remarkable that with Delius at this time having so little to show in support of his abilities, Grieg was 'so obviously impressed by his qualities and admitted him into an immediate companionship along with his countryman Christian Sinding. But they can surely never have dreamt that here in the process of finding himself was one of music's supreme originals.' [*Delius*, p. 24]

If the letters help to fill out the picture of the friendship between Grieg and Delius and between the male-dominated group at Leipzig that contained, at varying times, so many of Delius's — and indeed Grieg's — best-loved friends, they only allude from time to time to the women in Delius's life. Of his romantic attachments during the earlier years of his correspondence with Grieg, we would almost certainly have known more had not a number of the letters gone missing, probably — as has already been noted — because the Griegs judged it prudent to destroy such letters. Nevertheless, a few names can be salvaged from the documentational wreckage. Camilla Jacobsen, from Christiania, was Delius's fellow-student at the Leipzig Conservatory in 1886–87, and she may well have been one of the principal reasons why he went to Norway in the summer of 1887. During that same walking tour he had made the acquaintance of a girl called Anna Mohn, whom he met again when first visiting Grieg in 1889. Delius's interest in her seems to have persisted for some time, since there are a number of allusions to her in these letters. Another name that surfaces briefly is Petra Vogt, also in the Bergen area and evidently a girl in whom he displayed a more than passing interest. Another seemingly attentive friend at some stage during these early years was the musically gifted Charlotte Bødtker (1868–1920), who studied piano in Berlin. Marriage in 1892 to another Norwegian, Wilhelm Naeser, was to take her to the Americas, and any idea of a career in music was given up. Her husband died and she returned to Christiania shortly before remarrying, in 1904, the son of the musician and critic Otto Winter-Hjelm.

That Delius discussed his *affaires de coeur* with the Griegs — although probably more deeply with Nina than with Edvard — is evident, and Nina throws in an enigmatic reference to a Miss Whitehouse, who seems to have constituted an attraction for Delius in London. 'Rattling' was the Griegs' codeword for Delius's affairs, and a 'rattlesnake' was the object of his attentions; it is mainly Nina who uses these terms in writing to Delius.

Christian Sinding, on the other hand, seems to have been particularly attracted to married women. He fell for Adolf Brodsky's sister-in-law, Olga Picard, in Leipzig early in 1888; she was, at least, separated from her French husband by then. Sinding sought advice and help from both Grieg and Delius in respect of what seems to have been a rather complicated relationship, but by later 1889 the affair was over. He had a longer run-in, though, with Augusta Gade, who with her husband, a distinguished Norwegian doctor, entertained both Sinding and Delius at their home in Drøbak during the summer holidays of 1893. He got her in the end, marrying her within a month of her divorce in 1898, and they lived happily ever after.

Grieg himself led a rather more complicated romantic life than legend has allowed, and in recent years the rocky state, at various times, of his marriage has been much commented on. There is little reason to suppose that he or Nina discussed the problems of their marriage with the much younger Delius, but particularly close friends like Frants Beyer were well aware of the tensions that plagued it, and those in the know generally closed ranks protectively behind the pair. Benestad and Schjelderup-Ebbe suggest that Grieg 'allowed himself to be enticed into some questionable relationships' when his marriage was at one or other of its periodical low ebbs [*Edvard Grieg: The Man and the Artist*, p. 253] and Nina herself wrote privately of her husband's 'weakness for the fair sex'. He was strongly attracted to Brita Utne in Hardanger in the mid-seventies, to Leis Schjelderup in Paris in the early eighties and, briefly, to Bella Edwards in Copenhagen in the mid-nineties. But after each difficult phase of the marriage had been surmounted, he and Nina drew close together again. Beryl Foster has remarked how these periods of reconciliation and comparative tranquillity drew from Grieg his finest songs. When the relationship was undergoing one of its occasional convulsions, he either wrote no songs or those that he did compose tended to be inferior to those written expressly for Nina. There are perhaps some parallels to be drawn with Delius's marriage to Jelka Rosen, a nominal tie which certainly did not prevent the Englishman from 'enjoying himself with other women', as Jelka herself was later to put it. Such relationships inevitably placed a strain on their marriage, yet, rather like Grieg and Nina, as life went on each almost subconsciously seemed to realize that the one could not manage without the other. (There was also, I think, in the case of each pair a significant incompatability of temperament, something after all of an impediment to the married state.) In the final analysis, as with Grieg and Nina, one has to feel that love actually prevailed and that the nature of love ought not to be questioned too rigorously.

The title of this book implies a historical documentation of the relationship between two leading European composers of the modern era. Detailed analysis of and comment on the music must be sought elsewhere in the musicological literature so far published on each of the two men. Easily the most thorough comparative study known to me of the music of each is by Christopher Palmer, who devotes a whole section of his *Delius: Portrait of a Cosmopolitan* to examining Grieg's influence on Delius. Delius's debt to Grieg is clear enough, and he continued to acknowledge it almost to the end. Modern scholars, however, have seen that the debt is finite and that by the time *Appalachia* was composed, in 1902, Delius had worked Grieg out of his system. If his early work had leaned on Grieg and early Wagner, as that most perceptive of critical writers on Delius, Anthony Payne, has acknowledged, 'as time passed, and his poetic vision deepened, his models served him less satisfactorily until he finally dropped them.' ['Delius's stylistic development', *Tempo*, 60, Winter 1961–62, p.7] Not that one could ever say that all echoes of Grieg could ever completely disappear from the music of Delius's maturity. C.W. Orr [*A Delius Companion*, p. 59] maintained that there were certain harmonic passages in Grieg that might have been written by Delius at almost any time in his career, citing as an example the last six bars of Grieg's song 'On the water' ('Mens jeg venter', op.60, no.3, a setting of words by Vilhelm Krag). Orr was, it seems, on target in respect of this particular song, Benestad and Schjelderup-Ebbe singling out, as they do, its 'refined chromaticism combined with unexpected cadences' [*Edvard Grieg: The Man and the Artist*, p. 324]. Neville Cardus, writing about the opening pages of *In a Summer Garden*, drew another kind of comparison between the two composers and at the same time underlined a fundamental difference between them: 'The work begins with a melody which Grieg could easily have composed. Delius makes it his own by quickly drawing it into the tissue of his orchestra, until it is perceived only as we perceive a single thread of a texture.' [*A Delius Companion*, p. 89]

Perhaps the most succinct summing-up of what each of the two composers meant to the other has been offered by William Mead: 'Delius's acute sensitivity, his shimmering pointillisme give his art kinship with the impressionists. It was Grieg who first encouraged this art. There would have been a Delius if there had been no Grieg; because no personal restraints or misunderstandings could have frustrated such a will to create. That there was a Grieg meant that creation was easier. That there was a Delius means that Grieg is the greater.' [William R. Mead: 'A Winter's Tale: Reflections on the Delius Festival (1946)', *The Norseman* (Oslo), 1947, p.81]

My thanks in the first instance must go to the Bergen Offentlige Bibliotek and to the Delius Trust, in whose respective collections the letters from Delius to Grieg and from Grieg to Delius are to be found. I am particularly grateful for the advice and support of Karen Falch Johannessen, in charge of the Grieg Collection in Bergen, and of the Trustees of the Delius estate, Meredith Davies, C.B.E., and Martin Williams (for the Musicians Benevolent Fund), and I gratefully acknowledge their permission to reproduce the letters printed in this volume.

It was at a function hosted by the Norwegian Ambassador in London in April 1992 that Marion Boyars and I first discussed the possibility of basing a book on the Grieg/Delius correspondence. By that time the Embassy had decided to form a UK committee to advise on events for the forthcoming Grieg Year. I was invited to become a member of that advisory committee and it soon became evident that Grieg would take up a considerable amount of our time for the next year or two. With Grieg Year upon us, my colleagues and I duly metamorphosed into the committee of the newly-formed Grieg Society of Great Britain, and our discussions have thrown up many useful pointers for me during my work on the Grieg and Delius letters.

To Pål Moe, Press and Cultural Counsellor, Royal Norwegian Embassy, London, 1989–93, go my congratulations in respect of the degree of encouragement and support that he has demonstrated for the Grieg Year project in the UK and my gratitude for the continued interest and enthusiasm he has shown in respect of this book. I wish to thank Tania Hegge, Cultural Attaché, and Anne-Karin Stockinger of the Press, Culture and Information Section, too, for so readily coping with various of my queries. To Irene Garland, also of that Section, I owe a special debt of thanks and wish cordially to acknowledge her ever good-humoured, continuing, and intelligent advice and cooperation.

Torbjørn Støverud, formerly Cultural Attaché at the Norwegian Embassy and senior lecturer in Norwegian at University College London, and presently Chairman of the Grieg Society's committee, has kindly lent me background material and has furthermore read through and commented on this book in typescript. Robert Threlfall, Advisor to the Delius Trust and editor of the Collected Edition of Delius's works, has in his turn offered invaluable advice and has, too, read the typescript. To both these experts in their respective fields I am especially indebted — and not for the first time. Beryl Foster, author of an exemplary book on Grieg's songs and now Secretary of the Grieg Society, has also lent background material. The many and varied discussions I have had with her on the subject of Grieg and his music during the past year have been deeply appreciated and they have played their quietly valuable part in seeing this book through. Jonathan Maddox, of the Delius Society's committee, read through the material at an earlier stage of its development, and his perceptive comments have also proved invaluable.

To my further colleagues on the Grieg advisory committee, Roy Baker, Per Dreier, Robert Layton, Dr Gunnar Sundberg and Stephannie Williams, as to my further Delius Trust colleagues, Sir Thomas Armstrong, Felix Aprahamian and Robert Montgomery, I address my thanks for their kind interest and encouragement. Special thanks go to Marjorie Dickinson, Secretary to the Delius Trust, for many kindnesses and for the active support she has unstintingly given to me in my work. Rachel Lowe Dugmore, Delius Trust Archivist 1964–66, was the first to collate the Grieg and Delius letters and to set down a range of intelligent and informed comments on the material. For the working base that she initially provided me I remain grateful indeed.

I owe particular thanks to a number of individuals who have over the years willingly and often put their knowledge and expertise at my disposal, and in particular to Dr John Bergsagel, Dr Andrew J. Boyle, Dr Roger Buckley, Aud Dixon, Barbro Edwards, Dr Eric Fenby, Lewis Foreman, Evelin Gerhardi, Dr Don Gillespie, Stephen Lloyd, Lowinger Maddison, the late Norman Millar, the late John Boulton Smith, Malve Steinweg, Lena Svanberg and the late Sigmund Torsteinson, curator at Troldhaugen for nearly forty years. A number of institutions have been helpful, principally the Grainger Museum at Melbourne University, the Oslo University Library, the Munch Museum (in the persons of Arne Eggum, Sissel Biørnstad and Gerd Woll) and the *Anglo-Norse Review* (editor Ronald Harvey). I also wish to draw into this net my colleagues on the Anglo Norse Council, under its distinguished chairman Dame Gillian Brown; and members of the Delius Society and its committee, so many old friends and true.

Finally, I would like to express my gratitude to HE Mr Kjell Eliassen and Mrs Eliassen, under whose ever-hospitable roof this project was initiated and whose Embassy in London has consistently provided all the help one could have wished for.

Lionel Carley

GRIEG AND DELIUS:

The Correspondence

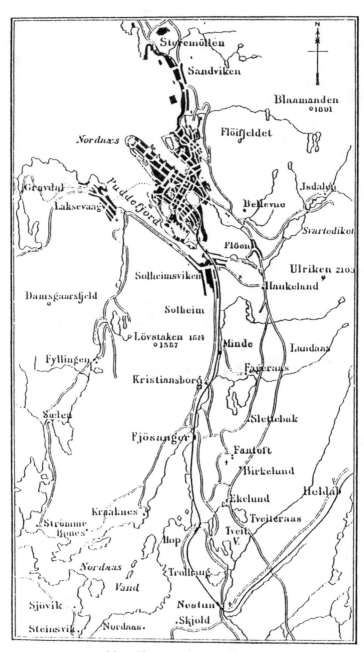

Map of Bergen and surroundings,
showing Hop and 'Trolhaug' to the south

When Delius was born on 29 December 1862, Edvard Grieg, born on 15 June 1843 and now aged nineteen, was gradually coming to the end of his student years at the Leipzig Conservatory. Grieg had shown exceptional musical gifts as a child and it had been on the emphatic recommendation of a celebrated figure in the cultural life of Norway, the violinist Ole Bull, that his parents had agreed to despatch their fifteen-year-old son to Leipzig to begin his studies there in October 1858. Among his teachers at the Conservatory were Ignaz Moscheles and Carl Reinecke, and although he subsequently declared that he had learnt very little at Leipzig, there is ample evidence that in fact Grieg had laid there the firmest of bases for the techniques he needed to draw on — both as composer and pianist — in future years. An unfortunate legacy bequeathed to him by his studentship was, however, the permanent injury to his health early in 1860 caused by an attack of pleurisy which left him with a severely damaged lung and consequent respiratory difficulties later in life.

Grieg had already composed piano pieces at school. More were to follow at Leipzig before his studies there came to an end at Easter 1862. He left the Conservatory with glowing reports. Back in his home town of Bergen (whose population at the time numbered around 25,000) there were to be occasional modest concerts in the year that followed, but Grieg's next major step was to set off for Denmark where, mainly in Copenhagen, he could associate with other young composers and devote himself more seriously to composition. To further piano pieces and songs was added the Symphony in c minor, written at the instigation of the doyen of Danish composers, Niels Gade. It did not please Grieg and although it was — in part or in full — to receive early airings (in Copenhagen in 1864 and 1865 and in Bergen in 1867), he subsequently suppressed it. During this period in Denmark, which lasted for the best part of three years, he met his cousin, Nina Hagerup (1845–1935). Two years his junior, she had been born in Bergen, but had grown up in Denmark. They became engaged in July 1864 and Nina, who had an attractive light singing voice, was from then on to be the inspiration and indeed the ideal interpreter of many of his finest songs.

Later in 1864, Grieg also met Rikard Nordraak (1842–66), a young Norwegian composer of extraordinary promise whose life was to be cut very short by tuberculosis. They became close friends, convinced that between them they embodied the spirit of the new Norwegian music — a music that would seek to reflect the history, folklore and natural scenery of their homeland. Nordraak's setting of a poem by his cousin Bjørnstjerne Bjørnson (1832–1910), 'Ja, vi elsker dette Landet' ('Yes, we love this land'), was to be his most enduring legacy, becoming, as it did, Norway's national anthem. His death affected his friend very deeply, leaving Grieg with a sense of responsibility that could no longer be shared. In Norway, the flag of national Romanticism in music would have to be borne by Edvard Grieg alone.

Grieg's *Funeral March for Rikard Nordraak* was composed for piano in 1866, the year that brought this period in Denmark to a close. His stay had been interrupted by an autumn and winter trip to Germany and Italy in 1865/66, which had added the orchestral overture *In Autumn*, op.11, to songs, piano pieces (including the Sonata in e minor, op.7) and the Violin Sonata no.1 in F major, op.8, all composed during his Danish sojourn. To all intents and purposes, Grieg was to remain in Christiania for the next ten years, although there would be various excursions, both in Norway (mainly to Bergen) and abroad. On 11 June 1867, shortly before his twenty-fourth birthday, he married Nina Hagerup in Copenhagen.

The Christiania decade was to be a period of substantial progress for the musician, if coloured darkly at the outset by the death of a daughter in infancy. There were to be no other children. On establishing himself in the capital, Grieg lost little time in getting himself noticed by the musical public. Mainly as a result of a programme of Norwegian music which he presented in October 1866, he was invited to conduct the Philharmonic Society — then an amateur body — and duly took charge of a series of concerts early in 1867. He became more deeply involved with leading Norwegian composers like Halfdan Kjerulf (1815–68), Otto Winter-Hjelm (1837–1931) and Johan Svendsen (1840–1911), and in 1867 he composed a second Violin Sonata, op.13. This was followed a year later by the piece that was, above all others, to bring its composer wide and lasting fame. Written while Grieg, Nina and the ill-fated baby Alexandra spent an idyllic holiday in the Danish countryside in the summer of 1868, the Concerto in a minor for piano and orchestra, op.16, was dedicated to the Norwegian pianist, Edmund Neupert, who performed it for the first time on 3 April 1869. The Copenhagen audience, which included Queen Louise, composers J.P.E. Hartmann and Niels Gade and pianist Anton Rubinstein, applauded several times during the performance, and thunderous and enthusiastic acclamation followed at the close.

A growing interest in the folk music of Norway manifested itself during this period of Grieg's life, and he was to draw frequently from this rich source for the remainder of his days. He and his friends would collect tunes during summer mountain tours and Grieg would harmonize and publish them. The culmination of this activity was to be the arrangements he began in 1902 of a series of Hardanger-fiddle tunes, published soon after as his forward-looking and often strongly dissonant *Slåtter* (*Norwegian Peasant Dances*) op.72.

The years in Christiania gave evidence of a heightened interest in compositions on a larger scale, although the writing of songs and piano pieces remained as ever an important undercurrent. Grieg collaborated with Bjørnstjerne Bjørnson in *Before a Southern Convent*, op.20, a cantata for soprano and contralto soloists, women's chorus and orchestra composed in 1871, and also in incidental music to the play *Sigurd Jorsalfar*, op.22, 1872. Together they conceived an opera, *Olav Trygvason*, for which Grieg wrote three scenes in 1873. The work progressed no further, however, and Grieg did not orchestrate his draft piano score until 1888, when he published it as *Scenes from Olav Trygvason*, op.50. In the meantime, there were other major works based on Bjørnson: the dramatic recitation *Bergliot*, composed with piano in 1871 and orchestrated as op.42 in 1885, and *Land-sighting*, op.31, composed in 1872 and revised in 1881, for baritone solo, men's chorus, orchestra and organ. The largest in scope of the works of the seventies was the incidental music to Henrik Ibsen's play *Peer Gynt*, op.23, mainly composed in 1874–75, but with later additions and reorchestrations. Together with the Piano Concerto, the two successive orchestral suites that Grieg was to extract from his incidental music in 1888 and 1891, as op.46 and op.55, were to be the most popular of his works for the concert hall, reflecting the favour that his albums of *Lyric Pieces* — of which there were to be ten in all — enjoyed in the home.

The *Ballade* for piano, op.24, was written late in 1875 in Bergen, when Grieg, having lost both parents in the autumn, was spending several weeks in his home town. Returning to Christiania after a series of travels in Germany in 1876, he resumed the round of conducting, choir-practices, piano teaching and — in between these money-earning activities — composition (which alone could not, it seemed, keep him and his wife). From the summer of 1877, however, the Griegs were to stay for much of their time in the Hardanger region —

mainly at Lofthus — where Grieg devoted himself more single-mindedly to composition. His String Quartet in g minor, op.27, dates from this period, as does *The Mountain Thrall* for solo baritone, strings and two horns, op.32.

The later 1870s — a time when tensions were becoming evident in his marriage — saw Grieg beginning to travel more widely from his base at Lofthus. His fame was growing and he was in demand abroad, particularly in Germany. Leipzig was duly revisited in the autumn of 1878 and 1879. During the second of these visits, Grieg would spend some of his time with the younger Norwegians then in the city, like fellow-composers Christian Sinding (1856–1941), who was just beginning a second period of study at the Conservatory, Iver Holter (1850–1941) and Ole Olsen (1850–1927).

In 1880, Grieg applied for and got the post of conductor of 'Harmonien', Bergen's symphony orchestra. During his two-year conductorship he composed relatively little, but the Cello Sonata, op.36, followed in 1883, and later that same year he set out on what was to be his longest foreign tour to date. It started in Bayreuth in the summer; in the autumn he gave concerts in various German and Dutch musical centres; and the year ended in Amsterdam, where he consolidated an important friendship with the composer/conductor Julius Röntgen (1853–1932), who was to become his protagonist in the Netherlands. During all this time Nina had been left at home, almost forgotten, and it is known that around this time Grieg had a relationship with Leis (Elise) Schjelderup, a 26-year-old Norwegian painter who lived mainly in Paris. However, a reconciliation with Nina was finally effected, largely through the efforts of Grieg's closest Bergen friend, Frants Beyer, and she rejoined him in the middle of January in Leipzig. She had travelled there with Beyer and his wife, and both couples then went on to Rome. The Beyers could only stay for two weeks, following which Grieg and Nina holidayed in Italy for the rest of the winter and returned to Bergen in the spring of 1884. Beyer had just had a house built on a promontory overlooking Nordaasvand, a lake at Hop, just a few kilometres from Bergen, and it was there that the Griegs first stayed. They determined to emulate their friends and Grieg purchased a site just across the lake from 'Naesset', the Beyers' house. During the summer in Hardanger, he drew up some preliminary plans for his new home. Below where it would stand was a deep hollow called 'Trolldalen', or the Valley of the Trolls, and it was Nina who proposed that the house itself should be called 'Troldhaugen' — the Hill of the Trolls. In the autumn more suitable plans were drawn up by an architect cousin of Grieg's, and in the spring of 1885 Edvard and Nina were able to move into their newly-built home. This was to be Grieg's base for the rest of his life, although for the most part he and Nina stayed there only during the summer months, when the companionship of the Beyers would be enjoyed to the full. That first summer, Grieg took time off with Beyer to make the first of what were to be many trips to the Jotunheim mountains, walking tours which would always have a recuperative effect on the composer.

1885 saw the publication of the suite *From Holberg's Time*, op.40, composed for piano in Lofthus during the summer of 1884 and then transcribed by Grieg for string orchestra. It was soon to become another public favourite. The first stop in the autumn was Christiania, where there were concerts and recitals. Wherever they went, Nina usually sang some of his songs. The winter of 1885/86 was spent in Denmark, with concerts in Copenhagen towards the end of the year and a notable performance of the Piano Concerto there in January, with Johan Svendsen conducting and Grieg as soloist. Ill health intervened and anaemia and nervous problems were diagnosed. It did not help that there were financial problems too, for the building of Troldhaugen had caused a heavy drain on Grieg's resources. After undertaking a recital tour of Jutland in March, Grieg returned for a while to Copenhagen before leaving for his new home once more in May. During the summer he completed another set of *Lyric Pieces* — the third, op.43 — which included 'To the Spring' and 'Butterfly'; he also made another Jotunheim tour, this time with a new friend, the Danish poet Holger Drachmann.

It was at Troldhaugen in the autumn of 1886 that Grieg finished his third Violin Sonata, in c minor, op.45, the last chamber work that he was to complete. There were to be revisions before it was first performed, at Leipzig on 10 December 1887. Following another Jotunheim tour in the summer of 1887 in the company of Frants Beyer, Grieg, thoroughly refreshed, could contemplate with equanimity the coming winter that he and Nina would decide to spend in Leipzig. Here, for the first time, they would meet Fritz Delius, a 25-year-old student from England in the first term of his second year at the Conservatory.

Delius was born in Bradford, in the county of Yorkshire. His parents were both from Germany, having emigrated from Bielefeld and taken out British nationality some years earlier. There could have been few greater urban contrasts than the grimy and smoke-stacked industrial inland city of Bradford and the picturesque port of Bergen, although each, in moorland or mountain, had attractive hinterlands. Opportunities in the wool textile business, of which Bradford was a major world centre, had provided the particular attraction for the immigrant Julius Delius, whose bride was soon to follow him. Of his son Fritz's numerous siblings, none was more musically gifted, but the boy's schooling in Bradford and London was not intended to fit him for musicianship, his father's design being that he should enter the prosperous family business. However, the home was unquestionably a cultured one and musicians of considerable repute had played there when Delius was a child. His own musical tastes were established early: 'When I first heard Chopin as a little boy of 6 or 7 I thought heaven had been opened to me — When also as a little boy I first heard the Humoresken of Grieg a new world was opened to me again.' Rather later, the young Delius was to come upon the operas of Wagner and again to be similarly affected.

An immigrant city, then as now, Bradford had an important German community with its own societies, musical and otherwise, and Julius Delius played a role there commensurate with his business and social status, serving, for example, on the committee which arranged concerts for the Hallé Orchestra. In 1880, his son's schooling came to an end and he was duly apprenticed to the family business. He worked for the firm until early 1884 and the period was marked by a series of travels abroad, representing Delius and Company, which took him to Germany, France and Sweden. From his father's point of view it would undoubtedly have been better if Fritz had stayed at home, for each trip became, in fact, a form of escape. Even in England, Fritz's first posting, to Stroud in Gloucestershire, had meant that he could all the more easily take himself off by train to hear concerts in London. In Germany, while based at a factory in Chemnitz, he sought out the violinist Hans Sitt and took lessons from him. In France, working at St Etienne, he found the lure of the Riviera too strong and so took his chances at the gaming tables of Monte Carlo. And in Sweden he had slipped the leash of the plain and practical manufacturing town of Norrköping and had crossed the border for the first time into Norway. It was here, in the summer of 1881, that he really began to find himself. None put it better than Thomas Beecham: 'The influence of the scenic grandeur of the Scandinavian Peninsula, particularly the western extremity of it, was profound, mystical and indelible. For the first time he realized his own secret affinity with high and lonely places. There he could breathe freely, and there could his spirit gain that just balance and serenity which seemed to have been banished forever from the crowded and noisy haunts of money-seeking men.' [Thomas Beecham: *Frederick Delius*, p. 21]

Very little is recorded of this first visit to Norway. We merely learn from Delius's first English biographer, Philip Heseltine, that 'an extended tour in Norway, ending up in Bergen and in no way connected with the buying and selling of wool, was the cause of considerable friction with the family when the truant returned to England in the autumn' [*Frederick Delius*, p. 9]. Of any detailed itinerary, there is no trace.

There was to be a series of bitter arguments with his father, leading to a virtual estrangement, before Delius was released from his obligations to the wool trade. They finally came to an agreement that he should try his luck as an orange farmer in Florida, a widely-advertised business opportunity at the time. A lease was taken on a parcel of land on the western bank of the St Johns River some 50 kilometres south of the fast-growing and flourishing town of Jacksonville, and Delius duly crossed the Atlantic in March 1884 to take up residence on his plantation, Solana Grove. He tried to make a success of his new occupation, but it was doomed to failure, largely on account of a chance meeting in Jacksonville itself. This was with a singularly gifted musician from New York, Thomas Ward, who like many others had come south to seek a cure for incipient consumption. His natural musicianship, coupled with an evidently excellent teaching ability, was what Delius needed above all else. This, the most important meeting of his life so far, could not have come at a more opportune moment. Ward was invited to Solana Grove and taught Delius all he knew. His pupil already played the violin proficiently and had quickly procured a piano. The sights and sounds of Florida around him, together with the negroes' four-part harmonizing that he could hear further inland on his grove, were all to imprint themselves indelibly in his mind and ultimately to find expression in his music. By the summer of 1885 he felt confident enough to desert the grove and strike north, to Danville in Virginia, where he taught music for the academic year 1885–86, giving lessons both privately and in a girls' school. His friends and mentors in the town were impressed by his ability and counselled training at the Leipzig Conservatory. Julius Delius, despairing of keeping his son away from music and no doubt privately impressed by the fact that Fritz had apparently succeeded for the first time in earning his own living, acquiesced. It was duly agreed that Delius should enroll at Leipzig for the autumn term of 1886. After a short visit to New York, he sailed for England in June.

Delius did establish in America a Norwegian musical connection, unexpectedly enough on a nearby plantation on the St Johns River. The wife of Lt Charles Edward Bell, another temporary English immigrant, was Norwegian by birth and upbringing. Her given name was Jutta Mordt, and her parents had apparently left Christiania and settled in the United States in the early 1880s, bringing their nine children with them. Several of the children received a musical training in Cincinnati. Of them, Jutta (?1857–1934) was possibly the most musically gifted. She left Florida for England around 1886 and later moved for a time to Paris, studying singing with Marchesi. In 1894, still very much in contact with Delius, she was advising the composer on aspects of the libretto of his opera *The Magic Fountain* — just as she may well have done in the case of his *Irmelin* a little earlier. By this time, she was separated from her husband. She moved back to England soon after, and there — under her professional name of Jutta Bell-Ranske — she taught singing and voice production. She was furthermore to publish in London, in 1901 and 1902 respectively, two books: *Peasant Lassies: Tales of Norway, with an appendix of folksongs* and *Health, Speech, and Song: a practical guide to voice-production*. Each was written in her own fluent English and the *Tales* brought in their train a series of favourable reviews in the British press (with Bjørnson in one case being cited almost in the same breath as their author). It seems that she returned, together with her daughter Catherine, to America in 1902, when to all intents and purposes contact with Delius ceased. She evidently continued to teach, and we find her giving public lectures on dramatic subjects ('Ibsen: His Message to the People' being one of them)* to huge audiences at the People's Institute in New York as late as 1917 and 1918. The family relationship to or friendship with Grieg that various sources have claimed for Jutta has not so far been corroborated.†

In Leipzig, Delius took lodgings at 8 Marschnerstrasse at the beginning of August, soon afterwards moving to what was to be his permanent address in the city: 5 Harkortstrasse. He had registered by the end of August and was actually admitted to the Conservatory on 7

* Information kindly supplied in part by Professor William Randel.
† The best-known Christiania Mordts of an earlier generation were the goldsmith Jacob Andreas Mordt (or Morth) (1796–1854) and his painter son Gustav Adolph Mordt (1826–1856).

October. Before long he was making friends with the Leipzig Norwegians, the first probably being the pianist daughter of a Christiania
merchant, Camilla Jacobsen, enrolled on the same day as he. She was
only to stay for a year, leaving Leipzig on 16 July 1887, but Delius got
to know her sufficiently well to visit her and her family when he went
to Norway in the summer of 1887. Also enrolling that autumn was
Johan Halvorsen (1864–1935), an exact contemporary at the Conservatory, leaving, as Delius was to do, after two years of study. Another
younger Norwegian with whom Delius was to establish a close
friendship for a number of years was Arve Arvesen (1869–1951), who
had enrolled in 1885 and was also, like Delius and Halvorsen, to leave
in 1888. A still closer friend-to-be was Halfdan Jebe (1868–1937), the
son of a doctor from Trondheim, who enrolled in the autumn of 1887,
only to stay for a year. Hjalmar Borgstrøm (1864–1925) also enrolled
in 1887. He stayed at Leipzig until 1890 and then moved on to Berlin.
Although apparently on cordial terms with Delius, he was not so close
as the other Norwegians. Borgstrøm is an interesting figure in that at
the time of Grieg's death in 1907 his reputation as a leading composer
of the successor generation in Norway was second only to that of
Sinding. He had come under the spell of Wagner and was very clearly
influenced by Grieg's contemporary, Johan Selmer. His late Romantic style, moving towards Impressionism, contributed to the early
success of his five symphonic poems, although his oeuvre, if uneven, is
considerably more wide-ranging. He lived mostly abroad until he
returned in 1903 to Christiania where he was then to gain a reputation
as a music critic. The first evidence for Delius knowing him comes in a
letter from Sinding on 27 November 1888: 'Borgström also asks me to
remember him to you [. . .] He's written some good stuff. Talented
lad.' Two more Norwegians were also to establish friendships with
Delius in Leipzig, although their own main periods of study there had
come to an end some years earlier. They were Christian Sinding, back
again in Leipzig in the autumn of 1886 and staying on there for some
three years, and Iver Holter, who revisited the city frequently in the
late 1880s and who met Delius there some time during the course of
the Englishman's first year of study.

At the Conservatory, Delius resumed violin lessons for a while with
Hans Sitt and studied theory and composition with Reinecke and
theory with Salomon Jadassohn, these being his principal teachers.
He seems to have made relatively little impression on them and
himself claimed that they had made little impression on him. His
musical education, which had started in earnest only in Florida, was

nonetheless licked into some sort of final shape at Leipzig. And his first major work, composed in Leipzig in 1886–87, the *Florida Suite* for orchestra (RT VI/1), represented an astonishing step forward from the few immature piano pieces and songs that immediately preceded it, already containing the essence of the sound world that today we recognize as almost unmistakably his own.

His first year at an end, Delius left Germany in the middle of July for Norway and was soon heading for the Hardangervidde (usually spelt -*vidda*, but I have retained the form favoured by both Grieg and Delius), the great mountain plateau to the east of Bergen in south central Norway. Here he took a walking tour through some of the region's finest scenery. He then made his way north to Molde, finding there a letter that he had been expecting from Camilla Jacobsen. From Molde he continued down the great valley tracts of Romsdal and Gudbrandsdal, walking for part of the time with Norwegians he had met en route. He reached Christiania on 13 August and on the 14th visited the Jacobsen family at their summer home on Malmøya. He stayed for two weeks in the area with Norwegian friends and seems to have spent a fair amount of that time in the company of Camilla and the Jacobsens. He left Christiania on 30 August on the first leg of his return route to Leipzig. He had sketched a series of *Norske Wiser* ('Norwegian Airs') (RT X(ii)3), little piano pieces with Griegian overtones, during his travels, and furthermore was on the way to gaining what Heseltine described as 'a very good knowledge of the Norwegian language.' Back in Leipzig for the autumn term, he renewed acquaintance with his Norwegian friends, including Christian Sinding.

Edvard and Nina Grieg left Bergen at the beginning of September 1887. They paid just a short visit to Leipzig before moving on to Karlsbad, where Grieg took a cure and devoted some time to revising and reorchestrating *In Autumn*, first composed in 1866. They then returned to Leipzig, where they were to remain for some six months from mid-October. In a letter to Frants Beyer on 22 November, Grieg related how he had just come home following a visit to Adolf Brodsky, when together the two of them had played through Grieg's new Violin Sonata no.3 in c minor, op.45. Brodsky, he told Beyer, was Johan Halvorsen's teacher at the Conservatory: 'I mentioned Halvorsen. A splendid lad, I like him more and more. He was up here the other evening and played the Sonata through with me, and he did so with such warmth and genuine artistry that I had a fit of pride at his being a countryman of mine. And then Sinding is here. Well, you just wouldn't believe what a remarkable man he is. We four, the Grieg pair (Nina included!), Sinding and Halvorsen, spend an hour after lunch nearly every day playing skittles.'

Delius had taken a great liking to Sinding. Heseltine tells us that he 'spent much of his leisure hours in the company of Christian Sinding, and when Grieg arrived towards the end of the year the three became almost inseparable companions' [*Frederick Delius*, p. 46]. It is unlikely that the meeting with Grieg took place much before the beginning of December, as Grieg's letter to Beyer would seem to indicate that it is still a closed circle of just four Norwegian friends who enthusiastically play their skittles after lunch. On 12 December, however, just two days after the first public performance of the new sonata, Grieg wrote to Beyer: 'This afternoon I have been for a long tour to Lindenau with Sinding and an English friend of his. The weather was glorious and the conversation full of substance, so I feel like new. We are shortly off to a big concert. . .' So Delius's own vivid memories of his first meeting with Grieg probably relate to just a few days before this particular occasion:

During my stay in Leipzig I had become great friends with Christian Sinding, the Norwegian composer, and we always took our midday meal together at the Panorama Restaurant. One day on our way thither suddenly Sinding said to me: 'There's Mr and Mrs Grieg', and I saw coming towards us two quite small people. Sinding knew the Griegs — already introduced.

I saw a little man with a broad-brimmed hat and long hair and on his arm a little woman with hair cut quite short. I was speedily introduced. We all four then made our way to the Panorama Restaurant to have dinner. I was very proud at having made his acquaintance, for since I was a little boy I had loved his music. I had as a child always been accustomed to Mozart and Beethoven and when I first heard Grieg it was as if a breath of fresh mountain air had come to me.

Grieg, learning how well I knew Norway and hearing that I had just returned from a mountain-tour, naturally took great interest in me and we soon found ourselves comparing notes of mountain trips in Jotunheimen* and the Hardanger Vidder.

After dinner, we all took a walk round the Promenade, Mrs

---

* Lit. *The Home of the Giants*. Both Grieg and Delius used the terms Jotunheim and Jotunheimen (i.e. Jotunheim and *the* Jotunheim) indiscriminately.

Grieg going home, and every day for many months we dined together, played a rubber of whist and then took a walk round the Promenade. Sometimes varying by going through the Rosental, a beautiful park. Then we all returned to our separate abodes to work. I lived at 5 Harkort Str and Grieg at 8 Hertel Str. He had then just finished his c minor Violin Sonata, which had its first performance during the winter season at the Gewandhaus chamber concerts, Adolf Brodsky playing the violin and Grieg the piano. It was a beautiful performance and I was very enthusiastic, and after the concert I wrote Grieg an enthusiastic letter with my impressions, enclosing in the letter a sprig of heather which I had gathered on the Hardanger Vidder. Next day I was very much moved to see what a deep impression this had made upon him.

We also very often went to the Opera together, for 'Nibelungen', 'Tristan' and 'Meistersinger' were constantly given and of course we never missed a performance. I was 25 then and he was a little over 40. After the opera, or wherever we had been, Grieg always took Sinding and me to a wine restaurant and gave us a nice supper and claret (Bordeaux — his favourite wine), talking a great deal and staying very late. Sometimes Johan Halvorsen, the Norwegian musician, would be of the party. [MS in the Grainger Museum, dictated to Percy Grainger.]

The young Ferruccio Busoni was also studying at the Leipzig Conservatory at this period and he too met Grieg there. Grieg in turn introduced him to Delius, telling the Englishman: 'This is a most remarkable pianist — and perhaps something more.'* Although the friendship developed little at the time, it was to be taken up again around the turn of the century, with Busoni beginning to promote — and to perform — Delius's music.

Before long, references to Delius began to appear in Grieg's letters to his friends. Indeed, he very quickly found a nickname for Delius: 'the Hardangerviddeman'. Christmas Eve 1887 was to be etched indelibly in the memories of those, including Delius, who spent it in the Hertelstrasse: 'Grieg invited me, Sinding and Halvorsen to spend Christmas Eve at his rooms, and a very delightful evening it was. After a hearty supper and a good deal of wine, we had music: Mrs Grieg singing all Grieg's Vinje songs most beautifully, Halvorsen

* Edward Dent: *Ferruccio Busoni*. London: OUP, 1933, p.67.

playing the c minor Violin Sonata, Sinding accompanying Mrs Grieg to several of his own songs, and I playing a piano piece I had just composed — a Norwegian Sleigh-Ride. We had all had rather more than was good for us to drink, and left in the early hours of the morning. As a Christmas present, Grieg gave me his Piano Concerto with a dedication.' [Grainger MS.]

That it was not actually Grieg's newest sonata that was played is made quite clear by Halvorsen and Grieg in their own accounts of the evening. First Halvorsen, who also gives a clue as to why the drink flowed so freely: Grieg's publisher Dr Max Abraham had 'sent Grieg a whole caseful of all kinds of liquors and other good things to celebrate Christmas with. Grieg invited us, i.e. Sinding, Delius and me, to keep Christmas Eve with him. And what a festive Christmas Eve it proved to be. I played together with Grieg his G major Sonata and then in the evening Bach's Chaconne. We had a little Christmas tree which stood on the grand piano, and all of us were in excellent humour, which gradually with the help of Dr Abraham's liquors rose to a state of sheer bliss. The Christmas tree caught alight, and Sinding, who scrambled up onto the piano to put the fire out, knocked the whole thing over. Luckily, all was well, just the odd tallow stain here and there. The drink that most contributed to our beatific state was called "Magenbehagen".' [*Edvard Grieg: Mennesket og Kunstneren*, p. 240]

But it was Grieg himself who, in a letter to Beyer written on Christmas Day, gave the most detailed account:

'Christmas Eve itself was a feast I shall never forget', he wrote, soon shifting, if briefly, into the present tense to convey a greater immediacy to the recounting of the occasion: 'now I'm busy again with preparations for Christmas Eve, have bought and decorated the Christmas tree myself, it sits in state in the middle of the Blüthner grand and I shall soon be lighting it, as I'm expecting Sinding, Halvorsen and Mr. Delius [. . .] at last my guests [arrive], so I have like lightning to climb onto the piano and light the candles. Jubilation all round. Then the handing out of presents. Then the banquet, to which Dr Abraham had sent a whole hamper of food and drink of the highest quality [. . .] Delius is "Norway-crazy" and has been to Norway 4 times [*sic*], staying out on the Hardangervidde for a fortnight and suchlike. After the meal we were, without exception, all plastered, but the programme had to be adhered to and it offered music, music and still more music! What a Christmas Eve! Indeed, had you been with us you would have said that you would never experience a more beautiful — a more interesting one! Firstly Halvorsen played Hallinger and Springere, then Sinding and Halvorsen a Suite by Sinding in the old style, that is to say in the spirit of Bach, so deep and full and rich, so genuinely entering into the spirit of the time, that I have no hesitation in calling it a masterwork. Among other things it made me take a closer look at my own Holberg Suite, which set beside Sinding's piece presents itself as very much French-influenced indeed, which anyway is precisely what it is supposed to be. But Sinding's piece lays claim to a profundity of a quite different order — and in truth it has it too. Then I played with Halvorsen my 2nd Violin Sonata, then Nina sang songs by Sinding and me, then Mr. Delius played a piano piece, which he calls "Norwegische Schlittenfahrt" with great talent, then again Sinding and Halvorsen a Suite in the old style by F. Ries, after which Sinding's Suite was repeated. By now it was past 1 o'clock. But even then Nina began again, and now it was the Vinje songs, songs by Elling and 3 of the new ones by Frants Beyer. You may rest well assured both in regard to their performance and their reception and Sinding said: "Well, I'm damned if I won't go there and see both Bergen and Frants Beyer and the Jotunheim and all that!" We broke up at half past 2.'

Grieg's often frail constitution evidently stood up well during the holiday season. He and Nina saw in the New Year in Delius's rooms, for example. And if the party on Christmas Eve could be said to have been with younger friends representing a new musical generation, it was outshone just a week later by a dinner party enjoyed with friends of an older generation. This lively occasion took place at the Brodskys' home, where Grieg was flanked at the table by Brahms and Tchaikovsky, the latter in particular being one of his greatest admirers. Again, the relaxed and convivial nature of the event is conveyed in a later recollection: Anna Brodsky felt that it had more resembled 'a children's party rather than a gathering of great composers.' Delius, a junior in all respects, was not present. 'During that winter season,' he later recounted, 'Tchaikovsky came to Leipzig, and also Brahms, but I never met them.'

Studies were resumed at the beginning of the new term, as was the regular pattern of socializing and music-making. In the middle of January the Griegs attended an evening of traditional plays from Upper Bavaria performed by a Munich company that was visiting Leipzig for a season. They quite literally wept with enchantment: 'Nina even spotted a tear in Dr Abraham's eyes!' Grieg told Beyer on 19 January. 'Yesterday I was there for a second time with Sinding and

Halvorsen and the "Hardangerviddeman" and we enjoyed ourselves so much that we stayed up till 2 o'clock, with oysters and wine.'

Grieg bears further witness, in a letter to Frants Beyer on 13 February, to shared pastimes: 'I'm just back from a long afternoon walk in lovely spring weather with Sinding and the "Hardangervidde-man".' At the same time he was looking forward with pleasure to a quiet evening to himself: 'something that hasn't fallen to my lot for a long time.'

1. FRITZ DELIUS TO EDVARD GRIEG

Harkort Str 5.^{IV} [Leipzig]
Saturday [18 February 1888]

Dear Grieg.

I should like to let you know what pleasure your Quartet¹ gave me & in what a strange mood it left me. It will be of little importance to you if I tell you how much I love & esteem you, but it is true & comes from my heart & so I thank you for all the pleasure that I feel in your works.

With affectionate greetings
I remain

Yours
Fritz Delius

Autograph letter, signed and undated.

1 Grieg's String Quartet no.1 in g minor, op.27 (1877–78), was given in Leipzig by the Brodsky Quartet on 18 February and again the next day. Loud applause followed each movement and, at the conclusion, drowned the hisses of one of Grieg's most entrenched critics, Edouard Bernsdorf, of *Signale*, and others in the Bernsdorf camp. Grieg described the event to Beyer on 20 February. From Beyer he had just received a picture of a favourite spot of his, the tourist hut at Skogadalsbøen, and in his letter of thanks Grieg told his friend: 'This English-American, deeply musical, splendid Hardangerviddeman, he understood my joy. You must get to know him. He is like us in nothing but feeling! But in the end that's everything!' The clear implication is that Delius was one of the few who would have been able to comprehend the profound love of his homeland that was such an essential characteristic of Grieg's make-up.

2. EDVARD GRIEG TO FRITZ DELIUS

[early 1888?]¹

Dear Delius,

Frau Brodsky² has just been here and has asked me to invite you to lunch tomorrow (Saturday) at 1 o'clock. We shall also be there

Yours
Edvard Grieg.

Correspondence card, signed and undated. Envelope addressed: Herrn Fritz Delius./ Harkortstrasse 5/ *4 Tr/ Hier* [?].

1   The probability is that this letter was written fairly early in 1888, no evidence having yet been found to justify an earlier dating.

2   Anna Brodsky, née Skadowsky, wife of Adolf Brodsky. Like his wife, Brodsky (1851–1929) was born in Russia. A fine violinist, he had studied at the Vienna Conservatory from 1860–66, taught in Moscow and Leipzig (as professor of violin) and played in orchestras in Russia and the United States. In Vienna in 1881, he had given the first performance of Tchaikovsky's Violin Concerto. A change in the direction of his career occurred in 1895, when he was appointed leader of the Hallé Orchestra. On Charles Hallé's death later that year, he was appointed principal of the Royal Manchester College of Music, a post he held until 1929. He first formed his celebrated Brodsky Quartet in Leipzig, reconstituting it in Manchester in 1895.

3. EDVARD GRIEG TO FRITZ DELIUS

Leipzig, 28/2/88

Dear Sir,

I was pleasantly surprised, indeed stimulated, by your manuscripts and I detect in them signs of a most distinguished compositional talent in the grand style, which aspires to the highest goal. Whether you will reach this goal only depends upon what turn your affairs take. If you will permit me, in the interests of your future, to offer you a piece of advice, (it is as an older artist that I take the liberty of doing this) it would be this, that you devote yourself now, while you are still young, fully to the pursuit of your art, rather than accept a formal position, and that you follow both your own true nature and the inner voice of your ideals and your inclinations. However, in order to achieve this it is essential that you choose the national and artistic environment as dictated to you by your genius.

It is my most fervent wish that you will one day find in your own country the recognition that you deserve, as well as the material means towards the achievement of your splendid goal and I do not doubt for a moment that you will succeed.

With the assurance of my warm sympathy

Yours very truly
Edvard Grieg.

Autograph letter, signed and dated.

Grieg's letter, in its careful phrasing quite distinct from the informal tone of the rest of his correspondence with Delius, was clearly intended for the eyes of Delius's father, back in England. One might go so far as to say that with the end of his time at the Leipzig Conservatory drawing nearer, Fritz saw that his life as a composer might well depend on a recommendation such as this, by a composer, moreover, of Grieg's standing. The 'manuscripts' referred to by Grieg probably comprised most of Delius's meagre production to date, the suite *Florida* and the tone poem *Hiawatha* being the only two finished works that might fairly at the time have been described as 'in the grand style'. As a letter of recommendation, it has curious echoes of the letter written to Grieg himself by Franz Liszt nearly twenty years earlier. Grieg had asked a friend to procure just such a note from the celebrated composer, who had earlier expressed appreciation for his first Violin Sonata: 'It bears witness to a talent [. . .] that needs only to follow its natural path in order to attain to a high level. I hope and trust that in your own country you will receive the success and the encouragement that you deserve' [*Edvard Grieg: Mennesket og Kunstneren*, p. 118. Liszt's original is in French]. Each letter was to play its own significant part in the life of each aspiring composer, Liszt's helping Grieg to secure a grant from the Norwegian Ministry of Education and Grieg's enabling Delius, at the end of his formal education in Leipzig, to get a further allowance from his father.

Having read through the manuscript of *Florida*, Grieg was shortly to hear it at Leipzig, as Delius later recalled: 'I was working at the time with Hans Sitt at orchestration and was working at an orchestral suite, which I called 'Florida', and it was arranged that it should be played at a rehearsal of a military orchestra in the coming spring. Sitt had arranged for an orchestra of about 60 to give me a 2 hour rehearsal in the Rosental Restaurant and all it would cost me would be a barrel of beer for the orchestra. This accordingly took place one spring morning, the audience being Grieg and Mrs Grieg, Sinding and myself, Sitt conducting. In the Suite was a very noisy nigger dance where I had used the trombones very noisily and *ff*, and Grieg after the performance said to me that he found it "scheusslich interessant".' [Grainger MS.]

In fact both Sinding and Grieg 'expressed their admiration for the work in the warmest terms', as Delius later told Philip Heseltine. [*Frederick Delius*, p. 47]

The 'Rosental Restaurant' was more properly Bonorand's restaurant in Leipzig's Rosental park, where students from the Conservatory could frequently arrange for their works to be played through for little more than the cost of the musicians' beer. Grieg himself was no stranger to the practice, having written to tell Beyer on 22 November: 'the other morning I got to conduct the Autumn Overture privatissimo with a military band.'

All good things have to come to an end and Grieg seemed to be somewhat prematurely rueful at the prospect of leaving Leipzig, when he wrote to Beyer on 13 February 1888: 'The time is passing, no it's rushing by, indeed it's fairly galloping past, and before I know anything about it we'll be packing our things and saying farewell to Leipzig, where we have been *so* well off, both in regard to health and to the company we've kept.' On 9 March, an urgent note was despatched to Beyer, the company having just drunk a bottle of champagne and Halvorsen having expressed a nostalgic craving for *rekling*, a dried fish dish from home: 'Send us some, dear friend, but immediately, immediately, because Halvorsen is leaving.' The note was signed in turn: *Edvard Grieg og Nina, Fritz (Hardanger Vidda man) Delius, Christian Sinding* and *Mr. Halvorsen (Konzertmeister)*. Halvorsen's idiosyncratic description of himself was due to the fact that he had just been appointed leader of the town orchestra in Aberdeen. (Grieg playfully recommended that he find a wife from among the descendants of his own ancestors, the Scottish Greigs, and bring her back to Norway. In the event Halvorsen was to find a 'Miss Grieg' much closer to home, marrying in 1894 Annie, the daughter of Grieg's brother John.) There is a postscript to the *rekling* story. The ever-loyal Beyer duly obliged, but in a letter of thanks dated 12 April, Grieg reported that the journey probably had not done it any good: 'I went to the customs station with Sinding and the Hardangerviddeman to fetch it (unfortunately Halvorsen had already left), and I couldn't even begin to describe their faces when they caught a whiff of it.' The customs officials, who should by rights have weighed the package, were so anxious to get rid of it that they pushed it over the counter to Grieg, begging him to take it away as quickly as possible. 'Neither Sinding nor Delius could work up any real enthusiasm for it, rather the reverse,' lamented Grieg.

The farewell for Halvorsen had had to go ahead without its malodorous centrepiece, as Grieg told Beyer on 21 March: 'You should have been with us yesterday evening at a little party that I arranged for Halvorsen at "Mutter Krause's" (you remember?) The participants were just the clique (we, Sinding and the Hardangerviddeman), but we enjoyed ourselves with oysters and hock till past midnight.'

Earlier in the year, Grieg had agreed to play his Piano Concerto at a Philharmonic Society concert in London. It was to be his first visit to England and Delius, one feels, must surely have played a part in encouraging Grieg to accept the engagement. At first it had seemed possible that they could travel to England together, as Grieg makes clear in his letter to Beyer of 21 March: 'We are off in the middle of April and hope to travel in the company of the Hardangerviddeman.' But, for whatever reason, this was not to be and the Griegs left about a fortnight after Delius.

The farewells stretched over a month. Halvorsen was accompanied to the station on 21 March by the Griegs, and more than probably by Sinding and Delius as well. Delius was off a fortnight later: 'Ah, the Hardangerviddeman! We accompanied him, too, to the station a few days ago,' Grieg told Beyer on 12 April. 'Now he is in England and our little colony has disbanded. Today we had our dinner quite alone.' Sinding was the only member of the group not to be crossing the North Sea, leaving Germany at around the same time as the Griegs, but for Norway rather than Britain. The Griegs were to leave on 22 April, by which time Grieg himself had already written the epitaph on what had clearly been one of the happiest periods of his life: 'When I think of how lucky I have been in my company this winter, I'm thinking mainly of Sinding, Brodsky and the *admirable* Hardangerviddeman, I can say without a lie that the trip has been worth it and that's really saying something.' [Letter to Beyer of 24 March]

4. FRITZ DELIUS TO EDVARD GRIEG

Claremont
Bradford.
12 April/88.   England.

Dear Grieg

I arrived here yesterday after rather an unpleasant journey. I got to Düsseldorf at 9 in the morning & left at 4.24 p.m., via Flushing; the Rotterdam train left too early for me as I had first to visit my sister. I believe this route will suit you best, it is fast & comfortable.[1] The ships are also very comfortably fitted out & only take 7 hours for the crossing. In Flushing I was so tired that I went to bed right away & noticed nothing until Queenboro', the crossing was very calm, too, just like on the Hardanger Fjord. We got to London at 8 o'clock in the morning. But the journey was very cold. Still, it is somewhat warmer in England than over there, even if you will not be able to pick roses in the streets. I do not think that I shall stick it out for very long here. I already miss you all very much & have suddenly arrived in so completely different an atmosphere that I feel rather depressed. If you should feel like spending a day or two here in Bradford I should be very pleased to make you & your wife welcome, but if not I hope we will meet at least once in London before my departure for Paris.[2] Please give your wife my best wishes & write me a few lines when you have the time & inclination. Hoping you are well & happy

    I remain

    Yours
    Fritz Delius

Autograph letter, signed and dated.

1   Grieg was a reluctant, if not fearful sea-traveller, and ever an easy prey to sea-sickness.

2   The decision must already have been taken that Delius, still without independent means of his own, might for a time undertake further travels. Some degree of parental support for the trip must have been agreed, perhaps as a reward for the completion of his course at Leipzig. He would initially travel to Paris, staying with his uncle Theodor — Julius's bachelor brother — in the rue Cambon. Delius seems to have intended this to be the first stage of a journey that would take him on to

Spain in the early summer. In the event it is quite possible that the lack of a suitable travelling companion aborted the Spanish trip, a clue lying in a rhetorical question from Christian Sinding on 27 June: 'How then am I supposed to get to Spain. Speak not to me of it.'

5. EDVARD GRIEG TO FRITZ DELIUS

Leipzig, 16th April
88.

Dear Delius,

You say I should write when I have the time and inclination. Well, I certainly have plenty of the second, but absolutely none of the first. At least, as you know, it's inclination that gets one down to work. I can well understand that in more than one respect you find it a quite different atmosphere to be living in. But that also goes for us too since *you* have been gone.[1] I really have to tell you that it is *very* rare that getting to know someone has given me such pleasure! Let us only hope that we meet again some time. Unfortunately we shall not be able to accept your kind invitation to come to Bradford. And our reunion in London? Well, that can hardly be much more than a quick handshake. But in Norway! That's where it must be — that is, when you are back from Spain bringing with you a whole world of new impressions. Then we shall sit ourselves down somewhere in the Norwegian mountains and listen to tales of Spanish eyes!

We are leaving here on Sunday via Calais and shall arrive in London on Monday afternoon. That is to say, provided I am ready, for I still have too many things to attend to. But I *must* be ready. I was at Sitt's[2] yesterday, and am going there again this evening. He was extremely kind and reveals enormous erudition. But I feel that his manner of orchestration is at times coarse. That is certainly the impression I got, although I will not pass final judgment yet.

We continue our lunchtime whist with Mr. Brown,[3] who seems to be a very attractive and natural person, — and as Sinding says, gifted too.

My wife asks me to give you all her good wishes. Farewell and don't forget the 3rd May and your devoted friend

Edvard Grieg.

Autograph letter, signed and dated.

1   If the Griegs missed Delius, so did Sinding, who wrote on 19 April to his recently-departed friend: 'You cannot imagine how much I miss you. I have hardly ever before met a person I could trust so completely, and at times an almost sentimental feeling comes over me when I think of you [. . .] Last night I went with the Griegs to Mr. Braun's, where we drank champagne. I proposed a toast to you, which was responded to with great acclaim. You really are very much missed here, you old Joseph. I am to send you many good wishes from the Brodskys [. . .] Greetings from the Griegs, who are leaving on Monday.' Sinding was on the whole a shy and reserved man, certainly not given to hyperbole, and his expressions of affection for Delius, like the Griegs', say much for the character of their English friend.

2   Hans Sitt (1850–1922): composer, violinist and teacher and a member of the Brodsky Quartet, in which he played the viola. He had been conductor of the town orchestra in Chemnitz when Delius had first taken lessons from him there in 1880. He taught at the Leipzig Conservatory from 1883 until his retirement in 1921. Sitt had himself made a new orchestral arrangement of Grieg's *Norwegian Dances*, op.35, and this was to be published by Peters in 1891. Presumably by then Grieg's 'final judgment' on his ability as an orchestrator had been modified.

3   Charles Braun (1868–?): English fellow-student of Delius at Leipzig, where he had some extra-curricular tutoring from Sinding, who found in him a promising musician. He enjoyed a brief success in his native city of Liverpool, two cantatas of his, *Sir Olaf* and *Sigurd*, being performed there in 1889 and 1890 respectively. During the final part of Grieg's stay in Leipzig, Braun was a welcome participant in the whist sessions of which Delius had so recently been a member.

6.   EDVARD GRIEG TO FRITZ DELIUS

[mid-April 1888]

G. Augener Esq.
Newgate Street 86
London E.C.

Edvard Grieg

Home:
5 The Cedars,
Clapham Common
London, S.W.

Printed visiting card, with addresses in Grieg's hand. On the reverse side Delius has written in pencil

Thal Str 10.
c.f. Peters.
Music publishers

The Griegs arrived in London on 23 April, staying at the Clapham home of music publisher George Augener, British agent for the C.F. Peters company of Leipzig. They were accompanied by Dr Max Abraham, head of the company, who had now become Grieg's patron angel. Augener had started his own business in London in 1853. (He was to retire in 1910.) Almost certainly Grieg introduced him to Delius during this visit, as before long Augener was to be the first to publish, under his own imprint, Delius's songs, starting with the *Five Songs from the Norwegian* (RT V/5). Composed in 1888, they came out as a set in London in 1890.

7. FRITZ DELIUS TO EDVARD GRIEG

Claremont
Bradford,
25 [April]/88.

Dear Grieg

Many thanks for your letter, which gave me much pleasure. At all events, you will now be in London & I hope after a pleasant journey. Our wonderful time in Leipzig has now melted away into the past. I have never lived through such a congenial time. It has been a cornerstone in my life, I hope there will be three more to come.

Next Saturday I am coming to London & go straight on to Reading where I shall stay with an acquaintance until Monday. On Monday I travel to London & will be staying at the Hotel Métropole where I shall be constantly at your disposal. I invite you & your dear wife herewith to supper with me at the Hotel Métropole on the 4th May & to spend yet another of our jolly evenings together. If you can, it would be a pleasure for me to show you various things of interest during the day. In short to be your guide. If the 5th should suit you better it would also suit me. On the 6th I travel to Paris. The weather here is very cold, I am freezing miserably. My father has delighted me by giving me the score of Tristan & Isolde. Please write me a few lines when you can.

Give my best wishes to your wife

Your devoted
Fritz Delius

Autograph letter, signed and dated '25/88'.

8.   NINA GRIEG TO FRITZ DELIUS

London 26th April
88. —
5, the Cedars
Clapham Common.

Dear Mr. Delius,

Many thanks for your kind letter from Bradford, which we have just received. Do forgive me if it is just I who answers it, but Grieg has such a frightful lot to do that he simply has no time at present for letter-writing.

I am afraid that he is not in a very good mood, he gets annoyed over everyone and everything and keeps wishing he had never come to London. I hope things will be better after the concert. The weather is atrocious, windy and cold almost like in winter, I can't tell you how frozen we are, and we long for our lovely Leipzig days again. —

How glad we shall be if we are all able to spend a little time together again here and by all means we accept with pleasure your kind invitation for the 4th May. — Grieg very much hopes that you will come to the rehearsal, although he doesn't know when it is to be, but that will all sort itself out when we meet here.

With warmest good wishes from us both

Yours sincerely
Nina Grieg.

The crossing from Calais to Dover was appalling, you certainly had a better one.

Auf Wiedersehen!
N.G.

Autograph letter, signed and dated.

Having accepted the London engagement, Grieg, fine pianist that he was, but aware that he was not among the very greatest, had done little but worry: 'Since the 1st of February [. . .] I have been practising the piano for several hours each morning so that I won't disgrace myself in London', he had told Beyer in his letter of 13 February. 'There is nothing to gain,' he complained some five weeks later, 'but a good part of my health to lose.' And on 12 April he informed Beyer that he had 'a sort of dark feeling that something will happen that is not good.' Having excused himself from a London invitation once before on the grounds of illness, he acknowledged that this tactic could hardly work again. 'The Hardangerviddeman suggested that I tell them that an old aunt of mine had died! That's just like him!' (This would have been just before Delius left Leipzig for England.)

In the event, however, Grieg himself was able to describe the evening of 3 May as a 'colossal success'. Apart from playing his Concerto under Frederic Cowen's direction, he had conducted the orchestra's almost sixty-strong string section in his *Two Elegiac Melodies*, op.33. 'I have never heard such a sound in Germany,' he reported to Beyer on 4 May, adding: 'An English singer, Miss Elliot, sang "The First Meeting" in German and then sang in English — well, what do you think: Farewell to Tvindehaugen! And how well she sang it!' He wondered over his success: 'I really believe that the English liking for my art must come from their liking of Norway, as I cannot explain yesterday's ovations in any other way [. . .] When I showed myself in the orchestra doorway there was a roar of jubilation in the huge hall (St. James Hall), which was filled to the last seat, and it was so intense and unending — I think for over 3 minutes — that I didn't know what to do. I continued to bow in every direction, but it just wouldn't stop. Isn't that extraordinary? In a country in which I'm a stranger [. . .] I was aware that I was known here, but not that my art was so highly thought of.'

On the evening of the following day came the supper party that was so important for Delius. 'My parents were in London at the time,' he later remembered, 'and we all had dinner together at the Hotel Metropole and Grieg persuaded my father to let me continue my musical studies.' What Grieg was evidently able to do was to convince Julius Delius that his son had considerable potential and that he should utilize his forthcoming stay in Paris to develop his musical gifts and to concentrate on composition. For this a continued allowance would be necessary. Julius's brother Theodor would for his part provide initial hospitality. (At a later stage Delius's benevolent aunt Albertine was also to help with an allowance.) There can be no doubt that this endorsement of Delius's abilities — following the laudatory letter of some two months earlier — by a now world-famous composer, was a crucial turning point in the younger man's life. He was to remain ever-grateful to Grieg for it.

Another successful evening for Grieg was to follow on 16 May, when at a chamber concert the composer played some of his piano pieces and accompanied Wilhelmina Norman-Neruda in his first Violin Sonata as well as in the last two movements of the c minor Sonata. Nina sang some of his songs. Following a short break on the Isle of Wight, where they arrived at Ventnor, in the company of Max Abraham, on 17 May, the Griegs left for Copenhagen. By this time Delius was living in comfortable circumstances in Paris at the home of his well-to-do uncle.

9. FRITZ DELIUS TO EDVARD GRIEG

43 Rue Cambon
Paris
[mid-May 1888]

Dear Grieg,

I have now settled down a bit & must confess that I feel very happy here. There is something in the atmosphere that is quite different from Germany or England. The hustle & bustle here is extraordinary, one just has to think that every street-urchin enjoys life. The concerts are over. I heard the last Lamoureux Concert & must confess that as far as ensemble & finesse are concerned the orchestra is far superior to Leipzig. I heard Parsifal Prelude, Tannhäuser Overture, Lohengrin Prelude to 1st Act, Women's March & Prelude to 3rd Act, Dance Marcabre Saint Saens, L'Arlesienne, Bizet & something from Bizet's opera The Pearl Fishers, quite excellent. I am meeting a lot of artists, musicians & writers. But I can't do much work. In a few weeks' time I am going to Spain, Seville or Granada, am already longing for it. It is beautiful, very beautiful here but I will soon have to have some peace &

quiet. I heard a new opera by Lalo at the Opera Comique, but found it utterly trivial.[1] Also Aida at the big Opera, quite excellent. How did your concert come off, did it bring in pounds stirling en masse for you. I have not heard anything from Sinding nor from Mr Braun. The weather is quite marvellous, not a cloud. My kind regards to your wife. I hope that you are both keeping well & happy. Please excuse this superficial letter, as soon as I have some peace you shall receive a much more detailed one.

Farewell & write me a few lines.

Your devoted
Fritz Delius

Autograph letter, signed and undated.

1   Lalo's opera *Le Roi d'Ys* was premièred at the Opéra Comique on 7 May and enjoyed considerable success — *pace* Delius's lack of enthusiasm.

10.   FRITZ DELIUS TO EDVARD GRIEG

43. Rue Cambon.
Paris. June 20/88.

My good, dear Grieg,

How are you, where are you? What are you doing? & how did you get on in London? You have no idea how much I miss you & have missed you since not seeing you any more. This evening I felt that I just wanted to say it to you. Yes! I think of you very often. I have been all alone here for the past 18 days. My uncle was in London & has only just come back today. I have been working the whole time & have written a lot, several songs, and Ibsen's *Paa Vidderne*,[1] for tenor voice, & an orchestral piece.[2] For you I have written two songs in remembrance which I should like to send as soon as I know your correct address. Next year I am certainly coming to Trollhaugen, if I am alive. Give my greetings to the North, until I am able to do so myself. It is very beautiful in Paris, but I would not like to stay here forever. The French are very artistic, but it is always merely art, the great vitality of Nature is missing, at least in music. It is all too refined & affected —

But one can learn much, very much here. The people are very free & have power, & everyone lives & is free: a great contrast to Germany. Moral freedom is widespread here too. In a few weeks' time I travel to Spain, Seville first. I will write & tell you all about it. From time to time I go to the Morgue where people who have died are laid out, suicides, or murdered. Oh, it's saddening to go in there. There are always 4 or 5 pitiful corpses looking so eternally wretched. Yes, you can very soon come across the two extremes here. The people of luxury in their fine carriages in the Bois de Boulogne & the wretched suicides in the Morgue. If only I had *you* here I could show you so very much. Things you could weep over, but also other things which would amuse you a lot. Now & again I also go where the very poorest people live. I dress shabbily & then go everywhere undisturbed. You can see 5 different worlds here in Paris, it is immensely interesting. If you have time write me a few lines. I shall continue to give you news of myself from time to time, until I can eventually greet you in your own home in *the North*. Yes, one day I think I shall come up & stay put there. Give my best wishes to your dear wife, & remember

Your friend
Fritz Delius

Autograph letter, signed and dated.

1   Ibsen's *Paa Vidderne* is a poem in nine sections. Written in 1859–60, its allegorical message is essentially that of Schiller's earlier-adumbrated 'Der Starke ist am mächtigsten allein.' The young man rejects his valley home and the prospect of a life to be spent in toil and banality and takes instead to the mountains, where he steels himself mentally and physically to the harshness of his surroundings, his purpose set to higher things. Delius here describes his setting of the work as 'for tenor voice', but he was shortly to adapt the piece as a 'melodrama', the poem being spoken rather than sung. *Paa Vidderne* (RT III/1) drew from Delius some of the very best orchestral music of his early years, but it had to wait until 1981 to be performed (as a television film made by NRK, the Norwegian Broadcasting Corporation) by the Oslo Philharmonic Orchestra under the baton of Charles Farncombe and with Svein Sturla Hungnes as speaker. The reasons for the work's neglect are various. Narrated, rather than sung, it belongs to a fairly esoteric genre; the poem itself is all but unknown outside Norway; Delius set it to a German translation, rather than using English or the Norwegian original; no suitable English performing translation was prepared until 1983; and the thirty minutes or so of Delius's music

require a large orchestra. Two performances in England, one in English and one in Norwegian, nonetheless followed in 1984. Described by Michael Meyer as perhaps one of the finest of Ibsen's non-dramatic works, *Paa Vidderne* in Delius's setting is fully worthy of its source.

2 The orchestral piece Delius refers to may well be *Hiawatha*, to which he has presumably put finishing touches. No other orchestral piece completed in the earlier half of 1888 would appear to have survived.

11. EDVARD GRIEG TO FRITZ DELIUS

Troldhaugen.
Hop Station
nr *Bergen*, Norway
9th August 88

Dear Delius,

I ought really to have told you before that I am a bad correspondent, otherwise you might perhaps find yourself capable of doubting my feelings of friendship for you. I ought long ago to have written, even if I had not got your last kind letter. I received it the day before yesterday and, to my surprise, see now that it was despatched from Paris on *20 June*, — a proof that the post, too, is a human institution! And you have set 'på Vidderne' to music! I can't tell you how curious I am to see the piece, however, on the other hand, I would rather not see it yet, for I have long had the idea of setting the very same poem to music. But — my curiosity is too great and I solemnly undertake not to steal from you!! That is, no *notes*, for I hope to have stolen your friendship once and for all, so that you shall never have it back. As a result I only need to tell you that you will be received in our house with open arms, if and when you come. Don't let the beauty of Spain make you forget Nordic nature and your Nordic friends! In a few days I am going to Birmingham[1] with my friend Beyer,[2] but I am afraid must first visit London for orchestra rehearsals. I am going by steamer from here to Aberdeen and am not really looking forward to the whole business. As soon as possible I shall return home, and shall stay at home until January, when I shall probably go to Berlin and London and perhaps also to Paris. But I have not yet learnt where to hide myself away in order to work quietly on my own. Every day I receive visits from all possible nationalities — well, that too has its interesting points — and indeed from all sorts of townsfolk seeking to be refreshed by an excursion to the countryside and making poor, unfortunate Troldhaugen their destination. — You have probably read that my final concert in London was a resounding success. The Music Festival in Copenhagen was also very successful. However, with the news of the death of my friend Edmund Neupert[3] in New York I have aged 10 years in the past fortnight. He was only 46 years old! One of the most genuine and most selfless artists who ever lived! How long am *I* to be spared? *Do* come next year. Sinding must join us too. (I dare say you know that he was in Copenhagen as well, and that next winter he is going to live at Brodsky's?)[4]

My wife sends you her kind regards.

As does your friend

Edvard Grieg.

Write soon!
I am looking forward to the songs!

Autograph letter, signed and dated. Envelope addressed: Fritz Delius *Esq.*/Claremont/*Bradford* /*England.* Postmark: BERGEN 9 VIII 88. Receiving postmark: BRADFORD AU 13 88. A musical phrase was pencilled by Delius on the back of the envelope.

1 Grieg had been invited to participate in the Birmingham Music Festival and was evidently eager to return to England to capitalize on his success in London in the spring and to earn some more British currency. He had re-scored *In Autumn* especially for the occasion and conducted it on 29 August; on the following day he conducted his *Holberg Suite.*

2 Frants Beyer (1851–1918) was Grieg's closest friend and neighbour. By profession a lawyer and by love and inclination a gifted amateur musician and musicologist, he was married to Marie ('Majs'), née Smith (1852–1925), who as well as helping him out at his office also shared his musical interests. No pair were closer to the Griegs, representing as they did an oasis of stability at home near Bergen while Edvard and Nina travelled widely and often lengthily elsewhere in Europe. Grieg's correspondence with Beyer is, in its affectionate spontaneity and authentic detail, a rich biographical resource.

3 Edmund Neupert (1842–88): Norwegian pianist, composer and teacher. The dedicatee of Grieg's Piano Concerto, he had given its first performance in 1869.

4 Gunnar Rugstad has dubbed Brodsky Sinding's 'angel of salvation' for having helped him not only by publicizing his work, but by offering him board and lodging in Leipzig during what was to be a decisive year

of his life, 1888–89. The impoverished Sinding was obliged to resist Delius's efforts to entice him to Paris, let alone to Spain or to Florida.

The Griegs, who had arrived back at Troldhaugen around the middle of June, had attended en route the first Nordic Music Festival, held in Copenhagen from 3–10 June. This was a pioneering event on a considerable scale, and at the opening concert Grieg had conducted the orchestra in a performance of his Piano Concerto, with Erika Lie Nissen as soloist. He also accompanied at a chamber concert some of his songs and the c minor Violin Sonata. Sinding's Piano Quintet, already highly regarded, was also performed at the festival, giving another important boost to its composer's reputation.

Delius, meanwhile, abandoning the idea of travelling to Spain, had taken himself off to spend the summer in Brittany, 'first at Perros-Guirec and afterwards at St Malo, where I did a good deal of work, only returning to Paris at the end of September.'

12. FRITZ DELIUS TO EDVARD GRIEG

chez Madam Chapalan
Sillon (Maison Insley)
St Malo.
(Ille & Vilaine)
[mid-August 1888]

My dear Grieg

Your letter was sent on here from Bradford, it came the day before yesterday & I cannot tell you how happy I was to hear something from you again. The same morning I got up thinking of you, as you had been wandering about with me the whole night. I also began to write a few things for string orchestra[1] & as I was at work your letter came. Now I ought to explain myself a little. I have decided not to go to Spain for the time being. I might not then be able to come to Norway next year, & that I am absolutely determined to do. Instead of going to Spain I calmly went to Brittany & I settled down at the seaside where I do a lot of bathing & a lot of work. It almost reminds me of Norway, there are so many cliffs, some places are very wild. I shall stay here until the middle or end of October & then go to Paris again, to my uncle's. Where I shall stay this winter I haven't yet decided. I hoped that you would want to come to Leipzig again & I would have come too, maybe I shall go there yet again. Perhaps I shall stay 2–3 months in Paris as there are the concerts to take in, & when I was last there they were over & I should like to hear the 9th Symphony at the Conservatoire, as they are supposed to do it tremendously well. I have also found a poet in Paris[2] who will write an opera for me, & I still have a lot to discuss with you. I shall write to you about this when everything is more definite. During the time I have been here I have dramatized *Zanoni*, the novel by Bulwer Lytton (I talked to you about it once) & am writing incidental music for it, as an opera it doesn't go well.[3] *Paa Vidderne* I will send to you as soon as I have finished some revisions. You say you will steal no notes from me. I believe that, Grieg. I really believe that you are incapable of stealing, notes at least. My friendship & sympathy you have already taken long since & I tell you frankly, never in my life have I met a nature which has won all my love as yours has. In my life I have been left so much to my own resources that I have become egotistic without realizing it & have really only cared about myself & worked for myself. You are the only man who has ever changed that & drawn my whole attention to you yourself & awakened the feelings which I now have for you. Now, take care of yourself, Grieg, & for a long time too, so that we may get to know each other still better. We must have many more splendid times together. Whenever you think of dying you must think that there is someone who holds you to this earth through the [strength][4] of his feelings. Poor Neupert, he must have been a real artist, now he too has joined the great host. I believe, however, that he would have lived much, much longer if he had only taken a little care of himself, I didn't know him, but heard a lot about him in America. How glad I shall be to set foot on Norwegian moorland again & to look out over the wide distances. Are we going to the Jotunheim? next summer? Yes! Sinding must come with us too — that will be splendid. You will receive the manuscripts as soon as possible. In the meantime farewell, & give my regards to your dear wife & also to your friend [Beyer?][4] whom indeed I do not know & write to me when you have the time & inclination. Good luck & a very pleasant stay in Birmingham is the wish of your friend

Fritz Delius

Autograph letter, signed and undated.

1   Probably the (since lost) three pieces for string orchestra (RT VI/4) referred to in Letter 14.
2   Unidentified.
3   The *Zanoni* incidental music was never to be finished, but an incomplete autograph draft score (RT I/1), with some cue lines, remains.
4   A number of words are obliterated in the original letter.

13.   FRITZ DELIUS TO EDVARD GRIEG

St Malo.
Bretagne.
chez Madam Chapalan
Sillon (Maison Insley)
[late August 1888]

My dear Grieg

I wrote to you at Trollhaugen after I received your last letter. Today I am writing simply to send you my sincere good wishes. I would just love to be with you now & hear I Höst.[1] Kind regards to your wife & Herr Beyer & fare well, I look forward to seeing you again at Trollhaugen

Your friend
Fritz Delius

Autograph letter, signed and undated.

1   *In Autumn.* In Norwegian in the original letter. Delius's letter was presumably addressed to Grieg in Birmingham. Frants Beyer had accompanied Grieg to the Festival.

14. FRITZ DELIUS TO EDVARD GRIEG

St Malo, (Ille et Vilaine)
chez Madam Chapalan
Sillon (Maison Insley)
[mid-September? 1888]

My dear Grieg,

Today I send you two more songs.[1] I am revising Paa Vidderne completely, as a melodrama in fact, with orchestral accompaniment.[2] I have already done the first two numbers. I was unhappy with it as it was. Would you like to see my first two numbers? in which case I will send them at once. But should you wish to wait you shall have the whole lot at the end of the month. I have also written three pieces for string orchestra & hope to hear them in Paris.

Are you coming to Paris this winter? I think I shall stay there & not go to Leipzig, I like it so much here in France. Please come & we shall explore Paris together. I have taken the liberty of dedicating 6 songs to your dear wife.[3] I have honestly never done so much as here in St Malo. I wish you were with me I have so much to show you & should awfully much love to see you again. Did you receive my telegram to Birmingham? along with letter? I am reading Peer Gynt again it really is sublime, in thought & execution.

Farewell until we meet again soon

Your friend
Fritz Delius

Kindest regards to your wife & also to the mountains
I am staying in St Malo until the end of October

Autograph letter, signed and undated.

1 See Letters 10 and 11. Delius appears to have sent Grieg a total of four songs. They will almost certainly have been from the two sets of *Songs from the Norwegian*, to be published in 1890 and 1892. None of the songs sent in the summer of 1888 was specifically identified by Delius by name (but see Letter 15, note 1).

2 'An original idea to make "På Vidderne" into a recitation. How did you hit on that?' asked Sinding on 6 October.

3 See Letter 38, note 1. On the autograph title-page of Delius's *Five*

Songs from the Norwegian, dated 1888, the figure '5' is written over an earlier '6'.

15.   EDVARD GRIEG TO FRITZ DELIUS

Troldhaugen
Hop Station
nr. Bergen, Norway
23 September 88.

My dear Delius,

Voilà! At last I sit in my distant corner of the world and have to thank you warmly for letter, for telegram, for songs and for all your expressions of friendly sentiments. Andersen says somewhere that man has talent or rather originality where an animal has instinct. But that is wrong. For man has both at the same time. My *instinct* told me from our first meeting that our sympathies were mutual. Very well then: next year! Yes indeed! I will do *all* I can to ensure that I have the pleasure of being able to receive you. No Music Festivals next summer! And Sinding must join us as well. Have you had any news of him? I have heard nothing from him for a long time. You have probably heard that he is supposed to be living at Brodsky's this winter. I think that is marvellous. — We are really delighted with your songs and my wife is most grateful to you for the dedication.[1] (Her name is *Nina*, not *Lina*.) How strange that I have set nearly all the texts too.[2] I find it very difficult to write and tell you all that I would like to say to you about the songs. But you will understand me better when we can meet and talk. There are so many beautiful and deeply felt things in them, — the passage

[3]

I just cannot forget, and will certainly show you one day that I

can steal after all. And then again there are other things which I find difficult to accept, not where ideas are concerned, for you never lack inventiveness, but in the form and in the treatment of the voice. A Norwegian melody and a Wagnerian treatment of the voice are dangerous things indeed to try to reconcile. But we can discuss this. Perhaps I am too narrow-minded. I am very much looking forward to the melodrama. There is much that is suitable for it, much that isn't. But the poem exerts such a strong appeal that one just cannot get it out of one's mind.

The overture 'In Autumn' sounded quite superb and its performance gave me great pleasure. After Christmas my wife and I will probably go to England again for a couple of months. I have been invited to conduct the suite from 'Peer Gynt' at the Philharmonic Society and to perform some of my chamber music at the Monday Popular Concerts. I shall try it once but I hope never again. I would much rather stay at home, but 'Troldhaugen' implores me most urgently to provide a few £ sterling![4]

Farewell, dear friend, and let us hear from you soon.

With our best wishes

Yours
Edvard Grieg

Autograph letter, signed and dated. Both envelope and notepaper bear the monogram EG. Envelope addressed: Monsieur Fritz Delius./chez Madame Chapalan/Sillon (Maison Insley)/*St Malo./France*. Postmark: BERGEN 24 IX 88. Receiving postmarks: Paris 28 SEPT.[88] and ST MALO 29[?] 9 [88].

1   The autograph manuscript of the *Five Songs* bears the title-page dedication 'Frau Nina Grieg gewidmet.'

2   See Letter 38, note 1 (*cf* also Letter 44, note 2).

3   The quotation is from 'Sehnsucht' (Longing), set by Delius to Edmund Lobendanz's translation of the original Norwegian poem by Theodor Kjerulf. It was to be published in 1890 as no. 4 of the *Five Songs from the Norwegian*. Kjerulf (1825–88) was brother of the composer Halfdan Kjerulf and was the leading Norwegian geologist of his time. Apart from his numerous geological writings and research studies, he found time to publish three collections of poems, in 1848, 1854 and 1866.

4   The cost of building and equipping his home had been considerably higher than Grieg had anticipated.

16. FRITZ DELIUS TO EDVARD GRIEG

St Malo, Oct 19/88

My dear Grieg,

Many thanks for your kind letter which gave me much pleasure. I definitely believe that mankind has instinct. My instinct has seldom led me astray, my reason often. When I first met you it was no longer instinct for I had already been acquainted with you so long through your music. I believe nothing reveals a human being so openly as music. A poet can (probably) dissemble but a composer must show himself, or nothing at all. You have absolutely no idea of how I look forward to next summer, when we will talk about all this. In the meantime I have written [. . .]¹ songs which I would like to add to the others as an album, since they are nearly all written in one mood. The poems appealed so much to me, & I was so much at home with them that I composed, without any hesitation, in the way which seemed most natural to me. All this we will discuss, so much do I attach to your criticism. Paa Vidderne was finished some time ago, next week I travel back to Paris & from there I will send you the score with some songs. I have a feeling that we will meet in Paris this winter. You must certainly see Paris one day: it is ten times more beautiful than London. My first Suite will be played in London this winter by August Manns.² You know that I prefer to live rather solitarily, that is, not in too big a place: One enjoys life more. Do you know what I have in mind, 'please don't faint': to live in Norway. That is 8 months in the year & 4 months in Leipzig or Paris. When I come to Norway I will look out for a nice place where I can live & work in peace. Perhaps you can help me find somewhere like this. Streets & smoke distort our ideas. One must breathe pure air before one can think purely. I feel so well in mind & body when nature is beautiful. Please take care this winter & do not exert yourself too [much]¹ for the sake of Pounds stirling. If you come to Paris I will take care of you & promise that you will have a wonderful time. My uncle is a splendid fellow. I can't do anything sensible in Paris, the environment is just not suitable.³

I hear from Sinding from time to time, he wrote to me a few

days ago & is happy at the Brodskys, they are, after all, splendid people. I am very glad that Brodsky has done this & has taken an interest in him. How he is going to get to Norway (he writes) 'the Devil only knows'. But something is bound to turn up. Well farewell, dear friend, & don't let me wait too long for your reply. Give my kind regards to your wife. I don't understand how I came to write Lina instead of Nina, I knew it perfectly well. My address is

43 Rue Cambon, *Paris*.

Stay well & write soon

Your friend
[Fritz Delius][1]

Autograph letter, signature missing, dated.

1   A number of words are obliterated in the original letter.

2   August Manns (1825–1907): German-born conductor of the Crystal Palace Saturday Concerts. He was to write to Delius on 14 March 1889 explaining that — at least for the time being — he and his orchestra could not spare the time for the *Florida* suite and that score and parts were therefore being returned. No other intimation that Manns ever intended to perform the work has been found.

3   Delius was to move early in November. 'As I found living with my uncle (his luxurious life) hindered me considerably in my work, I went out to Ville d'Avray and hired a small chalet on the lake and spent the winter there doing a great deal of work.'

17.   EDVARD GRIEG TO FRITZ DELIUS

Troldhaugen,
Hop Station nr. Bergen,
6th November 88.

My dear Delius,

Even without having received your kind letter, I would have written to you to say that on closer acquaintance I see your songs quite differently. The less flattering this fact is for *me*, the more so it is for *you* and for *your songs*. They show such fine feeling, and I shall never be so foolish as not to see that this is the main thing.

How delighted I am that your Suite is to be played by Manns this winter. You will then have more speedy success than most other mortals. But let us now talk of Norway. Your suggestion flatters my patriotism, as it does my feeling of friendship for you, but let us, however, turn the matter the other way around: 4 months in Norway (in summer) and 8 in Germany and France. We shall discuss in the summer which spot to choose in Norway. I hope it will be somewhere near me.

As far as sterling is concerned, it's all very well for you to talk, dear friend! It's precisely because of this that I *must* make every effort. I most certainly don't do so for pleasure. It is ridiculous that I should have to play, for I have no talent for playing in public. However, the Pounds sterling do not come in from conducting. — Your idea that we meet again in Paris this winter has no hope of being fulfilled, of this I am quite sure, for I am fully engaged during the winter months. At the end of January I am conducting at a Bülow Concert in Berlin, and from there it's straight on to Liverpool and London.

Yesterday at Troldhaugen I had the pleasure of spending a pleasant day with some distinguished artists. They were Herr Cesar Thomson (violinist)[1] and de Greef (pianist)[2], who are just now giving concerts in Scandinavia. A cosmopolitan breath of air like this does one good, but — I must confess — the peace and quiet of the countryside is even better for one afterwards! There is only one objection to my present existence: I can hear no orchestra. But that's just another inconvenience I suffer daily!

— I still haven't heard anything from Sinding. Well, if this is because he's writing more music, he has my forgiveness, but not otherwise.

Best wishes. From my wife too

Yours
Edvard Grieg.

Autograph letter, signed and dated. Envelope addressed: Mr. Fritz Delius./43, Rue Cambon/*Paris*. Postmark: BERGEN 6 XI[?] 88.

1   César Thomson (1857–1931): Belgian violinist, at this time professor at the Liège Conservatoire.
2   Arthur de Greef (1862–1940): Belgian pianist and composer, at this time professor at the Brussels Conservatoire. De Greef was to become a good friend of Grieg and a champion of his music.

18. FRITZ DELIUS TO EDVARD GRIEG

Chalet des Lilas
à la Chaumière
Ville d'Avray
(Seine & Oise)
[mid-November 1888]

My dear Grieg

Your letter gave me great pleasure & I thank you for your kind words concerning my songs. Indeed, you do not know how glad I am that you have had some pleasure from my songs, especially as *you* have given me so much enjoyment & pleasure through your music. So I will try to pay you something back. I have been in Ville d'Avray for a week now, 35 minutes by train from Paris. I have rented a small 2-roomed cottage, it stands quite alone on the bank of a small lake in a wood. So I am at work again. Close by there is a small restaurant where I eat. It is really lovely here, not a soul & all around woods & hills. You would think a 100 miles from Paris. The concerts have already begun. Next Sunday your Concerto is to be played at the Lamoureux[1] by René Chansarel.[2] I shall of course be there & give you a report. When will you leave Bergen — surely not before Christmas? I would love us all to be together again like last Christmas. Have you received Paa Vidderne? I have not looked through it carefully yet, & the songs too are the first sketches. I am already looking forward to next summer, do your gymnastics thoroughly & take care in London. I hope that the Pounds stirling will flow in. I am tremendously sorry that you cannot come to Paris, you really would enjoy it, it is 10,000 times nicer here than in Germany, more free, no comparison at all. Perhaps I shall come to London for a few days but I don't know yet. It would be lovely if you were already there.

I have heard nothing at all from Sinding for some time. He still hasn't replied to my last letter. But he likes it very much at Brodsky's. A young Norwegian Arvesen, a violinist, is studying in Paris with Marsick,[3] I think you saw him in Leipzig. When you were in Aberdeen you will certainly have seen Halvorsen. How is he getting on?

Farewell now, write soon. I hope that you & your wife are

in very good health. My best wishes go to both of you

Your friend,
Fritz Delius

Autograph letter, signed and undated.

1   Charles Lamoureux (1834–99): French conductor and violinist. In 1881 he founded in Paris the series of concerts that was eventually to bear his name.
2   René Chansarel: pianist at the Concerts Lamoureux and composer of piano pieces. He was the dedicatee of Debussy's *Fantaisie* for piano and orchestra.
3   Martin P. Jos. Marsick (1848–1924): Belgian violinist and composer, and professor at the Paris Conservatoire.

19.   EDVARD GRIEG TO FRITZ DELIUS

Troldhaugen, Hop Station
nr. Bergen, Norway
23 Nov 88

Dear D.

This card just to tell you that the score and the songs have arrived safely. It is probably your only copy of the score. I am very much looking forward to acquainting myself with the work, have up to now only skimmed through it. My heartfelt thanks for the dedication![1] How long am I allowed to keep it? We are off at the beginning of January via Kristiania[2] and Copenhagen to Berlin, where I have to conduct at a Bülow Concert.

With kind regards

Yours
Edvard Grieg.

I like the songs very much! Geibel's O schneller mein Ross! is splendid![3]
Write soon.

Autograph postcard, signed and dated. Addressed: Mr. Fritz Delius./ 43, Rue Cambon./*Paris*. Postmark: BERGEN 23 XI 88.

1   The title-page of the autograph full score of *Paa Vidderne*, dated 1888, bears the dedication 'Edvard Grieg gewidmet'.

2   Christiania (after King Christian IV of Denmark) until 1877; the K-form was then adopted by the government for administrative use. Twenty years later the city itself followed suit, Kristiania replacing Christiania in all official documents. Many older Norwegians continued to resist change, and the two forms co-existed until they were finally superseded, on 1 January 1925, by 'Oslo'.

3   'O schneller, mein Ross!' (RT V/7), composed in 1888, is a setting of three short verses from a poem by the German writer, Emanuel (von) Geibel (1815–84). Again it is not possible to identify the other songs.

20.   FRITZ DELIUS TO EDVARD GRIEG

Chalet des Lilas
à la Chaumière.
Ville d'Avray.
(Seine & Oise)
Tuesday. [27 November 1888]

My dear Grieg.

I enclose the programme of the Lamoureux Concert. Unfortunately I had a very bad seat, & could only really hear the fortissimos, all the delicate touches & nuances were lost to me. The soloist seemed to be well versed technically, but not much power & (so it seemed to me) not very musical. In short, for me it did not sound anything like as in London. It also seemed that the conductor & the soloist didn't understand each other very well, as the soloist continually came in more slowly than the conductor left off, which sounded very painful. Nevertheless there was very great applause after each movement. But the composition is so dear to me that I must hear it played in a quite different way. Where the orchestra was concerned it was splendid. Sinding wrote to me the day before yesterday in rather a sad mood, I fear he cannot work much at Brodsky's. His Quintet will be played on the 12th January. He writes, 'It will probably be drowned by whistles, should be a lot of fun for me'[1] I think that there will be a revolution here very soon — everything is getting ready for it. It will be interesting to join in. The reason is that Boulanger[2] has become tremendously popular & he wants to have a revision of the Government. You will see him becoming Dictator or Consul. Next Sunday is the anniversary of the death of a famous Republican *Baudin*[3]. They are afraid there will be a great deal of unrest. It is quite wintry here, all the leaves have already fallen, only a few birch trees look cheerful

Farewell my dear friend & please give my kind regards to your wife.

Yours
Fritz Delius

Autograph letter, signed and undated.

1   In their correspondence, Sinding and Delius were now also discussing the possibility of together visiting Grieg in the summer of 1889. On 6 October Sinding had written: 'I can say nothing yet about our getting together at Grieg's next summer. The Devil alone knows where I might be by then.' On 22 November he continued in the same vein: 'I don't yet know if I can come to Grieg's in the summer. The Lord leadeth me, or maybe it's the Devil. I don't care two hoots. But for the moment I certainly don't lead myself, and this annoys me mightily. Just how much I should like to come, if I can, I hardly need tell you.'

2   General Georges Ernest Boulanger (1837–91): French Minister of War. A nationalist and so-called 'révisionniste', he was to be accused of plotting and was forced to flee from his homeland in 1889 to Brussels.

3   Jean-Baptiste Baudin (1811–51): Deputy in the Legislative Assembly at the time of the Second Republic. Following a coup d'état, he was killed on the barricades on 3 December 1851.

21.   EDVARD GRIEG TO FRITZ DELIUS

Bergen, Norway.
9th December 1888.

Dear Delius,

I really ought not to write to you today, for I am in very low spirits. I am doing so nevertheless (avoiding, of course, effusions of pessimism) as I should like to say a few words about the melodrama. I have read it and re-read it and in it have found splendid music indeed. A pity that the general run of performance would fall short of your intentions. You see, you have composed with an unbelievable lack of consideration for the declaimer, and I am convinced that this lack of consideration will exact a cruel revenge if ever you should put the piece to the test. In my opinion this is precisely what is unfortunate about melodrama: namely that one cannot make *music*, absolute music. All the time fantasy has to lie on a

Procrustean bed. It is only if one does not disdain these considerations that one can make it effective, otherwise not. You have added a note, which is sufficient proof that you have entertained some secret fear.[1] But what are you to think, if the beautiful, passionate passages have to be played piano in order for the voice to be heard? You will not hear what you thought you would hear. I think that with regard to the way in which you have conceived the music, you ought rather perhaps to have taken a *singing* voice. Am I wrong? Possibly. But I do not think so, as far as my experience goes. In a melodrama I took every possible consideration myself, and yet, — after the first orchestral rehearsal I had to make alterations.[2] For the very *first* thing is: people must be able to follow the poem in an entirely natural and effortless way, otherwise the listener has no satisfaction. The conflict between *voice* and *music* is frightfully unpleasant. And how *fantastically* little it takes to mask the voice. How I wish we could hear a rehearsal together! One or two things will come over very well, — it is only as concerns the piece as a whole that I have my doubts. I hope that you will not only forgive me for speaking quite frankly, but that you will indeed expect it of me. Is this not so? For happily our friendly relationship rests on more than mere formality. And quite independently of this: whether rightly or wrongly: I have an aversion to kid gloves in any form!

How marvellously well you must have established yourself in Paris! Indeed it sounds quite ideal. Something like this I must do one day too. I heard from Sinding a few days ago as well. He certainly seems to feel quite at home at the Brodskys. But he doesn't mention his work there. Of course he must come to me in the summer. All in good time, as we say. I have acquired a little old square piano for my lonely room in the 'Troldthal',[3] on which he can hammer away. While on the subject of pianos: Just imagine my surprise: A few days ago the firm of Pleyel in Paris, which I do not know at all, sent me a wonderful grand piano as a present! The man can't be quite right in the head! I hope you will have the opportunity of admiring this beautiful instrument at Troldhaugen in the summer. It stands in my big room, alongside an old Pleyel grand, and really takes up far too much space. I hope I shall now be able to do a concerto for 2 pianos. I have just finished the instrumentation for a choral piece.[4] It is really the first act of an opera, for which Bjørnson wrote the text many years ago. I drafted the music immediately — and then I heard not a word more. In order to rescue this fragment, I am turning it into a choral piece, and it is going quite well. It deals with the Norwegian king Olav Trygvason, or rather with the Norwegian people awaiting this violent importer of Christianity.

At the beginning of January I move from here. From then on my address is: C.F. Peters, Thalstrasse 10, Leipzig. That does not necessarily mean that I shall go to Leipzig quite yet, but the letters will be sent on to me.

Write soon. And forgive me: The pessimism that was to have been avoided has perhaps after all crept into my discussion of the melodrama!

Kind regards

Yours
Edvard Grieg

Thank you very much for the letters, and for the news of the Concerto performance. When and where would you like the score of the melodrama to be sent?

Autograph letter, signed and dated. Envelope addressed: Mr. Fritz Delius./Chalet des Lilas/à la Chaumière/Ville d'Avray./*Seine & Oise/ France*. Postmark: BERGEN (date obscured). Receiving postmark: VILLE D'AVRAY 15 DEC 88.

1 'The conductor is throughout particularly requested to take into consideration the strength of the reciter's voice & whenever necessary to reduce slightly the volume of orchestral sound.'

2 *Bergliot*, melodrama for orchestra, op.42. It was originally set for spoken declamation and piano in 1871 to a poem by Bjørnstjerne Bjørnson published only the previous year; Grieg orchestrated the work in 1885. Writing to Max Abraham on 25 July 1886, Grieg expressed the view that it would be an honour to him if Peters would publish it: 'I quite see, however, that works like this do not sell as well as piano pieces at present. And yet I believe in their future.' Peters issued it in 1887, and Grieg told Julius Röntgen on 2 October that year: 'If you have a good tragic actress, I should like some time to try out my melodrama "Bergliot", which has just been published.' His setting certainly takes rather more care with the relationship and balance between human voice and orchestra than does *Paa Vidderne*.

3 Grieg had had a small wooden cabin constructed. It was sited well below the house and at the waterside, where he could compose without distraction. 'Komponisthytten' had little in the way of creature com-

forts, but a 'lonely room' (like that he had had at Lofthus) was almost a prerequisite for Grieg, who was particularly sensitive to sounds and sights that might disturb him while at work.

4 *Scenes from Olav Trygvason*, for soloist, chorus and orchestra. Grieg was to conduct the first performance in Christiania on 19 October 1889.

22.   FRITZ DELIUS TO EDVARD GRIEG

Chalet des Lilas
à la Chaumière
Ville d'Avray
(Seine & Oise)
[mid-December 1888]

My dear Grieg,

Thank you very much for your kind letter & candid criticism. It pleased me perhaps a lot more than you think for it has shown me that you are the person I always thought you to be. How good it does one to discover that about someone whom one esteems — & loves. What you wrote about the melodrama I rather thought myself, especially after having heard a piece at the Theatre Francais, the music almost always pp. I must tell you that I had not seen a single work in this genre before I composed 'Paa Vidderne', for that reason I wrote the whole thing so that I could easily write a voice part for it. Please keep the score until you come to England & if you will be so good as to bring it with you I shall, I hope, come & fetch it myself. I should also like to ask you to bring the songs as I should like to make a copy, since they are the only ones, & I do not even have any sketches. I was so glad to hear that you have a short work ready, perhaps you will have it performed in London? & I hope I shall get to hear it then. Were you really serious when you wrote to me about writing a double concerto or rather a concerto for two pianos, that would be simply marvellous. I hope you have already started it. I think that you could get splendid effects. To get a grand piano like that as a present is not bad at all, you ought rather to say that Pleyel must be perfectly right in the head. I have a String Quartet[1] ready & have sent it to Sinding to give it to Brodsky. In the summer Sinding & I will turn up in Bergen. How I long for the summer. It's pretty cold here & I've caught a fine old cold.

It's marvellous in my chalet, but rather damp, & as I have just finished my Quartet I am staying here for a few days. (Perhaps you don't know that I am at the moment at my uncle's in Paris) Please write to Ville d'Avray. I wish you & your dear wife a merry Christmas & *many* more New Years.[2] Farewell & I hope to see you again soon.

Yours
Fritz Delius

Write a few lines soon. I think the only improvement that Christ & Christianity have brought with them is Christmas. As people really then think a little about others. Otherwise I feel that he had better not have lived at all. The world has not got any better, but worse & more hypocritical, & I really believe that Christianity has produced an overall sub-mediocrity & really only taught people the meaning of fear.

Farewell, dear Grieg.

Autograph letter, signed and undated, written on notepaper headed 23 RUE CHAUCHAT (crossed out by Delius).

1   String Quartet (RT VIII/1). Of the sole autograph manuscript of this work of Delius's, only the last two movements — and some eleven bars of the second movement — have survived. Sinding thought it 'damned good', but proposed a number of alterations — some double-stops, for example, being unplayable as Delius had originally written them. He did not succeed, however, in getting Brodsky and his quartet to give it an airing.

2   Seasonal greetings went from Delius to Sinding, too, with instructions to pass them further, as Camilla Jacobsen was to visit Leipzig. 'I'll go and see Frl. Jacobsen today and give her your regards', wrote Sinding on 22 December. 'Shall much enjoy seeing her again. I also much enjoyed what you wrote about the female altruist. I might have guessed it would turn out like that.' Sinding added that he was 'reasonably sure' of being able to join Delius at Grieg's in the summer. He was to write again, with a note of regret, on 13 January 1889: 'Had very much looked forward to seeing Frl. Jacobsen here. But I'm afraid she didn't come, went to Bremen I believe it was, according to what Frl. Holmsen told me.' Any guess about the episode of the 'female altruist' would be idle speculation, but Sinding's mention of Borghild Holmsen (1865–1938) is a rare reference to another of the 'Leipzig' Norwegians who came into Delius's orbit. She was a composer and pianist from Ekeberg who, following studies in Leipzig and Berlin, made her debut in Christiania in 1888 with a concert of her own compositions.

23. EDVARD GRIEG TO FRITZ DELIUS

Bergen, Norway
30 December 88.

My dear Delius,

At the same time as I send you these lines I am posting to your address a parcel containing 'På Vidderne' and 'I Höst'. The songs are not with them, I am afraid, the reason being as follows: We left Troldhaugen a fortnight ago owing to an outbreak amongst the local countrypeople of an infectious disease (diphtheria). I was there this morning and looked for the songs, but in vain: they are lying about somewhere under legions of other scores, and I just could not find them, in spite of a good deal of hunting around. Do please forgive me. If only I had known that you needed the songs, then I would have put them on one side with the melodrama. The songs stood open on the grand piano for months — proof that they have not been mislaid. So you will have to be patient until the summer. Just think what Dr. Abraham[1] has sent me: the Tannhäuser score printed from Wagner's own handwriting, (exists in only a few copies)[2] but that's not all, for this copy is a present from Wagner to a friend of his youth. Not only has he himself written in it, but he has also drawn on the title-page a picture of himself when young.

We are leaving Bergen on the 2nd January, and going via Kristiania and Copenhagen to Leipzig. After a few days there we are going on to Berlin.[3] I hardly know what will happen after that, for I feel much too run down. Is there any medicine in Paris to strengthen a weak stomach that can keep nothing down? Should there be one, I shall turn up in Paris personally 'out of gratitude'.

And you have written a string quartet! Wonderful time, this time of youth, when it just pours out of one's heart in one long stream! 'Oh, if only it were to stay like this for ever!' And now farewell, and I wish you from my heart a happy New Year 'mit Wiedersehen'

Yours
Edvard Grieg.

Autograph letter, signed and dated. Envelope addressed: Mr. Fritz

Delius./Chalet des Lilas/à la Chaumière/Ville d'Avray/(*Seine & Oise*)/ *France*. Postmark: BERGEN 3 [. . .]. Receiving postmark: VILLE D'AVRAY 5 JANV 89.

1   Dr Max Abraham (1831–1900): head of the publishing house of C.F. Peters, of Leipzig. His relationship with Grieg was close, devoted and productive, but with Grieg's piano pieces being so eminently saleable, Abraham's pressure on the composer to produce ever more in the genre may ultimately have deprived us of more orchestral works. Sinding, too, was to complain of the demands made on him in 'the song and piano piece factory'.

2   The first full-score edition of *Tannhäuser* was made by the relatively cheap method of auto-lithography, as opposed to engraving. This was the only case where Wagner made the lithograph masters himself, and just 100 copies were printed. Max Abraham's gift was indeed a generous one. (I take the opportunity here to set right an error, based in part on an earlier translator's version of this letter, which occurs in my *Delius: A Life in Letters* 1, p.36, where the *Tannhäuser* score is simply described as 'autographed' by Wagner.)

3   'Grieg and his wife are coming here in a fortnight,' Sinding was to tell Delius on 16 January. 'He is conducting at a Bülow Concert in Berlin on Monday, I believe. Am much looking forward to seeing him again.'

24.   FRITZ DELIUS TO EDVARD GRIEG

Chalet des Lilas
à la Chaumière
Ville d'Avray
(Seine & Oise)
[31? December 1888]

My dear Grieg,

Just a few words to say 'Happy New Year' to you & your wife & to wish & hope that you will enjoy very good health throughout the coming year, both of you. How time passes! a whole year has gone by since we were together at my place on the 4th floor in the Harkortstrasse & drank Benedictine punch & the ringing of bells filled the room when we all raised our glasses, & we shall, I know, be together at many more New Years.[1] Let's see now whether I am not right. I might almost go so far as to say that I would eat 'Reckling' with pleasure if only I were up there in the North with you now. It is not impossible that I shall meet you in London 'at the beginning of February', didn't you say? & not impossible too that you may get to hear my symphonic poem 'Hiawatha'.[2] I have written to Herr Manns about it, & I should very much like you to hear it. I am about to start on something about which I shall write a little later. In the meantime accept my very best wishes & give my kindest regards to Frau Grieg

Yours
Fritz Delius

Autograph letter, signed and undated.

1   Grieg, too, was in nostalgic mood when he wrote to Halvorsen on 31 December: 'I also remembered that last splendid Christmas Eve we had together at Leipzig. That was surely once and for all. But — never mind! We'll fix a Summer Eve at Troldhaugen instead. Delius is coming. Sinding, don't know [. . .] And Halvorsen will come too! [. . .] Time and place to meet we can decide later.' [Autograph letter in Bergen Public Library. 'Never mind' is in English in the original.]

2   *Hiawatha*, 'a tone poem for Orchestra after Longfellow's poem' (RT VI/6), exists in a now defective autograph manuscript dated '1888 Januar'. As noted earlier, Grieg presumably saw the score while in Leipzig. There is no record of August Manns' reaction to the piece.

25.   FRITZ DELIUS TO EDVARD GRIEG

Chalet des Lilas
à la Chaumière
Ville d'Avray
(Seine & Oise)
[early January 1889]

My dear Grieg,

I was delighted with i Höst, really delighted, & thank you very much for it: I was tremendously interested to look at the work in score form & how I should love to hear it: Many thanks too for PV. The songs can wait up there until I fetch them, I am in no hurry: I am very sorry that you have taken so much trouble about them; had I known this, I wouldn't have written to you about them, for whether I have them now or in 6 months' time is immaterial. The Tannhäuser score must be colossally interesting & I will be mindful to take a good look at it. That's what I call a lovely Christmas present. I am delighted with Dr Abraham. Please give him my regards. Just you come to Paris & try at least to get rid of your stomach complaint. Paris is splendid for stomach complaints & some very famous specialists live here. You must come; you won't regret it. I have a proposition to make: come here at the beginning of May; then we will see the World Exhibition[1] as well; afterwards I shall travel to the North with you. But if you cannot wait so long, come as soon as you can & I promise to show you things which are really *only* to be seen here. Please write & tell me if you can come. Latterly I too have not been well & little inclined to work. Please give my regards to your wife & let me hear very soon from you with best wishes

Yours
Fritz Delius

Have you read 'Brand' by Ibsen & 'Beyond Our Power' by Bjornsen?[2] What a different interpretation of the same material. In my opinion Ibsen is one of the greatest minds of this century, if not *the greatest.* He is the *only one* who handles the Christian religion & its history without kid gloves & says what he really feels without beating about the bush & without regard for anything at all.

Autograph letter, signed and undated.

1   The Universal Exhibition of 1889 in Paris. Its lasting monument was the Eiffel Tower.
2   Delius's persistent misspelling of Bjørnson's name is to be found frequently in all but the most recent editions of his songs.

26.   EDVARD GRIEG TO FRITZ DELIUS

Leipzig, 4th February
1889
Hentschels Hotel.

My dear Delius,

Just imagine: at noon today I was sitting with my wife for the first time again in the Panorama! It really was melancholic! The same surroundings, the same waiters, who addressed us as old friends, the same bowing proprietor, the same good roast hare and bad red wine, all very full of atmosphere, and yet, as I said, melancholic, for we just could not rid ourselves of our memories. Did we think of you, you may ask? On the whole Leipzig seems surprisingly quiet to me this time round. But that is by no means unpleasant, as I do need a rest. I have come from Berlin, where I much enjoyed conducting some of my works. Just imagine, the rush to attend the last concert was so great that *hundreds* were turned away. The critics were abusive, but it was a success nevertheless, and a very considerable one. And I have become so blasé that the approval of an unbiased audience is worth more to me than all the critics put together, no matter whether they rage or praise. In the middle of February we are going to London where, come what may, we stay until the middle of March. My address there is: 5, the Cedars, Clapham Common, c/o Mr. G. Augener. But after that we must have some peace and quiet, and no Paris, at least for this winter. We are thinking about perhaps going back to Leipzig for a while, until spring returns to the North, but all that has yet to be decided. Anyway, as you can well imagine, we have certainly had a hard time of it.

We left Bergen on the 21st January, went by sleigh over the mountains in a dreadful (but magnificent) snowstorm and after 6 days arrived in Kristiania, where my wife fell ill, indeed seriously so. We were supposed just to be passing through, but I stayed for a week, after which I had to go on alone because I had rehearsals in Berlin. I felt very dejected on the journey. Fortunately, however, my wife came on a week later.

We consulted celebrated doctors, but it's always the same story: the learned ones are unable to agree! Have you read Tolstoy's 'Thoughts on the Purpose of Life'? He has a word or two for the learned gentlemen. You ask if I have read Brand! 20 years ago! And 'Beyond our Power'! That too, I should think about 5 years ago, when it came out. It is an ingeniously conceived work, but in its execution nowhere near as consummate as Ibsen in his dramas. His latest work is 'The Lady from the Sea', an original, characteristically Ibsenish thing, which must have a tremendous effect on the stage. And the strangest thing is: it has a mystical, almost romantic keynote, which is certainly at least influenced by Hypnotism.

You must keep well! For goodness' sake: don't do anything silly! Think of the wonderful summer and our reunion in Norway. Sinding is looking forward to it immensely. Isn't it wonderful that his Quintet has had such an outstanding success. It is probably decisive for his whole future.[1] Yesterday (just between you and me) I wrote an application to the Norwegian Parliament for a Civil Pension of the same sort as I have (i.e. for life) for him. One must strike while the iron's hot. I really am hopeful that it will work.

And now fare well (and carefully, despite your youth) so that we can enjoy meeting again.

My wife joins me in sending warmest regards

Yours
Edvard Grieg.

Autograph letter, signed and dated. Envelope addressed: Mr. Fritz Delius/Chalet des Lilas/à la Chaumière/Ville d'Avray/(Seine & Oise.)/ *France*. Readdressed: *43 rue Cambon*/Paris. Originating postmark obscured. Receiving postmarks: VALENCIENNES [. . .] 6 FEVR 89 and PARIS DÉPART 7 FEVR 89.

1 Sinding had written to Delius on 21 January about the performance: 'The Quintet has been played and was a complete success, something I would never have considered possible here. Even had the honour of being called to the directors' box with Busoni after the performance, and both of us had many nice things said to us. [. . .] I doubt that I shall experience quite such a performance again. As for Busoni, he's a devil of a fellow, a genius. He's going to be an artist of tremendous importance.' Sinding returned to the subject in his next letter, dated 26 January: 'I saw for myself that Reinecke was deeply offended. And Frl. Holmsen told me that Jadassohn was trembling with fury during his lesson, although he wasn't even at the concert.' Sinding left Leipzig for Berlin on 27 January to meet Grieg and Erika Nissen, who was to play Grieg's Concerto there. 'Shall also call on Frl. Jacobsen.'

27. FRITZ DELIUS TO EDVARD GRIEG

43 Rue Cambon
Paris.
[February 1889]

My dear Grieg

I was delighted with your letter: that you are well & had such great joy & success in Berlin. If one asks oneself just once, What have the critics ever done that is great or good one must honestly say, nothing, & they therefore have no significance: perhaps an apparent one but certainly not a real one.[1] It is like the gravy from a good roast hare, if it is good you leave it & eat it with the meat, but if it is bad you can pour it away.

The roast hare itself is always there. When I read about your dinner at the Panorama, the whole scene came back to me again, I played whist again, drank Benedictine & joined in our walks together along the Promenade. What wonderful memories. Last Saturday Arvesen a violinist, & Soot[2] a Norwegian painter came over to me at Ville d'Avray. We played your C minor Sonata together, which also brought back many memories to me. At midnight we took a walk in the woods, there was very beautiful moonlight & a hard frost. I am now staying in Paris again for a few days to get rid of my cold, & am much better. I am looking forward to our meeting in Norway as never before. I should think it quite certain that Sinding will come too. Yes, as you said, it is marvellous that he has had such a brilliant success, & it is also marvellous that you have done what you write to me about. That is what I love about you Grieg & you do not know how highly I esteem you for such an act. I believe too that his success will have a great influence on his whole career. If only he can get an Author's Pension![3] I shall acquire Tolstoy's work. If you have not yet read it, please buy '*The Conventional Lies*' by *Max Nordau*[4] right away. You *must* read the work, it is magnificent. Perhaps I am crazy, but I am writing incidental music for Emperor & Galilean[5]. I believe I shall work quietly in Ville d'Avray until, døde piene,[6] I sit myself down on the steamer to Norway.

I hope that your wife is better now. Was it the same kind of attack as she had in Leipzig? These damned experts always make me angry when I hear about them. They act as if they could do heaven only knows what & at the end they can do nothing. Find out oneself what one can & cannot put up with, live moderately, eat little meat, lots of fish & vegetables & I think one would seldom need a doctor. For these learned gentlemen only look wise & try one thing & another, until they try you into the grave itself. Adieu dear Grieg. Give my kind regards to your wife & Sinding as well, I will be writing to him too as soon as possible

Yours
Fritz Delius

Autograph letter, signed and undated.

1   Grieg had conducted on 21 and 29 January two Berlin Philharmonic concerts which had included *In Autumn*, the *Peer Gynt Suite* no.1, the *Two Elegiac Melodies* and the Piano Concerto. In spite of his complaints, reviews had on the whole been very good.

2   Eyolf Soot (1858–1928): Norwegian painter. He had spent his younger years in America, but after art studies in Norway and Germany he moved in the early 1880s to Paris to study with Bonnat. He was now painting not very far away from Ville d'Avray, in and around Saint-Cloud. In 1889 he was awarded a silver medal at the Paris Exhibition and painted an excellent portrait of his aunt and uncle, *Jonas Lie and his wife*. He was to marry Bjørnson's niece Inga Bjørnson in 1892.

3   *Dichter Gage* in the original letter.

4   Max Simon Nordau (1859–1923): born in Budapest, he trained as a doctor. His *Conventional Lies of Society* was published in 1883 and attacked current ethical, religious and political principles. Two later works, *Paradoxes* (1886) and *Degeneration* (1893), added further to his reputation.

5   *Emperor and Galilean*, Ibsen's largest-scale drama, was published in 1873. None of Delius's work on it appears to have survived.

6   *By Jove*. In Norwegian in the original letter (but more properly *død og pine*).

28.   EDVARD GRIEG TO FRITZ DELIUS

5, the Cedars
Clapham Common
London.
24 Feb. 89

Dear Delius,

You have been working too hard. That's what's behind it all. Or else: Où est la femme!? You must do gymnastics every morning. It is gold most precious because it puts one in a better frame of mind and improves one's powers of resistance.

I had my first Popular Concert yesterday. Played my Cello Sonata with Piatti,[1] as famous as he is boring (between you and me). It was absolute torture for me. The hall was crowded and the enthusiasm great. My poor wife was not well but nevertheless had to sing, as well as she could in the circumstances. But it is also so very cold inside the houses here that any singer is bound to catch cold. Tomorrow I have my 2nd Popular Concert, I am playing with Mad. Neruda.[2] Thank goodness there is fire and vitality there. On Wednesday we go to Manchester, Queens Hotel, in order to perform with Hallé[2] (you will probably recall that his wife played with me last year, and — noblesse oblige!) The concert is on Thursday. Hallé is playing my Concerto(!?) which I have to conduct, along with the Elegiac Melodies, then I have to play a sonata with Mad. Neruda and my wife is to sing.

On Friday we go to London again, where on the 9th March I have the 3rd Popular Concert and on the 14th the Philharm. Soc. Here I am conducting my Peer Gynt Suite. How nice if you were to be here then. On the 9th March, when I have finished with the damned piano playing, I'll be as happy as a sandboy. I hope you will be here by then, in order to spend a little time with the boy.

Kindest regards from us both.

Yours
Edvard Grieg

Regards please to your parents and to your little sister, who looked so much like you.

Autograph letter, signed and dated.

1   Alfredo Piatti (1822–1901): Italian cellist and composer. From 1844 he was a frequent visitor to London, settling there in 1880. One of Delius's boyhood memories was of hearing Piatti, whom his father had entertained — just as he entertained the violinist Joseph Joachim — at home in Bradford.

2   Charles Hallé (1819–95) had married the Bohemian violinist Wilhelmina (Wilma) Norman-Neruda (1839–1911) in 1888, the year of his knighthood. For each it was a second marriage. Both had been child prodigies, Hallé as a pianist. Born in Hagen, Germany, he settled in Manchester in 1848, founding some ten years later the great orchestra and series of concerts that bear his name. One of the most vivid memories of Delius's boyhood years was of hearing the Hallé Orchestra play, under its founder, Wagner's *Ride of the Valkyries*.

29. EDVARD GRIEG TO FRITZ DELIUS

Mr F. Delius and Compagnon is admitted to the *artist-room* this evening.

Edvard Grieg

14/3/89

Autograph pencilled note, written in English on printed visiting card, unsigned and dated.

A degree of chronological confusion reigns over this particular period of Delius's life. We know that around the middle of December he had caught a chill and had gone up to Paris to stay with his uncle for a few days. Early in January he had told Grieg: 'Latterly I too have not been well & little inclined to work.' A month or so later, he had informed Grieg that he felt much better, but was nonetheless in Paris for a few days once again, specifically to 'get rid of' his cold. At just this stage, it may well have been that Theodor Delius took alarm at his nephew's precarious state of health and wrote to his brother and sister-in-law recommending a return home, at least for the time being. So Delius was probably packed off to Bradford around the middle of February to spend, as he himself put it 'a few weeks with my family' and presumably still unable to shake off what seems likely to have been a respiratory infection of some kind. During this period he had 'spent a fortnight at Ilkley at the Wells House, a hydropathic establishment.'

When Grieg met one of Delius's sisters, presumably together with her parents (see Letter 28, postscript) and perhaps even at his London concert the day before, Delius was possibly recuperating at Ilkley at the time. We cannot be sure, since no envelope that might have confirmed his current address has survived, but it seems very likely. Delius did, however, manage to get to Grieg's concert at the Free Trade Hall in Manchester on 28 February, when the main item on the programme was the Piano Concerto, with Hallé as soloist.

Unfortunately, much later in life Delius managed to confuse the picture by remembering, when talking to Percy Grainger, his return home to Bradford (as well as his attendance at Grieg's Manchester concert) as having taken place in March, rather than February. He made no mention of seeing Grieg again in London at the Philharmonic Society's concert of 14 March; and he furthermore remembered 'going back to Paris in April, when I stayed with my uncle again.'

Letters from Sinding in March do however contain one clue to Delius's whereabouts. Writing from Leipzig on the 16th, he addressed his friend at 43 rue Cambon: 'Are you dead or are you still alive? Grieg told me that you had gone to Paris because of your health, and I begin to fear that you are really ill. Do send a few lines and tell me how you are.' Sinding's envelope, notable in that it was not re-addressed to England, bore a Paris receiving postmark of 17 March. Only three days later he again wrote from Leipzig, having clearly already received a reassuring reply from his friend: 'I was very glad to hear from you once again, and that you are not ill, as I had feared. But you are tired, too?' His letter ends: 'Do you know that Grieg is coming to Paris shortly? I suppose you saw him in England?' This would seem to indicate that Delius must have been back in Paris by around 18 March at the latest. In other words, he could well have been able to attend Grieg's important London concert on the 14th and been admitted to the 'artist-room' as Grieg's note suggests. If he did meet Grieg in London, he did not report it at the time to Sinding nor, very much later, to Grainger. At all events, it can be reliably affirmed that his visit to England took place in February/March rather than a month later.

30.   FRITZ DELIUS TO EDVARD GRIEG

Chalet des Lilas
Ville d'Avray.
(Seine & Oise)
[May 1889]

Dear Grieg,

I suppose you will be at Troldhaugen again, it must be marvellous in Norway now, real Spring. It's delightful here too & not too hot yet. The time is approaching when I shall begin the tour I have so much longed for & I hope the elements will be kind to us & help by sending fine weather: It will be my first visit to Jotunheim & I am very glad that it is *you* of all people who will introduce these magnificent natural surroundings to me. I shall leave Paris towards the end of June & look up Sinding in Christiania. (So far he has not sent me a single word about this tour) I hope he can come too? I shall [probably]¹ arrive in Bergen on the 25 July [so that]¹ I can get to know your home a little.

I hope you are both in the best of health & am looking forward enormously to seeing you again where there is not so much dust & dirt but more air.

I very seldom go to Paris now, it's too lovely here.

Farewell, dear Grieg, & give my regards to your wife

I look forward to seeing you soon

Yours
Fritz Delius

Autograph letter, signed and undated.

1   A number of words are obliterated in the original letter.

31.   EDVARD GRIEG TO FRITZ DELIUS

Troldhaugen, Hop Station nr Bergen
1 June 89

Dear Delius,

I have been meaning to write for some time, but I don't know what is the matter with me: since coming back here I have been overcome by idleness, something which makes me feel distinctly uneasy. This much I do know, that I look forward to our getting together again here more than ever before, like a child even. Make sure you are here by the middle of July. And another thing: if you call for Sinding first in Kristiania, do go *by sea* to Bergen and not overland. Sinding has already promised to do so, not just to save time, but so that we shall be in a position to enjoy the scenery together all the more. I thought we should spend the first week or so here at Trold-haugen and then travel to Hardanger, from where we will go on at the beginning of August to the Jotunheim. Incidentally, it is absurd for you to pick Sinding up in Kristiania. The easiest thing for you is either to take the ship from Hamburg to Bergen or to go via Hamburg Friedrichshafen (Jütland) Christiansand. And for Sinding there is nothing easier than the sea voyage here. But do consult the German time-table, as the services on the routes I have mentioned do not operate daily.

We have had a quite wonderful time here. Ideal summer weather, the like of which is a rarity here. Today for the first time the temperature has dropped and a storm has broken out. I hope you will bring back to us the good weather that we all need very much for our adventure. The well known surgeon, Professor Nicolaysen[1] in Kristiania has placed at our disposal his little hut in the Jotunheim (on Lake Gjendin). That should be marvellous.

What are you doing? Are you working hard or are you going to the Exhibition? We had better discuss personally your situation as far as god Eros in all his glory is concerned. But write to me soon. I am preparing my new concert piece, the Scenes from Olav Trygvason, for a performance and the choral parts are giving me plenty to do. It has become a strange crude thing, nothing less than Wagnerian and yet it treats of the Nordic gods. That is of course a mortal sin, but then we are all guilt-ridden creatures anyway. A dozen sins more or less don't make any difference. Peer Gynt quite rightly says: the good Lord may be very good, but — he is not an economist! When I have done with all this Nordic crudity, I shall try to cleanse myself again in some refined songs. I hope I shall have managed to do this by the time we meet again. Your songs are here and they look forward impatiently to being reunited with their rightful owner. So then: write soon.

With best wishes

Yours
Edvard Grieg

Please give our regards to your uncle.

The original of Grieg's letter has not been found, and this translation has been made from a typed transcript in the Delius Trust Archive. Envelope addressed: Mr. Fritz Delius./Chalet des Lilas/à la Chaumière/*Ville d'Avray*/(Seine & Oise)/France. Postmark: BERGEN 1 VI 89. Receiving postmarks: PARIS 7 JUIN 89 and VILLE D'AVRAY 8 JUIN 89.

1   Julius Nicolaysen (1831–1909): Bergen-born professor of surgery at Christiania University and senior physician at the National Hospital, where he introduced new antiseptic and aseptic procedures. Nicolaysen, a music lover, had been a close friend of the composer Halfdan Kjerulf, in whose quartet he had played. He is referred to briefly in a contemporary English travel account (*Three in Norway by Two of Them*

(4th ed., London: 1888): 'there are no fish in any parts of Gjendin except the extreme ends and the waterfall where Professor N. is living.' Later in the same book, he is mentioned again: 'Leirungsö is nearly four miles from our camp, and the professor's hut is an extremely comfortable and convenient little dwelling, in a most charming situation. Only one thing has been wanting, reindeer.' (pp.83 and 176–77) The 'Three', incidentally, who are the subjects of this book, spent their Norwegian summer more or less indiscriminately slaughtering anything — bar people — that moved, whether on land, in water or in the air, a salutary reminder of a particular and not at all uncommon variety of tourist exported by England to Norway at this time. Apart from indulging in some occasional angling, Delius seems not to have shared such deadly predilections.

32. FRITZ DELIUS TO EDVARD GRIEG

43, Rue Cambon
Paris
[early June 1889]

My good, dear Grieg

Your kind note made me feel happy: but you can't be happier than I am. For months now our meeting in Glorious Norway has been my be-all & end-all. How I long once again to wipe all the dust & dirt from my feet, & to set foot on the fresh, fragrant moorland! How marvellous if we can live for a while in this hut & enjoy something of the uncivilized life. I will of course come direct to Bergen from Christiania by sea & not overland. It is a bit far to go via Hamburg from here — but one can travel quite well via Havre or Amsterdam. I expect to travel from here in about 10 to 14 days' time & spend a day or two in Christiania & then stay in Hamar[1] for a few days with Arvesen the violinist. Then I shall go direct to Bergen via Christiania &, if all goes well, arrive in the middle of July. I am just reading Peer Gynt for the 5th time, this time however in Norwegian with the help of a dictionary, & am making good progress. Is Olaf Trygvason a new dramatic work? I only know Landkennung,[2] although I have never heard it. Where is the performance to take place? Just now I am busy with your C minor Sonata (violin). I am going to play the first & second movements with Arvesen. It is already going well. This is a splendid work & the better I get to know it the more I like it. I myself have not been lazy. I have sketched out something from Emperor & Galilean. Then a little Suite d'orchestre in 5 movements — Marche, Berceuse, Sckerzo, Duo & Tema con Var^{en}, which has come off quite well.[3] Then I am completely revising my Florida Suite & have finished two of the main movements. It was clumsily done with many unnecessary orchestral brutalities in it. Only here do I feel I have really learnt how to orchestrate. I hope you & your wife will regale me with your new songs. Farewell, dear Grieg, & my kind regards to your dear wife. I look forward to the pleasure of seeing you again in the near future

Yours
Fritz Delius

Autograph letter, signed and undated, written on headed notepaper.

1   Hamar, some 120 kilometres north of Christiania, was Arvesen's home town.
2   *Land Sighting (Landkjendning)*, op.31.
3   *Petite Suite d'Orchestre* (RT VI/6). The unpublished autograph full score is signed and dated 'Fritz Delius Mai 1889'.

The Griegs left London at the beginning of April. Sinding had been right and their first destination was Paris. Once again Delius had played a part in getting them there, the evidence being found in a letter from Grieg — in London at the time — to Max Abraham on 2 March 1889: 'I'm thinking about going to Paris in April, but am still undecided. Delius, to whom I spoke recently, strongly advises me to do so.'

Following his return from England, Delius stayed at first with his uncle, but evidently returned to Ville d'Avray some time during the month of April. The fine spring weather, coupled with his restoration to full health, would have made his chalet and its semi-rural surroundings once more a potent attraction to him.

Meanwhile Grieg made arrangements in Paris with the conductor Edouard Colonne to return to the city in December, when he would conduct Colonne's orchestra in concerts of his own works. While Grieg was in Paris, Delius saw to it that his uncle Theodor was introduced to him. The Griegs then travelled on to Leipzig, where they were just in time to see Sinding before he set off for Norway for the summer. 'I am having Grieg over this evening,' Sinding told Delius on 15 April, 'and then I leave at 4 o'clock in the morning.' The

Griegs stayed in Leipzig for two weeks, after which they were on the move again, first to Berlin, then to Copenhagen and Christiania, before they arrived back at Troldhaugen by the middle of May.

Delius was now trying to pin Sinding down on the matter of the summer holiday arrangements. Had Sinding's letter of 20 May not mysteriously been misdirected by the post to New York, Delius would have learnt what he needed to know in reasonable time. The letter finally reached him on either 17 or 18 June: 'I can't say how much I am looking forward to our trip, and all the more so because I still don't know my own country at all. Just one thing — I can't leave here as early as the middle of June [. . .] I therefore prefer your first plan — to set off not before the middle of July. I've also told Grieg that we'll arrive about this time, and he agrees. I have been asked to send you best wishes from him and his wife. They stopped for two days in Chr.ania on their way through, and both looked very well. — Busoni has written to tell me that he would like to come too, and Johan Svendsen also intends to come. But Grieg was afraid that at this rate the party might well become too large for convenience to undertake the tramp through the Jotunheim.' There is little doubt that it would have been the most singular event in musical mountaineering history had all five of these composers made the trip. But Busoni and Svendsen did not, in the event, join the party.

33.   FRITZ DELIUS TO EDVARD GRIEG

Hamar
July 1/89

My dear Grieg

I arrived here yesterday with Sinding & shall stay until Thursday when we will return again to Christiania. On the 12–13 we'll be going by steamer to Bergen: shall write a card beforehand. If all goes well we shall meet on the 15th in Bergen: I have never looked forward to anything as much as I do to this meeting & tour in Jotunheim   Sinding too is delighted as never before. [. . .]^{1} has also placed a hut at my disposal [. . .]^{1} I am sending you what he has [. . .].^{1} If only the weather [. . .]^{1}

85

Kind regards to your wife

Yours
Fritz Delius

Autograph letter, signed and dated.
1   A number of words are obliterated in the original letter.

Communication had actually been re-established with Sinding on 15 June, when Delius received a letter from him written three days earlier: 'I shall be at Grieg's at Troldhaugen on the *15 July*. He wrote and told me that he had advised you to go direct to Bergen. But if you can come here it will give me enormous pleasure.' Two days later he wrote again: 'I shall be very glad if you really do come here [. . .] It is really shameful for me as a Norwegian to need to be guided in my own country by you, a foreigner. Arvesen writes to me that it's decided that we visit him in Hamar. I should very much like to do this, and if it's agreeable to you we can pay a visit to Bjørnstjerne Bjørnson in Gausdal as well.' At the end of this letter, Sinding again took pains to remind Delius that he was welcome to come to Christiania first, but added: 'Grieg wants you as much as I do.'

There can be no doubt that Grieg was excited at the prospect of the visit by these particular friends: 'The day after tomorrow,' he told Max Abraham on 13 July, 'Sinding and Delius are coming, a few days later Augener and then we are off by way of Laerdal to the mountains and Jotunheim. You have no idea of just how much my brain, taken up by so many demands recently, is longing for a break! And how I look forward to it! There's just one thing missing for me. That you won't be with us!' In neither of his own accounts of the trip does Delius mention Augener, with whom he must shortly, at least, have been dealing: the *Five Songs from the Norwegian* were, after all, published the following year.

Delius arrived in Christiania in the early hours of Monday morning, 24 June, to be met at the pier at two o'clock by Arve Arvesen and his father Olaus, well-known in Norway as a leading educational reformer. The night was spent at the Britannia Hotel. Johan Halvorsen joined the party the following morning, and before lunch Delius and Arvesen together played a sonata of Grieg's at Warmuth's — presumably the c minor that they had played together at Ville d'Avray in February. His friends flooded in to greet him over lunch. Besides Arvesen and Halvorsen, fellow guests were Iver Holter, conductor at the Christiania Musical Association (or *Musikforening*), and the painter Eyolf Soot. The 'Wisdal' who made up the party and who had also been up the night before to welcome Delius, must have been the artist Jo Visdal (1861–1923). Visdal was already a fine portrait sculptor: a bust of his fellow-student Edvard Munch, which he had executed in 1886, had made such a favourable impression that he was awarded a scholarship which had enabled him to travel to Paris. Here he had studied with Bonnat and Alfred Roll and subsequently with Puvis de Chavannes, before returning to Christiania in 1889. In Norway again, he was to confirm his reputation with a series of portrait busts of the great and the good over the years, including Bjørnstjerne and Karoline Bjørnson at Aulestad in 1890, Johan Selmer in 1894, Henrik Ibsen, the Lies, Arne Garborg and Erika Nissen. Delius must surely have first met Visdal in Paris during the time they overlapped in the city.

Delius spent the rest of his first week with Sinding at the home of Sinding's brother-in-law Glør Mejdell, a lawyer and writer. On Sunday, he and Sinding travelled by train to Hamar, staying at Arvesen's home, Sagatun. Sinding left at some stage of the week, rejoining Delius briefly in Christiania during Monday, 8 July. That night Delius embarked on a coastal steamer for Fredriksvaern, where Holter met him on arrival the following morning. Sinding joined them there for three further days on Wednesday. Late on Saturday evening, Sinding and Delius boarded a Bergen-bound steamer at nearby Larvik.

Later in life, Delius gave a partial account of the trip to Grainger, confining himself, however, largely to memories of the time spent with Grieg:

> I left for Norway via Havre to Christiania, and having stayed with a relation of Sinding's for a few days at Nesodden, we both left for Bergen by boat round the coast. On arriving at Bergen we were met by Grieg, who conducted us to his home near Bergen at Hop Station. He lived in a very comfortable little wooden house called Troldhaugen, situated rather high up on a promontory jutting out into the fjord. Here we spent a very agreeable week fishing and walking, Grieg playing some of his latest compositions to us, and making excursions to Bergen to buy the necessary knapsacks and provisions for our projected walking tour in Jotunheimen. A friend of Grieg's, Prof. Nicolaysen, had lent Grieg his hut on Gjendin and it was thither we were bound. When we had completed our arrangements, we left for Voss in Hardanger and thence via Gudvangen and the Sognefjord to

Laerdalsøyri. From there we drove to Nystova, which is at the opening of the Jotunfjeld, and walked to Framnaes on Lake Tyin. From Framnaes we rode to Tvindehaugen and then made the ascent of Skineggi and had a wonderful view of the range of the Bygdin mountains. At Nystova we had made the ascent of Stugunøsi, creeping along its back to the top, and got a wonderful view of the Jotun mountains. Grieg and Sinding went down the proper way, but I went down a more direct and very much steeper way and almost came to grief. When I arrived at Nystova they were just on the point of sending out after me. From Skineggi we descended on the other side to Eidsbugaren on Lake Bygdin and from there we walked over Høistakka to Lake Gjendin, lying in the midst of mighty mountain peaks; it was a very beautiful walk. At Gjendeboden we were met by our guide, Viste Kleiven, who rowed us to our hut, Leirungshytte, a row of several hours. The hut was situated at the border of the lake and at the foot of a waterfall, and opposite was Besseggen and Besshø.

Here we spent a very pleasant time, fishing, boating, walking. Our principal food was trout from the lake, wonderful trout. Milk and cream we got from a saeter [i.e. a hill farm] at Memurudalen on the other side of the lake a few miles away. We ate flatbrød, the flat Norwegian oatcakes, and every evening we had hot whisky toddy and played cards.

At last Grieg returned to Bergen via Laerdalsøyri. We went together to Nystova, where we had a nice supper together with a bottle of port wine and we drank many skaals for the last time. Next day Sinding and I returned by slow stages to Christiania via Valdres. I went from there to Fredriksvaern for a week's sea-bathing and fishing with Musikdirektor Iver Holter. Then I returned to Havre on the Kong Dag and thence to Paris. [Grainger Museum MS.]

Delius also kept a diary of his trip, and in this he expanded a little on the above account:

Monday 15th. Arrived at Bergen at 2.30 p.m. Met by Grieg on the pier, went at once to Troldhaugen, delightfully situated on a fjord.
Tues. Bathed, walked & fished.
Wed. Bathed. Went to Bergen to do some shopping. Met a Miss Anna Mohn, who I had met in Eide 2 years before. Very nice.
Thurs. Went to Mohns to dinner. Went over their stores of stockfish.

Friday. Bathed, fished. In the evening Franz Beyer & wife came to supper.

Sat. Went to Beyers to supper.

Sund. Bathed & fished.

Mond. Did some shopping.

Tues. Left in the afternoon by Voss Banen for Vossevangen. Train crowded with English.

Wed. Left at 7 a.m. in carriage for Gudvangen & Laerdalsøyri. Delightful day. Dinner at Gudvangen. Laerdalsøyri at 7.30. Nice hotel. Drank Toddy on the balcony.

Thurs. Left in carriage at 8 a.m. for Nystova via Maristova. Delightful scenery. Stopped for dinner at *Borgund* (a very interesting church). Arrived at Nystova at 8 p.m. after a magnificent drive over a Vidde. Slept on the floor in the drawing room.

Frid. Made the ascent of Stugunøsi & had a grand panorama of Jotunheim.

Sat. Left for Framnaes (Lake Tyin). Stayed the night & left early next morning by boat for Tvindehaugen. Left at once for Eidsbugaren via Skineggi. Grand view of Bygdin & mountains from the top. Arrived at Eidsbugaren at 4½ p.m. Dinner, Prof. Sars & Dutch lady, Miss Jilsine. Slept with 8 others in same room.

Left at 12 next day, *Mond.*, for Gjendin. Grand march on a vidder. Arrived at Gjendeboden 6 p.m. Dinner 7.30. Quiet chat with Grieg & Sinding. Slept with Grieg.

Bathe in the morning. Met by our guide, Vistiklewin, & left in a boat for the hut of Dr Nicolaysen. After delightful row, arrived at 2.30. Dinner I cooked.

Wed. Went on long walk. Fished in the foss nearby. Splendid trout (Had a dangerous walk with Sinding).

Thurs. 1st Aug. Went to Gjendesheim in boat. Had dinner, received letters, rowed back.

Frid. Fine, lovely day. Long walk on the hills. Rain in afternoon.

Sat. Rowed with Vistiklewin to a Saeter across the lake to fetch eggs & milk. Got back at 3.30. Dinner. Delightful day again (Leirungs Hütte).

Sund. Quiet day. Not a cloud. Caught fish.

Mond. Rain all day.

Tues. Rain all day. Took a walk at night in the hills. Got very wet.

Weds. Rain & sunshine. Took a walk with Grieg & Sinding. Delightful view.

Thurs. 8ᵗʰ. Started at 11 a.m. for Gjendeboden with Visticlewin. Rowed half way. Arrived at 2 p.m., got letters, started with knapsack over the Vidder. Grand view & weather. Descended Høistakka at 7. Met by a boat. Arrived at Eidsbugaren at 8. Met 2 Frenchmen. Good beds.

9. Started early for Tvindehaugen. Arrived at 11. Took leave of Visticlewin. Rowed with 2 men to Framnaes. Dinner. Walked to Nystova, arrived at 7. Last night with Grieg, he going next day back to Laerdalsøyri. We (S & I) thro Valdres. Cards & portwine, for last time.

Sat. 10ᵗʰ. Left at 9 a.m. in skyds for Skogstad. Grieg the other way, after a hearty farvel!*

Having parted from Grieg, Delius continued his tour, arriving at Fredriksvaern — where he was again met by Holter — on 14 August. He stayed for a week before leaving for Christiania, where he finally embarked for home — seen off by Christian Sinding — on Thursday 22 August.

During his Norwegian tour of 1887, Delius had jotted down in a small notebook† a series of 'Norske Wiser', as well as a first setting of Ibsen's 'Cradle Song'. The same notebook returned with him in 1889, and it includes an incomplete orchestral piece dated 'Aug. 1889, Leirungs Hytte, Jotunheim, Norge'. Undated sketches headed 'Feast at Solhaug', after the title of Ibsen's play, are also to be found in this notebook. The 'Small piece composed in Jotunheim (Norway) jointly by Grieg, Sinding and Delius, MS', which was found among Delius's papers in 1935 and so described, has long since disappeared.

34.   EDVARD GRIEG TO FRITZ DELIUS

Christiania, 6ᵗʰ October
1889

Dear Delius,

I have *three* letters from you,[1] but not one contains what I deserved to hear: that I am a silly ass, who has not yet replied. So you are working again at full pressure! Well, one ought to work while the pressure is on. I imagine that the pressure will produce something à la Jotunheim. I have been here for 2

* From a notebook (known as the 'Red Notebook') in the collection of the Grainger Museum, Melbourne University. Delius wrote his diary in English.
† Now bound up as Delius Trust Archive Vol.38.

days and am preparing several things for performance,[2] among them the Scenes from Olav Trygvason on the 19th. There will be a repeat on the 27th and then on the 15th November in Copenhagen. After that on to Brussels, where I have 3 concerts at the beginning of December. I come to Paris in the middle of January or a little later.[3] Then in the middle of February to Stuttgart and afterwards Prague. As you see, I am using to the full the strength I gained in the Jotunheim. I have a frightful lot to do here, but I have the strength and so it should be alright. But most of all I should like to be, like you, in some quiet village, just working! Oh well: the time must come. Then we shall go walking and philosophizing again!

Yours
Edvard Grieg.

I spoke to Sinding yesterday. All's well with him. He's off to Leipzig in November.

Autograph letter, signed and dated. Envelope addressed: Mr. Fritz Delius./Croissy/Seine & Oise/8 Boul[d] de la Mairie/*France*. Postmark obscured. Receiving postmarks: PARIS 11[?] OCT 89 and [CROISSY?] SEINE ET OISE 11 OCT [89].

1 Grieg uses, in German, the more intimate form of address for the first time, and the (capitalized) *Du* and *Dein* forms are now maintained for the rest of his correspondence with Delius. With letters to and from Nina, the *Sie* and *Ihr* forms — as would have been appropriate — continue throughout.
2 'Greetings from Grieg, who had his first concert yesterday', wrote Sinding from Christiania on 10 October. 'Great acclaim.' On 17 October, Sinding sent 'regards from Holter, who will be writing to you soon, and from the Griegs.'
3 In fact the Griegs continued straight to Paris on 9 December, the day after Grieg's third and last Brussels concert.

In September, Delius had initially stayed with his uncle again, but October saw him established in rooms just across the road from the town hall in the small rural town of Croissy-sur-Seine, some six or seven kilometres north of Ville d'Avray.

35. NINA GRIEG TO FRITZ DELIUS

[Paris, mid-December 1889]

Dear Delius,

Grieg asks me to tell you that had he not been ill already on arrival in Paris, he would have written to you at once. The worst does seem to be over, but he is still too weak to see anyone. When he is better you will hear from him. We both send our kindest regards.

Yours sincerely
Nina Grieg.

Autograph letter, signed and undated, written on the reverse of a visiting card printed *Edvard Grieg*.

Early in March 1890, Delius was to write to a former pupil of his in America: 'We had "la grippe" quite badly here in Paris.' Grieg was an early casualty of the 'flu epidemic. He wrote to Beyer on 14 December: 'You can imagine how strange it is to be here, to be lying sick here, and to have no idea that I am in Paris.' A Danish doctor visited him daily. Although fit enough in time to conduct Colonne's orchestra in two concerts of his own works and to play chamber pieces at a third, Grieg continued to be troubled by influenza symptoms and was unable to be present at the two performances of his String Quartet on 28 December and 11 January.

Meanwhile, Delius had set himself the task of orchestrating Grieg's 'Norwegian Bridal Procession', op.19, no.2. His autograph pencil draft score, which is preserved complete in the Delius Trust Archive, is dated 'le 2 Dec^bre 1889', and it could be that this act of homage to his friend and master was intended as a Christmas gift. If a fair copy was indeed handed over to Grieg, it would not appear to have survived. In due course, Grieg's piece was orchestrated by Halvorsen and it is his 1903 version that has since been played in the concert hall.

Score and parts of Delius's version, prepared by Robert Threlfall, were published by Boosey and Hawkes in 1993, and the piece was given its first performance by Per Dreier and the Royal Philharmonic Orchestra at the Royal Festival Hall on 15 June 1993, appropriately commemorating the 150th anniversary of Grieg's birth. It is, perhaps extraordinarily, the only known case of Delius's having orchestrated a work by another composer.

36. EDVARD GRIEG TO FRITZ DELIUS

[Paris, 23 December 1889]

Dear friend,

We are invited to Jonas Lie's[1] tomorrow, Christmas Eve. So I am afraid it is not possible. What a pity that you live so far away that everything has to be worked out so long beforehand, as I find that very difficult. But I will write to you, just as soon as I possibly can.

Yours
E.G.

Autograph letter, initialled and undated, written on the reverse of a visiting card printed *Edvard Grieg*. Envelope addressed: Mr. Fritz Delius/8, Boulevard de la Mairie/Croissy. Postmark: PARIS 23 DEC 89.

1   Jonas Lie (1833–1908): major Norwegian author and poet. He lived in Paris from 1882 to 1906 and had been a friend of Grieg's for some time. Grieg had set his 'Upon a Grassy Hillside', publishing it in 1884 as one of his *Six Songs (Older and Newer)*, op.39.

Before he left Paris, Grieg gave Delius a letter of introduction, written on one of his visiting cards, to Vincent d'Indy, the conductor and composer. It is addressed on the reverse to 'Mr. Vincent d'Indy/7, Avenue de Villars', and the text runs:

May I introduce to you my talented friend Mr *Fritz Delius*.
With best wishes and respects

Yours
Edvard Grieg

Paris
26 January 90

As this card was retained by Delius, it would seem that the introduction was not actually effected at the time. Rather more than eleven years later, d'Indy was to conduct in Paris two of Delius's orchestral songs and Delius must surely have met him by then.

The Griegs stayed in Paris until the end of January. On leaving, they travelled first to Stuttgart and then on to Leipzig for further concerts, staying there for a few weeks. They finally returned to

Troldhaugen early in April, remaining in Grieg's beloved 'Westland' until October.

37. FRITZ DELIUS TO EDVARD GRIEG

Croissy (S & O)
1 April 90

My dear Grieg,

How are you?[1] & how much longer will you be in Leipzig? I have not had a reply from home yet, which means that I cannot come: but it is lovely, wonderfully lovely here now. Spring has come & everything is beginning to blossom. In the garden the fruit trees are in full bloom & the weather! is warm & sunny. I go for long walks every day & am remarkably well & fresh [I][2] have now ordered my life according to my own nature & the truth at least [. . .][2] it is *World [Joy?]*[2] instead of *World Woe*.

I do not know what I shall be doing this summer, either Norway or Germany. Farewell, dear Grieg. Kind regards to your dear wife

Your friend
Fritz Delius

Regards to Dr Abraham too.

Autograph letter, signed and dated.

1   This is the first (extant) letter in which Delius addresses Grieg using the familiar *Du* form.
2   A number of words are obliterated in the original letter.

A visit to Leipzig was certainly in the air, although it is not clear what Delius might have been expecting from 'a reply from home'. Money perhaps? Sinding had written to him on 15 March, on his way back from Germany to Norway, where a performance in Christiania of his Symphony was to be conducted by Holter: 'What are you doing? Have you given up your trip to Leipzig. If not, then hold on till I come back in three weeks' or a month's time. I spent a lot of time with the Griegs. Borgström had taken your place at whist. Grieg made a great impression at the Gewandhaus with his "Olav Trygvason". And it's a magnificent work, particularly the first two parts, in which he pulls off some colossal effects.' Shortly after returning to Leipzig, Sinding wrote again to Delius, on 29 April: 'I met Grieg a few hours before my departure from Christiania. He looked well and also asks to be remembered. You talked about coming here. The Nibelungen will probably be performed in May, you really shouldn't miss it.' Another letter followed on 23 May: 'I am very glad that you really are coming.' Johan Selmer was in Leipzig too: 'We are waiting for you impatiently,' he wrote to Delius on the 24th, adding: 'Molard *must not* miss "Meistersinger", which will be given on 30 May.'

William Molard (1862–1937) was to play a central role in Delius's life in the 1890s and a minor role in that of Grieg in the middle of the decade (see Letters 70n and 72–74). The first mention of him to be found in the Delius literature comes in a letter from Delius to Johan Selmer on 9 April 1990: 'Through Molard I have had the opportunity to see one of your scores' [ALS in Oslo University Library]. However, a letter written by Molard's wife-to-be, the Swedish sculptress Ida Ericson (1853–1927), makes it clear that the initial acquaintance may well have been struck up as early as 1889. She wrote to her friend Hilma Ahlgrensson on 26 March 1890 from Paris and referred to photographs taken in her studio by an artist friend: 'Boutet de Monvel (the bachelor) took them as he has a camera. One of them shows Molard (mon amour) playing the piano and on the piano stands a bust I did of a friend, whom I like very much indeed. (It's an Englishman, composer and one of the most intelligent musicians I have met in my life).' [ALS in the collection of Thomas Millroth, Stockholm; the whereabouts of Ida's bust of Delius remains unknown].

Molard himself was a civil servant working in the Ministry of Agriculture, where his duties do not seem to have been particularly onerous. His mother was French but he was of Norwegian descent on his father's side. His great love was music, for which he had more than a little talent, and he played the piano and composed. Early in 1887, he had got in touch with Grieg, apparently to see if he could help get some of Grieg's songs published in France and offering at the same time to translate them. In his reply, Grieg gently suggested that Molard might care to get in touch with Peters, as he himself did not have the rights to his music for France: 'I well remember your father, whom I regret not knowing more closely. Is he still alive? I also remember going into his music shop once in Kristiania, (Akersgaden) to buy some music paper.' [ALS in Bergen Public Library, dated Troldhaugen, 21 January 1887]

In the event, the Molards are remembered less for their own not inconsiderable artistic gifts than for the fact that they kept their studio home — just off the rue Vercingétorix in Montparnasse — open to all and sundry, in particular to Scandinavian artists, writers and musicians who either lived in Paris or were just passing through. The result was that their casual, bohemian and above all welcoming household attracted during the nineties and beyond an extraordinary array of visitors, among the sometime regulars being Delius, Edvard Munch, August Strindberg and Paul Gauguin. A long-overdue evaluation of their impact on Parisian cultural life — and on the careers of the many talented Scandinavians they went out of their way to help — now appears in Thomas Millroth's *Molards Salong* (Stockholm: Forum 1993).

38. FRITZ DELIUS TO EDVARD GRIEG

8 B^d de la Mairie
le 26 Mai 90.
Croissy (S & O)

My dear Grieg

I suppose you will be at Troldhaugen again now: I hope that you and your wife are well. I am sending with this post a volume of songs.[1] In a few days I'm off to Leipzig for a couple of weeks in order to hear various things there. You will probably be doing a lot of bathing & fishing now. I have got a devilish wanderlust again & would like to see the sea again. Farewell, my dear Grieg. I am sending a few lines herewith to your wife.

Yours
Fritz Delius

Please give Franz Beyer my best wishes ogsaa hans Kone.[2]
I shall send him a volume of songs too.
If you have time, write me a few lines
Poste Restante
Leipzig

Autograph letter, signed and dated.

1   Delius's just-published *Five Songs from the Norwegian* were settings of

German translations of 1) 'Slumber Song' by Bjørnstjerne Bjørnson, 2) 'The Nightingale' by Theodor Kjerulf, 3) 'Summer Eve' by John Paulsen, 4) 'Longing' by Theodor Kjerulf, and 5) 'Sunset' by Andreas Munch. One of the principal influences governing his choice of poems is already clear. Although Grieg had made no settings of Theodor Kjerulf, he had composed four songs to poems by Andreas Munch, including 'Sunset' in the mid-1860s, and had written several songs to texts by Bjørnson soon afterwards. Compared with Andreas Munch and Bjørnson, John Paulsen was a lesser figure, but this Bergen poet had been a good friend of Grieg's since youth, and Grieg first set five of his texts in 1876. 'Summer Eve', or 'Jeg reiste en deilig Sommerkveld', had been the second of these. No fewer than eleven more songs to Paulsen texts were to follow in 1893–4. The other main influence at work on Delius seems to have been the matter of the availability of Norwegian poems in German translation (virtually all of the Scandinavian-language texts he chose were set in German). Apart from the Paulsen, Delius's other four songs from this set use the translations he had found in Edmund Lobedanz's *Ausgewählte Gedichte [. . .] von anderen neueren nordischen Dichtern*, published in Leipzig in 1881.

2   *Also his wife*. In Norwegian in the original letter.

39.   FRITZ DELIUS TO NINA GRIEG

Croissy le 26 Mai 90
8 B^d de la Mairie

My dear Frau Grieg

I am sending you today an album of songs: you know them already. I have taken the liberty of dedicating the album to you & I should like at the same time to express my thanks for all those lovely days we have enjoyed together. When I first became acquainted with Grieg's music, it was not only that it made a deep impression on me, it was as if I was hearing something quite new, a curtain went up. So it was too when I heard you sing. I had never heard anyone sing like you, it was also something quite new to me. My very best wishes to you, Frau Grieg. With kind regards I remain

Yours sincerely
Fritz Delius

Kind regards to your sister[1]

Autograph letter, signed and dated, addressed 'Frau Grieg' and written at the same time as (and enclosed with) Delius's letter to Grieg of the same date.

1   Tony (Antonie) Hagerup (1844–1939), Nina's sister, who often lived with the Griegs at Troldhaugen. Her happily-accepted role there was as a kind of housekeeper who would, moreover, look after Troldhaugen when the Griegs were absent. Grieg would jokingly refer to her as his 'second wife'. She stayed on with Nina after Grieg's death.

40. NINA GRIEG TO FRITZ DELIUS

Troldhaugen 6th June 1890.—

Dear Delius,

Since it is likely to be some time before Grieg can get round to writing, I send you these lines in advance in order to convey to you my warmest thanks for the lovely songs. I am enormously pleased to have them, and to trill away a little to myself at the piano, they must sound wonderful when they are sung beautifully, something which I can unfortunately no longer do. Many thanks too for the letter and for the fact that my little bit of singing found in you so warm an audience. —

Good that you are going to Leipzig again, I have always thought that it was a little too lonely for you in Croissy. Of course I do not know if this was really the case, but some time ago in Paris I very definitely had that impression. Let us hope that you will spend some happy days with Sinding in Leipzig, so long as you do not both die from the heat. I cannot imagine it being particularly agreeable there at this time of year and there is nothing to hear either. No, this is a time when it is much lovelier in Norway, so fresh and fragrant. You too will, I hope, feel the same when you eventually begin to 'jotunolo-gize'.[1] But you mustn't forget us and Troldhaugen, we shall always be delighted to welcome you here. I have not yet seen the little rattlesnake,[2] but do not doubt that she will be visiting her relatives this summer too. —

For the present Grieg sends you all his good wishes, he is tolerably well, I feel he would love to be getting on with his work, but am afraid he often gets disturbed.

And now farewell, dear Delius, and accept kind regards from my sister and from

Yours sincerely
Nina Grieg.

Regards to Sinding please?

1 Christian Sinding   2 Delius at Leipzig

3 Arve Arvesen, by Edvard Munch

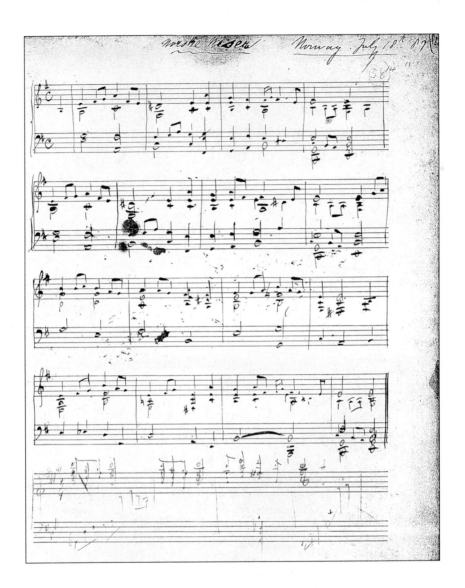

4 The first of seven short pieces, *Norske Wiser*,
sketched by Delius during his holiday in Norway in 1887.
It was composed on the steamer between
Stavanger and Sandeid on 18 July.

5 Halfdan Jebe

6 A card party at Leipzig: Nina and Edvard Grieg,
Johan Halvorsen, Fritz Delius and Christian Sinding

Harkort-str 5. III
Sonnenland

Lieber Grieg.

Ich möchte Ihnen schreiben
was eine Freude Ihr Quartett
mir gegeben hat & in was eine
sonderbare Stimmung es mir
gebracht hat. Daß ich Ihnen
sage wie ich Sie liebe & schätze
ist von wenig Bedeutung für
Sie, aber es ist war & kommt-
Herzen & so danke ich Ihnen
für alle die Freude daß ich
an Ihre Werke fühle
mit liebevolle Gruß
verbleibe ich
Ihr
Fritz Delius

7 Letter from Delius to Grieg, Leipzig, 18 February 1888

8 Troldhaugen

9 Grieg's hut at Troldhaugen

10   Delius with four of his sisters, c. 1888

11   Grieg goes to fetch the post at Hop Station

12   Edvard and Nina Grieg in London in 1888

14 Title-page of Delius's autograph score of *Paa Vidderne*, 1888, with its dedication to Grieg

ST. JAMES'S HALL.

HERR

EDVARD GRIEG'S

Evening Concert,

ON

WEDNESDAY, MAY 16, 1888,

AT HALF-PAST EIGHT O'CLOCK.

Programme of Works by Edvard Grieg.

PART I.

1. SONATA in F major, Op. 8, for Piano and Violin.
   a. Allegro con brio.
   b. Allegretto quasi Andantino.
   c. Allegro molto vivace.
   Madame NORMAN-NERUDA and THE COMPOSER.

2. SONGS ... { "Two eyes of brown."
   { "I love thee."
   { "Wandering in the wood."
   Madame NINA GRIEG.

6. PIANO SOLO ... { a. "On the mountains"
   { b. Norwegian Bridal procession passing by (from Op. 19)
   THE COMPOSER.

PART II.

4. ROMANCE and FINALE (Piano and Violin) (from Op. 45).
   Madame NORMAN NERUDA and the COMPOSER.

5. SONGS ... { a. "My song shall be thine, sweet springtime."
   { b. "In the summer evening."
   { c. "Good morning"
   Madame NINA GRIEG.

6. PIANO SOLO { a. "Alla Menuetto" (from Op. 7)
   { b. "Humoresken" (from Op. 6)
   { c. Norwegian folk-songs and dances (from Op. 17)
   jätertog—national dance.
   Stabb-Låt—national dance.
   a.—Pastorale.
   THE COMPOSER.

Sofa Stalls, 10s. 6d.   Stalls, 7s. 6d.   Balcony, 3s.

Admission One Shilling.

Chappell & Co. 50, New Bond Street, and at Austin's Ticket Office, St. James's Hall.

13 Programme of Grieg's concert in London on 16 May 1888

Autograph letter, signed and dated.

1 One of the Griegs' favourite coinings in respect of a part of the world that was particularly dear to Grieg himself. In a letter to Julius Röntgen dated 19 June 1892, he refers to Röntgen and himself as 'Jotunologen' (Jotunologists), a perfectly legitimate word that has been used elsewhere, for example, to describe such experts on the region as Professor Ernst Sars (1835–1917), the distinguished historian whom Delius had encountered at Eidsbugaren during his summer tour of 1889 (see p.89). Another verbal coining Grieg used in writing to Röntgen was 'Jotunisieren' ('to Jotunize'). Röntgen himself went a step further by giving the mountains musical form in his *Jotunheim Suite*, an outcome of one of the tours he made with Grieg in the region.

2 As so often, the identity of the girlfriend referred to here is concealed, but Nina presumably means Anna Mohn.

41. EDVARD GRIEG TO FRITZ DELIUS

Troldhaugen,
17th June 1890

Dear Delius,

I suppose I can say, like Jacobson the brewer in Björnson's A Bankruptcy: 'I'm a real scoundrel!'[1] for not having written to you ages ago. And now to cap it all the telegram arrived. Many thanks to you and to the others who joined in sending it, please pass on my best wishes.[2] I spent my birthday at Lofthus in Hardanger, having fled there in order to escape the numerous people bringing congratulations. For I do not like such affairs. You just cannot imagine how the Sörfjord looked! I have never seen it looking so beautiful.

Thank you very much for the songs too. The one I did not know before is very pretty, quite steeped in poetry. You will have my new songs when we meet.[3] I hope this will be in Norway and moreover this summer, don't you agree?[4] It is a quite wonderful year here: a mixture of sunshine and mild rain. I am doing a little work and walking a great deal. Write soon.

With best wishes, also from my wife

Yours
Edvard Grieg.

Autograph letter, signed and dated. Envelope addressed: Herrn Fritz Delius./*Poste restante*/*Leipzig*. Readdressed: Harkortstr. 5^{IV}. Postmark: BERGEN 18 VI 90. Receiving postmark: LEIPZIG 22 6 90.

1 'Ein grosser Schweinehund bin ich!' The original Norwegian in Bjørnson's play runs: 'Ja, jeg er en svinepels, jeg.'
    Grieg was inordinately fond of quoting from literary and other sources in his letters, and the same quotation would frequently be recycled for different friends. On 15 December 1884, Röntgen had been on the receiving end of the same line: 'Ich sage,' wrote Grieg, 'wie der Brauer Jacobsen in Björnson's Fallissement: Ja, ich bin ein grosser Schweinehund!' This weakness for quotation could, when really quite unnecessary, verge on bathos as, for example, in a letter to Röntgen dated 19 March 1897: 'John Paulsen is more than right when he says: Indeed what more can I say.'

2 Grieg had just celebrated his 47th birthday.

3 Either the *Six Songs* to various German texts, op.48, and/or the *Six Songs* to Drachmann texts, op.49. Both were published by Peters in 1889.

4 Encouragement was to come from another Norwegian friend, the painter Gudmund Stenersen, who wrote to Delius on 12 July: 'Now I can better understand Ibsens Brand and Peer Gynt, when I have seen those wild tracts [. . .] I hope to see you here in Norway this summer.' (Original in English.) Stenersen (1863–1934) studied in Paris with Bonnat (like so many other Scandinavians) from 1889–90 and then with Fernand Cormon from 1891–2.

42.   FRITZ DELIUS TO EDVARD GRIEG

[Havre de Pas]$^{1\ et\ seq.}$
St Heliers
Jersey. (Channel Islands)
[July 1890]

My dear Grieg,

I was very glad to hear from you again & I thank you very much indeed for your letter. I would have really loved to go to Jotunheim again but must be content with Jersey for this summer.^{2} But next summer! will you be there? Jersey is very beautiful & there is good bathing. [I] have lodgings near the beach & am also doing some work. The [island] lies only 2 hours [from the] French coast, it [. . .] everything is dead & everyone looks [. . .] pious. I was in Leipzig for over three weeks & am very pleased with this trip. I saw of course quite a lot of Sinding, all goes well with him, although he has been working a little too hard recently. I also heard a rehearsal of his Symphony. The 1st movement is the best, in my opinion: Movement III sherzo is also very good. I like movements II & IV less. I find that the symphony as a whole doesn't hold up, & is [. . .] too thickly orchestrated; although [. . .] in my opinion [this may be due to a] bad rehearsal.[3] Holter [. . .] in Leipzig for a few days too. I must confess that for me Selmer is an extremely [disagreeable] [. . .] person. Just listen to how he [. . .] behaved. I had a mind to have a rehearsal [. . .] & had to pay 50 marks for it, which is quite a good idea, for one can rehearse better [. . .] wanted to arrange it so that I could rehearse for at least 2½ hours, as I had 5 things to rehearse. Selmer had already rehearsed 2 or 3 times with [. . .] a Finnish March or something like that. Nevertheless [he came] to me & asked me if he could rehearse his March [at my] rehearsal, he wanted, Heaven knows how, to make it popular etc! I said [no] as I only had time to rehearse my own things. So I went out to Gohlis where [. . .] was to play; the orchestra was an hour & a half late & just as I was about to begin [. . .] Selmer & asks me if he could play his [. . .] once. I said 'You know what I [already] told you', so he takes the baton & [. . .] begins to rehearse. Not just straight through [. . .] but the violins alone, the violas alone etc. [. . .] 25 minutes of my time that was already [. . .]. As he went off he said to me, 'You know [each] must know how to help himself'. Afterwards he wrote me such a fawning letter where he apologized in such an abject way.[4] It is quite [. . .] that such a thing happened for I have never really liked him. [I am] quite content with my rehearsal as far as the orchestra is concerned. I had just enough time to [. . .] the things through. Farewell, dear Grieg. Please give my good wishes to your dear wife & thank her [. . .] kind letter. Auf Wiedersehen!

Farvel!

Yours
Fritz Delius

Autograph letter, signed and undated.

1 *et seq.*   Many words are obliterated in the original letter.
2   In spite of the blandishments of his Norwegian friends, Delius had elected to spend most of July in Jersey. It is not clear why he should

have done so, but it can probably be assumed that he had made friends in the area during his summer holiday in nearby St Malo in 1888. He returned to Paris on 26 July.

3 'You were right in your criticism—' wrote Sinding on 23 December 1890, 'the finale is a failure, quite out of style with the rest, but at least I'll have a try at making a better one.' Max Abraham was also critical of the work and Grieg wrote to him on 5 July obliquely questioning his judgment and saying that he himself only knew the first movement but found it 'quite magnificent'.

4 The 'fawning letter', in Selmer's slightly fractured English, begins: 'I hope you do not feel too much offended by my behaviour today. Trusting in your friendship and noble colligality I dared to do it [. . .] At least, I hope, that you have not lost *too* much time by my playing my short, modest composition.' The Norwegian composer and conductor Johan Peter Selmer (1844–1910) was a pupil of Ambroise Thomas in Paris and of Friedrich Richter and Oscar Paul in Leipzig. He wrote colourful programme music, and Delius had written in April 1890 a short letter of unreserved praise to him in respect of his *Nordens Aand (Spirit of the North)*, op.5, 1872, a work that had been given at the Nordic Music Festival in Copenhagen in 1888. Delius had borrowed the score from William Molard. One other letter from Delius to Selmer is preserved; dated 18 April 1890, it expressed admiration for Selmer's *Scène Funèbre*, op.4, in particular for the quality of its orchestration. [Originals of both letters are in the Oslo University Library.] With such complimentary remarks having been made about his works, Selmer may well have imagined that he had a new disciple ready to make sacrifices on his behalf. Grieg himself had more reservations. He had been at the première of *Nordens Aand* in 1872 and immediately thought Selmer to be talented, but he also felt that his music was rather too 'demonic' as a result of French influences. Much later, writing to Gottfred Matthison-Hansen on 29 August 1905, he was to quote a Danish composer friend: 'In his time Emil Horneman said of Johan Selmer, after the performance of his choral piece "Nordens Ånd" [. . .] "The mountains heave, a mouse is born!" ' Grieg evidently by then fully endorsed Horneman's view.

43.   EDVARD GRIEG TO FRITZ DELIUS

Troldhaugen
11th August 1890

My dear Delius,

How sad that you are not coming to Jotunheim. On the day after tomorrow I am going by steamer to Skjolden in Lyster-fjord (Sogn) and from there to a saeter 'Turtegrösaeter' on the threshold of the Holy of Holies, with a view over to the Skagastölstindene.

Frants Beyer is coming with me as far as that, but his doctor has forbidden him to indulge in any mountaineering at all. So he stays there, and I have no travelling companion from then on. If I find none that I like, then I too will stay there for my 3 weeks. How wonderful it would be if you were to surprise me. It would certainly be very good for you, especially for your nerves, for I'll wager that Cupid is active on the island of Jersey too.

I have completed a piece for 2 pianos[1] and now am enormously looking forward to no music-making! That is, of course, only in Jotunheim, for otherwise it is quite impossible to be without music! We must fix something for the winter. I have declined all invitations, because I want to work. I thought at first of Copenhagen — but I cannot get Rome out of my head either!

Write soon. With many good wishes

Yours
Edvard Grieg

What is your address in future?

Autograph letter, signed and dated. Envelope addressed: Herrn Fritz Delius/Ceylon Villa/Havre de Pas/St Heliers/*Jersey*/(Channel Islands). Readdressed: 43 Rue Cambon/*Paris*. Readdressed: Croissy/8 B^d de la mairie/Seine et Oise. A whole series of postmarks begins with BERGEN 12 VIII [90] and continues: NEWCASTLE-ON-TYNE AU 16 90, JERSEY AU 19 90, BREST A PARIS 20 AOUT 90, PARIS R.CAMBON 21 AOUT 90 and CROISSY 21 AOUT 90.

1   *Old Norwegian Melody with Variations*, op.51.

44.   FRITZ DELIUS TO EDVARD GRIEG

(Maison Insley)
Sillon
St Malo.
(Ille & Vilaine)
14 September 90

My dear Grieg,

'Mange tusend Tak för Breven'.[1] I got it only a few days ago for it had been readdressed 3 times. At the end of July I left

Jersey & went to Paris   from there to Normandy for a short time again to Croissy & then here where I have been for a month & will stay until 15 October. How I regret not being with you! to Jotunheim the Holy of Holies & glory of glories. I expect you are back at home again now. How was it & what sort of weather did you have? I now have a double longing for Norway (as Björnsen would say) & must definitely come next summer. This winter we will arrange something for next summer, won't we? You speak of my nerves. I assure you I don't have them any more & have never been so lively & active. Cupid has been very quiet never quite absent but more platonic at least. I have been bathing almost the whole summer; here in St Malo it is absolutely marvellous & suits me & my work very well. You have written a piece for 2 pianos. You spoke some time ago about it; Dr Abraham also spoke about it when I was in Leipzig   Is it a fairly long piece? I am looking forward to getting to know it this winter, I hope. Dr Abraham was eagerly awaiting it. He was enormously kind & friendly & I liked him much more than I did before   He talked a little about Rome too, do you really mean it? When we next meet I shall really have something to show you, for I have done a lot: I shall soon publish another volume of songs.[2] It must be lovely in Troldhaugen now. Here the weather has been absolutely marvellous for 3 weeks; not a cloud to be seen. Give my best wishes to the little rattlesnake, as to Frøken Pétra Vogt, should you meet her quite alone. Now farewell & do give my kind regards to your dear wife & to Franz Beyer too.

Write soon.
With all good wishes

Your friend
Fritz Delius

My address after 15 October
8 B^d de la Mairie
Croissy
(Seine & Oise)
but I hope [St Malo][3]

Autograph letter, signed and dated.

1 *Many thousand thanks for the letter*. Delius's Norwegian is faulty.

2 *Seven Songs from the Norwegian* (RT V/9), composed in 1889–90 and published by Augener in 1892. The set is made up as follows: 1) 'Cradle Song' by Henrik Ibsen (the autograph manuscript being headed 'To Madame Grieg'), 2) 'The Homeward Journey' by Aa. O. Vinje, 3) 'Twilight Fancies' by Bjørnstjerne Bjørnson, 4) 'Sweet Venevil' by Bjørnson, 5) 'Minstrel(s)' by Ibsen, 6) 'Hidden Love' by Bjørnson, and 7) 'The Birds' Story' by Ibsen. All but no. 4 had already been set by Grieg in his op.15, op.25, op.33 and op.39. Grieg's version of 'Twilight Fancies' ('Prinsessen') is without an opus number. Other songs set by both Grieg and Delius (apart, that is, from those included in Delius's *Five Songs* and *Seven Songs*) were 'Two Brown Eyes' ('To brune Øine') (Hans Christian Andersen), set by Grieg as op.5, no.1, in 1864–65, and set by Delius in 1885 (RT V/3); and 'Hör' ich das Liedchen klingen' (Heinrich Heine), set by Grieg as op.39, no.6, in 1884–85, and by Delius in 1890–91 (RT V/11, no.3). Other poets from whose works both Grieg and Delius found song texts were Emanuel Geibel, Holger Drachmann and Vilhelm Krag, although each composer set different poems.

3 '*but I hope*' is in fact followed by a rudimentary drawing of a hand pointing to the address at the top of the first page of this letter.

Sinding, who had been summering at Nesodden, near Christiania, wrote to Delius with news of friends on 17 September: 'Grieg will soon be coming here to give a concert. A couple of new works by him have come out.' Arvesen, he said, had also been to Christiania: 'He'll probably be going to France soon, and said he would submit himself to your influence. He had to be pushed, he said, and you were always good at keeping tabs on him. I gave him a good talking to.'

The Griegs spent their winter in Copenhagen, staying there until the middle of April 1891. It was an unproductive period for Grieg himself, who could only manage to write two movements of a second String Quartet that was in fact never to be finished. Delius, during the same period, was probably working mainly on his first opera *Irmelin* (RT I/2) at Croissy, before leaving to spend much of the month of March in Bradford and in London. Sinding had gone to Berlin in November and he was frequently to winter in that city in the years that followed. Writing to Delius on 23 December he mentioned that Hjalmar Borgstrøm was there too, together with 'several others from the Norwegian colony in Leipzig; unfortunately Frl. Holmsen as well.' He could not afford to come to Paris yet, but asked Delius to pass on his greetings to Arvesen.

Even though Sinding was to remain in financially straitened circumstances for some years, at least his music was getting published, Wilhelm Hansen having already given out a number of his works. Delius's difficulties in interesting publishers in his music were to continue for some 15 years before he would finally enter into an agreement with the Berlin firm of Harmonie in 1906. One of the earliest of a good many letters of rejection came in February 1891. Presumably on Grieg's recommendation, he had sent some songs to Max Abraham. Abraham returned them with friendly but firm advice to the composer first to make a name for himself with piano pieces or short chamber works. Songs, of which several thousand were being published annually in Germany, would not win him recognition. Abraham hoped to come to Paris in April: if he did so, he would pay a call on Delius and talk the matter over.

45. EDVARD GRIEG TO FRITZ DELIUS

Copenhagen 22nd Decbr
90.
Hotel König v. Dänemark.

Dear Delius,

I have been intending to write for so long and then came your kind letter this evening.

I am very moved — a few hours ago I was told in the street that *Gade*[1] was dead, (he had visited me the day before) I hurried to his home — and there lay the handsome old man, stiff and cold, but he looked gentle and happy. Carried off quite suddenly by a thrombosis.—

I have been travelling for 2 months, conducted a few concerts in Christiania and am now living here quite quietly without giving any public performances. Whether we shall go anywhere south in the spring is still undecided. I should love to hear your overture 'På Vidderne'[2] — and what about the opera material?[3] It must surely contain much that is capital. Ibsen is in Munich and has just enriched the world with a play. — It is called: Hedda Gabler and is in some respects a masterpiece, but — too coldly and carefully calculated. No matter, it's marvellous that the old man can still produce something of this quality.

Farewell, my dear chap! And a thousand Christmas greetings and New Year dittos from my wife and from your

Edvard Grieg

The new year must see us in Norway, mustn't it?

Write soon!

How are your prospects for the future? I am very eager to hear about them.

Autograph letter, signed and dated. Envelope addressed: Monsieur Fritz Delius./8 B^d de la Mairie/Croissy/(S & O.)/France. The removal of postage stamps has obliterated a Copenhagen postmark. Receiving postmark: CROISSY 25 DEC 90.

1   Niels Wilhelm Gade (1817–90): Danish composer. Grieg had first met him in 1863 in Copenhagen and, although never formally studying with him, had come to appreciate his advice and encouragement. Grieg's youthful Symphony in c minor was a direct outcome of Gade's advice to him to write a symphony rather than piano pieces and songs, the earliest of which Gade had considered to be mere trifles.

2   Delius could evidently not get Ibsen's poem out of his head. Presumably convinced that his *Paa Vidderne* melodrama stood little chance of public performance in prevailing circumstances, he wrote a completely new work of the same name — effectively a symphonic poem even if he called it a 'concert overture'. Tending to the bombastic, the piece is at times heavily scored and one wonders if recent study of some of Selmer's work may not have exerted some influence on him. At all events, this latest piece was now in Iver Holter's hands, and Holter liked it well enough to programme it for the Christiania Musikforening's following season.

3   Sandwiched as it is in Grieg's letter between references to *Paa Vidderne* and to Ibsen and *Hedda Gabler*, this allusion must surely be to a further Ibsen work. Delius had already discarded *Emperor and Galilean*, the subject of his interest nearly two years earlier, but while living at Croissy he had written to Emma Klingenfeld, Ibsen's German transla-tor, whose version of *The Feast at Solhaug* (a play first published in 1856) had been published in Leipzig in 1888: 'A short while ago I wrote to Herr Henrik Ibsen on the subject of my plan to adapt "*The Feast at Solhaug*" as a lyric drama. He replied to me saying that I should apply to you & that you own the German publication rights. I take the liberty herewith of asking you if you will permit me to adapt your translation to music' [ALS in Oslo University Library]. No reply from Klingenfeld has been found, but three pages of a pencil draft score for full orchestra, evidently intended as a prelude to the proposed opera, survive among various sketches for the work in the Delius Trust Archive. No more progress was made on this particular project, but Delius had by now begun work on *Irmelin*, his first opera, which was to be completed in 1892 and for which he would write the libretto himself.

46. FRITZ DELIUS TO EDVARD GRIEG

Claremont
Bradford
10 March 91.

My dear Grieg

Many thanks for your kind letter, please forgive me for not answering it earlier, I have been very busy for the whole winter & now I have come to Bradford for a few days. This winter has been really cold-hearted & dragged a lot of good artists away with itself into eternity. You ask me about my prospects! All goes well as concerns my spiritual development & my material affairs trouble me little. I have enough to eat & for the present I am satisfied with that. How I should love to come back to Norway this summer! & to wander a little in Jotunheim. If it weren't for all that marching through storms etc. I would be there at once. Shall we go together & have a jolly time? Write & let me know. I am staying at home here for another 10 days & then go to London for a few days, then back to Paris, where I am after all quite at home & can work very well. The whole race is surely higher & nobler, more adept & more ingenious than the ham-eaters.[1] How I would love to be with you for a while, just to live for a little in your atmosphere again. You really know nothing of mine, apart from my very earliest efforts. I must bring a few scores to Norway with me.

Farewell my very dear Grieg & best wishes to your dear wife. Write soon!

Yours
Fritz Delius

8 B^d de la Mairie
Croissy
(Seine & Oise)

Autograph letter, signed and dated.

1   *Schinkenfresser* (i.e. Germans) in the original letter.

47. EDVARD GRIEG TO FRITZ DELIUS

Christiania 1st May 91.

Dear Delius,

Yes, I really am still alive and am looking forward very much to seeing you again. So you are coming to Norway this summer? That is marvellous! We are setting off for home in about a fortnight's time and will be staying put there. It would be best if you were to come around the middle of July. I shall be at work until then, and then perhaps we shall go up into the mountains for a while. My wife says you have a straw hat to pick up! So you are obliged to come! We are expecting Brodsky and his wife & perhaps Novacek too.[1] So, if by chance there should be no 'lodgings' available at Troldhaugen, we shall find something suitable nearby and have a splendid time fishing, bathing and climbing. And to cap it all you have some new scores! I spent a lazy winter in Copenhagen. Began various things, but finished nothing.

I am sitting here like a painter's model. Interesting but boring?! — I am looking forward as never before to my lovely Westland! You are heartily welcome and must write soon.

Yours
Edvard Grieg

We see a good deal of Sinding daily. He has written some beautiful songs.

Autograph letter, signed and dated. Envelope addressed: M. Fritz Delius./8 B^d de la Mairie/Croissy/(Seine & Oise)/France. Postmark obscured. Receiving postmark: CROISSY 5 [? MAI 91].

1 Ottokar Nováček (1866–1900): Hungarian violinist and composer. He was a friend and contemporary of Delius's at Leipzig, where he was for a time a member of the Brodsky Quartet.

Plans for another summer tour to Norway were developing. Sinding had written from Christiania on 16 April to tell Delius that Grieg, who had just arrived from Copenhagen, was proposing that they all go into the mountains again. 'The Brodskys are perhaps coming here too, and Grieg is naturally very keen to show them the splendours of Norway. Whether I can join you I don't yet know [. . .] The Griegs and Holter send their regards.' By 5 May, however, Sinding's personal position had changed: he had too much work to do and would have to stay in Christiania. Before long, he was arranging the passages from Antwerp to Christiania of both Delius and Arvesen, sending tickets to Delius on 21 May. He apparently had a source of free tickets for this route, a letter from William Molard to Delius in August 1893 providing another piece of evidence for this: 'We might perhaps have gone to Dröbak if Mors Lil ['Mother's boy', i.e. Sinding] had got the free trip he promised for us from Antwerp to X^{ia}.' The source was, as it now appears, Sinding's friend Augusta Gade, to whom he was evidently becoming more and more attracted and whose father was in the shipping business. That Grieg was once again hugely looking forward to the holiday is clear from a letter to Abraham dated 11 June: 'You really are coming! Bravo!! [. . .] Stay for a few days with us in Bergen, along with the Brodskys, before we all of us together, maybe with Delius and Beyer too, go to Jotunheim.' And on 17 June he wrote to Holter: 'Everybody will be mucking in at Troldhaugen: Brodsky with his wife and sister-in-law fru Picard, dr. Abraham, Delius, Holter and, I hope, Sinding.' Since Olga Picard had earlier been the object of Sinding's affections but had already split with him in 1889, it was probably a good thing that all did *not* come to Troldhaugen. Sinding may have got wind a little earlier of Olga's possible visit to the Griegs and so pleaded too much work as an excuse for himself not to put in an appearance.

Delius arrived in Christiania on Sunday 28 June, and after spending a few days in the capital travelled north to Gjøvik, a small town facing the rather larger town of Hamar across Lake Mjøsa. Arvesen was to participate in a recital the following evening, 4 July, as was the distinguished operatic soprano, Gina Oselio. Arriving at his hotel at Gjøvik, Delius met Bjørnstjerne Bjørnson and other members of the Bjørnson family. Bjørnson's daughter Bergliot was the link between him and the family. Like Gina Oselio, she had studied with Mme Marchesi in Paris, and it was in Paris that Delius had first met her, almost certainly through their mutual friend Arve Arvesen. Oselio herself was to marry Bjørnson's son Bjørn in 1893.

On Sunday 5 July, it was on to Aulestad, Bjørnson's home, where Delius was to stay for six days as the great man's guest. The time was spent sightseeing, walking, bathing, making music and, on one notable occasion, listening to Bjørnson reading aloud his recently-completed *Peace Oratorio*. This work had been written at Grieg's express request as the text for what was intended to be — in Grieg's own words — a 'modern Requiem, without dogmatism' (an interesting pre-echo of Delius's concept of a 'pagan' Requiem of nearly a quarter of a century later). Bjørnson had first read the finished text to Grieg in Copenhagen at Easter, but Grieg, in spite of his admiration for it, was unable to find either the inspiration or the energy needed to tackle the task. 'Just at that time,' he later wrote to Bjørnson, 'my health received the serious blow that shook the very foundations of my creative energy.'

On the day that Delius left Aulestad, he inscribed for Bjørnson a short musical quotation, signing it 'Fritz Delius. Aulestad. le 11 Juillet, 91.' This was a result of Bjørnson having sent a poem in manuscript to Bergliot in Paris over a year earlier. It began 'Skogen gir susende, langsom besked', had been written long before, and had just been found among his papers by his wife. 'Someone should set it to music,' he had written to Bergliot. She evidently passed the poem to Delius, and shortly thereafter he made a setting of it which remained in manuscript during his lifetime, but which was finally published as no.1 of a set of *Four Posthumous Songs* in 1981. It was the first four bars of this song that Delius wrote out for Bjørnson as a farewell thankyou.

It seems that it may have been something of a rarity for Bjørnson to entertain Englishmen at his home, for if he raised the appropriate national flag for foreign visitors, he obviously lacked the Union Jack, asking Delius to procure one for him. Delius wrote to him from Troldhaugen on 29 July: 'The English flag will very soon arrive at Aulestad, but please use it with care otherwise you will be overrun by English tourists. I shall always think back with pleasure on my delightful stay at Aulestad and I thank you and your wife for your kind reception [. . .] The Griegs send many greetings.' [ALS in Oslo University Library]

Delius stayed the night of 11 July in Lillehammer, spending the evening there with Bergliot Bjørnson and other friends; and then, having passed a further night in Christiania, took a steamer down the Christiania Fjord to Drøbak to see Sinding. He stayed for two nights there at the home of Augusta Gade and her husband. On 15 July he continued to Fredriksvaern, where he was to spend much of his time with a painter friend, Hjalmar Johnsen, as well as with 'the Backers', one of whom would have been the painter Hans Henrik Sartz Backer (1865–1948), who had studied with Johnsen at Fredriksvaern in 1888–89. He was related to a considerably more famous artist, Harriet Backer, and spent some six months painting together with her in the early 1890s. (Harriet herself was sister to the celebrated pianist and

111

composer Agathe Backer-Grøndahl (1847–1907).) Hans Backer had studied for some five months in Paris in 1889–90 and it is conceivable that he may then have met Delius. He had also helped, with conspicuous personal success, to set up the Norwegian section of the 1889 Universal Exhibition.

48. FRITZ DELIUS TO EDVARD GRIEG

Fredrichsvaern
16 July 91.

My dear Grieg

I arrived here yesterday from Aulestad where I spent a very pleasant week at Bjørnsen's. Holter isn't here but on a sailing tour, & I expect him back any day. I fear that I haven't enough money to come to the Jotunheim with you this year. Are you quite sure that you are going there? I really don't know what to do. If I could perhaps spend a few days with you when you come back from the Jotunheim, then I would stay on here quietly until then. Please write a few lines to me at Wasilliofs Hotel. I should so much love to see you again & to stay with you for a while, I have much to tell you & much to show you. Write & tell me how we can best arrange it, I am staying for a fairly long time in Norway this year in order to hear my overture which Holter is going to perform.[1] Best wishes to you & your wife & Troldhaugen

Yours
Fritz Delius

Wasilliofs Hotel
Fredrichsvaern

The Björnsens send their best wishes & hope to see you soon at Aulestad.

Autograph letter, signed and dated.

1 *Paa Vidderne.*

Grieg evidently invited his friend to come straight away to Bergen, as Delius left Fredriksvaern on Sunday 19 July, having spent just four nights in the town. Holter joined him at Kristiansand and they continued to Bergen by coastal steamer, though making a short rail diversion en route. Grieg came in to Bergen to meet them off the steamer and then accompanied them home to Troldhaugen. He wrote to Bjørnson on 23 July: 'I have just got one of your guests in my home. — the Englishman Delius, a talented and modern musician — with an exceptionally likeable nature. I am now going with him to Jotunheim.' For some reason or other the Jotunheim project was almost immediately shelved, as Delius's rather short diary entry makes clear:

Spent a delightful week sea-bathing, fishing & taking walks. Then all of us — Griegs, Holter & I, left for Hardanger — Lofthus on the Sørfjord — where we stayed a few days. We all left for Odda, where we stayed the night, leaving by carriage next morning for Haukeli via Røldal — a lovely spot, where we stayed the night, visiting an old church down in the valley. Next day a heavenly drive in the sunshine to Haukeli Saeter, where we had a good dinner & a good bottle of Burgundy. Next morning, Grieg being rather unwell, I took a walk with Mrs Grieg on the Vidder — picking lovely blue & brown gentian flowers. Again a lovely day. Next day said farvel to the Griegs & left in the pouring rain for Grungedal, Botn, Vinje, Dale. [Autograph MS in Grainger Museum]

While Delius's route, if continued more or less in the same direction, would have taken him back to Fredriksvaern, the Griegs turned north again. The Röntgen family had arrived at Lofthus and Edvard and Nina were to join them there. Röntgen and Grieg then continued up to the Jotunheim, where they were shortly to be joined by Frants Beyer.

It was either during this visit to Troldhaugen or during Delius's earlier visit to the Griegs in 1889 that young Annie Grieg's modesty had needed to be protected. She recalled to Sigmund Torsteinson, then Troldhaugen's curator, many years later how, while visiting her uncle and aunt, the manly young Fritz Delius had suddenly been spotted from the house serenely walking up, on his way back from bathing in the lake, without a stitch of clothing on him. Nina had dashed out to envelop him in a large towel and Annie's honour was — more or less — preserved. The incident, remembered by Fru Halvorsen with amusement, throws an interesting sidelight on the evidently very easy-going friendship with the Griegs.*

Although the diary entry does not specify it, Delius and Holter must surely have kept company all the way back to Fredriksvaern. Holter may not have stayed on much longer at what was one of his favourite summer resorts, but Delius certainly seems to have done so — very likely at the well-known hotel run by Wassilioff, and his sister Tatjana, a Polish couple. He had stayed at Wassilioff's earlier in the summer, as well as during his 1889 trip.

Why Fredriksvaern? An old naval port with a fortress, Fredriksvaern was little more than a village close by the modern port of Larvik. As a summer resort it was ideally situated, looking out to the open sea with hills behind and with a good railway link to Christiania, little more than 100 kilometres — as the crow flies — to the north. Vilhelm Krag called it the 'poets' village': the stillness and serenity of Fredriksvaern, he said, had a character of its own and one could be alone there, but never lonely.† The writer Nils Collett Vogt (1864–1937) had been the first to discover it and painters like Hjalmar Johnsen, musicians like Iver Holter and poets like Krag himself soon followed.

Delius certainly seems to have been content to stay there well into the autumn, and the Griegs even came down to see him. Their own autumn was to be spent in Christiania, and one wonders if they were present at the concert given by the Christiania Musikforening on Saturday 10 October, when Holter conducted two notable orchestral premières. One was of a work of his own: *Suite for large orchestra from the music to 'Götz von Berlichingen'*, which opened the concert, and the other was of Delius's *Paa Vidderne*, which the programme described as a 'Concert Overture for large orchestra'. The final work on the bill, it was the first orchestral piece of Delius's to achieve a full public performance, and Delius had prolonged his stay in Norway specifically to hear it. He probably stayed in Christiania a few days beforehand so that he could attend rehearsals. He would certainly earlier have made excursions to the city to see new friends like Randi Blehr, wife of the prominent Liberal politician Otto Blehr and well known for her pioneering work in the field of women's rights. Around this time she had written him a letter from Holmenkollen, above Christiania, saying that she hoped he would visit her there soon: 'I stood "på vidderne" and from there I sent you my greetings *above* the

* Oral evidence, Sigmund Torsteinson/Lionel Carley, Troldhaugen, 2 May 1976.
† Vilhelm Krag: *Dengang vi var tyve Aar*. Oslo: Aschehoug, 1927, p.152–3.

Christiania mist over to Nordstrand' (Nordstrand was just some six kilometres south of the city on the Bundefjord). The introduction to Randi Blehr had probably come about through Grieg, whom she knew well, but she had many other artist and composer friends and Hjalmar Johnsen and Christian Sinding were among them.

49. NINA GRIEG TO FRITZ DELIUS

Kristiania 24th Oct.
91. —

Dear Delius,

Many thanks for your letter, it gave me *such* pleasure. The reason why I write at once is that you must not expect us on Sunday. There is so much for Grieg to do here just at present that he just cannot get away. But I hope that we shall meet here again one day — would simply like to know *when* you are coming, so that we are not taken up with something silly. — Yes, I can quite understand that you are still staying quietly in Fredriksvaern, it was quite horrible weather on Thursday evening. I thought of you so much when I heard it whistling through the stovepipe and — no, enough of this nonsense! —

What you say about 'lonely people' I don't understand, I have a lot of objections to what you say, but would rather chat it over with you than write it.

— It was so glorious in Fredriksvaern that I am quite unable to forget it. Such scenery is very much to my taste, how I would love to live there for a while! Such contrasts as 'Krabbehullet'[1] in a storm, 'woodbines' smelling so sweetly, moonlight through wild, hurrying clouds and sunshine through trees in gold — God, isn't it all wonderful! And then to look out far, far into the sea!—

Do forgive me, dear Delius, just say with Ibsen 'one sees you are a woman, you have so many words'—

Well, I look forward to seeing you again, for we shall see each other here, shan't we?
Best wishes from Edvard and from

Yours very sincerely
Nina Grieg.

Autograph letter, signed and dated.

1   Lit: *Crab-hole*. In Norwegian in the original letter. According to local
expert Stig Hatlo, the reference is likely to be to a summer chalet —
across the bay to the south of Fredriksvaern — 'Rakkehuset', which is
still owned and used by descendants of the Grieg/Halvorsen family.
(Information kindly supplied by Liv Andresen, Chief Librarian, Larvik
Bibliotek.)

50.   NINA GRIEG TO FRITZ DELIUS

Kristiania 16th November 91.—

Dear Delius,

Well, what a faithless one you are! Do you know the old
saying: out of sight, out of mind? Does that apply to you as
well? — I suppose that you have finally become so absorbed in
rattling that you can think about nothing but the mutual
rattle. Well, — if that is the case I suppose I must be patient
and wait until you have calmed down enough to be in a
position to spare a few thoughts for us again.

— But seriously: how are you? why have you sent no word?
I must confess that I have long been expecting a few lines from
you and am just a little bit disappointed that it has so far been
in vain. Do you find me too demanding? Who knows! —

There was a concert again on Saturday at the 'Musikforening', a Grieg Concert.[1] I sat up there in the guests' box with
Sinding and we talked also of you, which you certainly did not
deserve if you can forget us for the very first 'rattlesnake' that
comes along. The pieces 'Olav Trygvason', 'Peer Gynt' Suite
II, 'Before a Southern Convent' etc. went quite well, but it can
never really sound right in the Circus, one always has to use
one's imagination to have any idea as to how it should really
sound. But there was great enthusiasm with laurel wreaths,
torches and all the rest of it. Next Saturday is Edvard's own
concert, the 28th Sinding's and then at the beginning of
December we are off from here in snow and ice over the
mountains. So we shall have to endure the winter storms up
there at Troldhaugen, — well, I don't know, I am not afraid,
would rather have that than just walk up and down here on
the Karl Johan. Nevertheless — I would most of all love to go
to the South!

almost summer-like, the fields quite green and the trees full of fat buds. The path from Hop is quite soft and wet, and the big stones are still lying there   you remember, down where it was always so muddy. Snow and sun and sledging are all over with here, but up there in the mountains I often had to think of you and your Sleigh Ride. Heavens, how I chatter! A merry Christmas and a happy New Year to you with all my heart. We both send all our good wishes.

Yours very sincerely
Nina Grieg.

We are sending you a little book of poems by a young Norwegian poet called Kragh.[1] There is so much feeling in them.

Just imagine, we have received a charming little picture from Hjalmar Johnsen too, done from his window in Fredriks-vaern, although a winter scene I really am incredibly happy to have a souvenir from down there.[2]

Somewhere I expect you will have read about Edvard's Jubilee celebrations and the students' torchlight procession? It was wonderful.

Van Druten has translated Jonas Lie's 'onde Magter' (boose Geesten)[3] and sent them to Edvard.

Autograph letter, signed and dated.

1   Vilhelm Krag (1871–1933): Norwegian author and poet. He came into prominence in 1891 with the publication in Bergen of his first volume of poems (*Digte*). Sinding wrote six songs to his texts later in the year, Gina Oselio being the first to sing one of them, 'Moderen synger', in Christiania on 19 November. Grieg himself set five of Krag's poems as his op.60 in 1893–94, and Delius just one, 'Jeg havde en nyskaaren Seljefløjte', almost certainly in 1893 when Krag visited him in Paris. It is probable that this particular poem has survived only in Delius's score (and posthumous publication in 1981), as no publication of the poem *per se* has been found.

2   Delius was to stay in touch with Hjalmar Johnsen for a time: 'I have heard now & then from Johnsen,' he wrote to Randi Blehr on 3 March 1892. 'He is a very kind man & his letters are full of feeling: his brother also has sent me his poems. Unfortunately I don't understand them very well.' Peter Rosenkrantz Johnsen (1857–1929), Hjalmar's brother, was to be better known for his prose writings and journalism.

3   A Dutch translation of *Evil Powers*, Lie's novel first published in 1890.

52.   FRITZ DELIUS TO EDVARD GRIEG

33 Rue Ducouëdic
Montrouge
Paris   25 Dec 91.

My dear Grieg,

I wish you & Frau Grieg much good fortune in the New Year
& very good health too. I will think of you on New Year's Eve
& of all the lovely times we have had together.

It has been terribly cold here; today, however, it is raining
& has become quite mild again. Last Sunday Colonne[1] gave
the Ninth Symphony & also Wagner's Bacchanalia from
Tannhäuser   I have never seen Colonne conduct like that.
Quite remarkable. On Sunday he gives the same concert.

Are you staying in Bergen for the whole winter, or are you
going to Copenhagen again? Lamoureux twice gave a symphonic poem of Richard Strauss, there were splendid things in
it but also frightful echoes of Tannhäuser's Bacchanalia. It
was *Don Juan*   Never have the Concerts been so interesting as
this year. Come over here for a while, you will perhaps enjoy it
better than last time. Farewell, dear Grieg   Give my best
wishes to your dear wife & write to me soon.

Yours
Fritz Delius

Autograph letter, signed and dated.

1   Edouard Colonne (1838–1910): French conductor and violinist. He
founded in Paris in 1873 the series of concerts that was eventually to
bear his name. From 1894–97, Halfdan Jebe played the violin in
Colonne's orchestra.

53.   NINA GRIEG TO FRITZ DELIUS

Troldhaugen 2nd March.
92. —

Dear Delius,

So in other words: the old 'uns are jealous, they say: All or
Nothing, so they strew snow between you and the dangerous
girls. It all looks very serious, and yet, you can quite easily

overcome this difficulty because — *it is just as easy to rattle along on 'Langski',*[1] the greybeards have forgotten that, for all their wisdom. If you spend a winter here in Norway, it will soon be seen who is the stronger. You may in the meantime write a fairytale about it if you like, fairytales have a wonderful way of saying everything in a veiled way. Can you not make it into a libretto, — say about an unhappy young man on whom a spell has been cast by the mountains? Is he eventually to escape, or are the mountains to keep his heart forever? I believe he will become free in the end, but only when he finds the right woman, she who can break the spell.

— What is happening this summer? What are your plans? How I would love it if we could all go together somewhere on the 'Vidde'. Well, Sinding is in Paris now too,[2] — can't you two think up something nice? I have never longed for the spring so much as I have this year, the winter has been so unendingly long, so icy cold and so unfriendly. Just imagine the whole of the Nordåsvand frozen as far as the eye can see, — we go for walks in all directions across it, an endless white plain, which disappears far, far away in the mist. God, *how* slowly spring comes to us in the north! In the Bois I expect it will soon be looking lovely, won't it? Please write soon and tell me a little about it, what it is like there, not where the world idly comes and goes, but deep in the woods, where it is dark, where it is lonely and still. — And how are you? So you are working hard, — what are you writing? Do you hear anything from home, does the sun of favour shine on you or not? You are very naughty really, a very wicked fellow because of 'Little Håkon'.[3] And I, always so confident when it was a matter of a promise from you! But I dare to make one more request. I should so much like to have a portrait photograph of you, a really good one, will you make me a present of one? In the autumn I received a splendid one of Sinding, in which I take a daily delight. It stands here and looks at me, a little crossly actually, and yet I did make the portamento from E flat to C — quite *against* my own feelings.[4] How well I now understand why he raved so much to us about Rich. Strauss's 'Tod und Verklärung'. Edvard sent for the score and the arrangement for four hands, and we have had such fun with it. I would dearly love to hear it, it must sound magnificent. There is, by the way, some Wagner in it, and even more Liszt. — All good

wishes from Edvard, — I don't know if he may perhaps write
to you himself — he has had to do some unforeseen work on
'Peer Gynt' recently. Björn[5] wanted to have more music.

And now adieu, dear Delius, all good wishes to you and
Sinding from

Yours very sincerely
Nina Grieg.

I have just heard from Milly Augener that you are in
England.
We don't think we shall be so keen on spending another
winter at Troldhaugen for some time. I have the feeling that
we have both been really longing to get away from the place,
but haven't talked about it.

Autograph letter, signed and dated.

1   lit. *long ski*. In Norwegian in the original letter.
2   'Sinding arrived in Paris a fortnight ago,' Delius wrote to Randi
Blehr on 3 March, 'to see something of Parisian life. He seems to like it
very much here.' A month earlier Sinding had written to ask Delius to
help him during the first part of his stay, as well as to find accommodation 'at a hotel near you' and to meet him at the station.
3   'Cradle Song' ('Vuggevise', from Act 3 of Ibsen's *The Pretenders*),
composed in 1889, was shortly to be published by Augener as no. 1 of
the set of *Seven Songs from the Norwegian*. It was dedicated to Nina Grieg,
who was evidently waiting impatiently for this particular song's arrival
in printed form. *A very wicked fellow because of* is in English in the original
letter.
4   Presumably a reference to Nina's interpretation of one of Sinding's
songs — perhaps at the concert of 28 November 1891?
5   Bjørn Bjørnson (1859–1942): son of Bjørnstjerne Bjørnson and
distinguished in his own right as actor, director and author. Later to
become director of the National Theatre, he was at this time instructor
at the Christiania Theatre. For his production of *Peer Gynt* at the
Christiania Theatre in 1892 he not only directed the play, but designed
the sets and took the title role. He had asked Grieg for more music for
the scene with the 'Great Bøyg', and Grieg — under protest — had
complied.

54. NINA GRIEG TO FRITZ DELIUS

Troldhaugen 1st April
92. —

Dear Delius,

We have had a wonderful day today with spring air and spring sun, soon the summer will come, soon, — well, if only it were not the first of April, il se moque de nous — perhaps! — So you want to keep working till the end of July, well, I suppose that means that you are thinking of Troldhaugen for the end of July?

That ought to be just right for Grieg, for he too will be free then. Then, as soon as we have finished at Troldhaugen we shall go somewhere and enjoy the last of the summer together, shan't we?—

You gave me a lot of pleasure with your last long, kind letter; for once I got to know something about you. You seem to be frightfully industrious, is this really true? And, you know, I was already beginning to think it might be a second or even indeed the real Miss Whitehouse[1] who had drawn you to London.[2] So you see how one can do a rascal an injustice, as we say in Norway. Women really do seem this time to be quite out of the picture, Endymion is the dangerous one who has taken their place.[3] Dangerous enough, since even Diana the chaste goddess kissed him. But that is the only thing that I know about him, who Cynthia is I haven't the faintest idea. Perhaps I here reveal an abysmal mythological ignorance, but please be considerate if this has to be so and come to my aid with your superior knowledge.

— I am most impressed that you are actually writing an opera and even dare to speak of it yourself, — but I am delighted that I know about it and hope you will keep me a little à jour with your progress. It would be delightful if we could hear it in London next winter, but unfortunately the idea of spending some time in London next winter happens to be just one of those things that came into my head. Perhaps I have been building castles in the air as so often before and as I shall continue to do as long as I live, one must, after all, have such small pleasures if they can make one happy, it does no harm even if the happiness is only of the imaginary kind. —

But it was the opera I was talking about. Why don't you write the libretto yourself? You yourself spoke about this some time ago and surely one then works much more freely? Of course I find your little poem 'Northern Nights'[4] beautiful, so poetic and evocative, it shows moreover so much understanding for our wonderful summer nights and their luminous twilight. Yes, there we agree, that too is the time for me, and I would not want to miss it in any year, returning as ever to exercise the same magic over us. The same with 'den Bjergtekne'.[5] The piece conjures up for me the pure Norwegian scenery, so primordial that it impresses itself upon us malgré nous whenever we wander in summer in lonely valleys through chasms, thickets and river spray. Of all that Grieg has done, this is perhaps the piece I like best of all, — am not really sure — and I am absolutely delighted that it has been performed in Paris, although of course the people there cannot possibly understand it. How was the performance, by the way? One cannot judge by the fact that the piece moved you, you are a musician and can use your imagination and knowledge. —

Last but not least,[6] many thanks for the picture. You made a poor job of packing it, with the result that it suffered badly in transit. Do make a better job of it when you send your own picture — with cardboard on both sides. Your two little sisters are charming, but I believe, if I am to judge by what you have told me, that they are far from being flattered. Is that not so?

No, I cannot imagine you without a moustache, in particular I cannot conceive of how you manage to get by without having a moustache to stroke. — Every time I write to you I find myself alarmed at how long my letter grows, — Grieg makes fun of me too — it is also a great failing not to be able to express oneself briefly and concisely, it does not come naturally to me, at least not when I write in German. Forgive me, dear Delius; I will mend my ways if possible. Farewell and write and tell me how you are and what Paris looks like in its spring dress.

With all my good wishes

Yours very sincerely
Nina Grieg.

Grieg is sitting downstairs and working, he is looking forward to seeing you here in the summer and sends kindest regards.

Poor Sinding, getting such a chill and not being able to speak. I too was fearfully vexed at my helplessness when we were in Paris.

Can you remember a summer evening last year when we went to Tveteråsskoven[7] and you picked a bunch of flowers? They are still behind the mirror in the dining room and will stay there until you bring a new bunch in the summer.

Johannes Wolff[8] is giving some concerts here now. He came to lunch with us the day before yesterday and played right through the day until eleven o'clock in the evening. He is a fantastic player. That youthful tenor tone and rhythmic verve carries one utterly away.

Autograph letter, signed and dated.

1 No other reference to Miss Whitehouse has been found.

2 In his letter to Randi Blehr of 3 March, Delius had told of having 'so much to do' in London recently.

3 Together with other British newspapermen, Richard Le Gallienne (1866–1947), the poet and journalist, had been invited by a Norwegian steamship company to visit Norway in the summer of 1891. During the course of his trip he befriended Peter Rosenkrantz Johnsen and Rosenkrantz must have mentioned Delius and the fact that he was anxiously looking for a writer with whom to collaborate on an opera. Le Gallienne and Delius were soon corresponding and when the composer stayed with the poet and his wife in their home on the outskirts of London in February 1892, a subject was chosen. 'We have sketched out the plot of a little opera together on the story of Endymion — and he has gone back full of it', Le Gallienne noted at the end of the month. Until recently all trace of this work was lost, but some sketches at last came to light in 1982. Nothing, unfortunately, was to come of the collaboration, but the search for a librettist — now for *Irmelin* — continued. In the end, Delius decided to write his text himself. It was something of an act of faith for Le Gallienne, who knew little about music, to accept so readily the idea of teaming up with a composer of whom scarcely anyone had heard, but it had apparently been enough for him to learn that Delius was a friend of Grieg and that he had more than once been Grieg's house guest.

Le Gallienne was to return to Norway in August 1892, together with his publisher John Lane. Rosenkrantz Johnsen gave them a letter of introduction to Bjørnson, whom they duly visited at Aulestad (welcomed, one hopes, by 'Delius's' flag). And Rosenkrantz himself conducted Le Gallienne to the Grand Café in Christiania and introduced him to Ibsen, acting as interpreter for the occasion.

4   Possibly a translation into German of Holger Drachmann's 'Lyse Naetter', a first attempt at which is to be found in Delius's 'red notebook'.

5   *Den Bergtekne (The Mountain Thrall)*, for baritone, string orchestra and two horns, op.32, composed 1877–78.

6   *Last but not least*: in English in the original letter.

7   Tveiteraas and Tveit Vand lie a little to the east of Hop. Nina is referring to the wood at Tveiteraas.

8   Johannes Wolff, the Dutch violinist, had played Grieg's Violin Sonata no.3 with the composer in London in March 1889 and again in Paris in January 1890. Grieg probably effected his introduction to Delius. Wolff was to ask Delius in 1896 for a full score of his *Légende* (RT VII/3), as he was scheduling a London performance of the work for January 1897.

55.   NINA GRIEG TO FRITZ DELIUS

Troldhaugen 16th May 92.

Dear Delius,

Will you be so kind as to give Sinding the enclosed letter, I don't know his address. — We have not heard from you for ages, since the beginning of March in fact! How are you? Is it possible that you have not received my last letter? Thank goodness we are getting on better now, but we have been through a really miserable time. Came the day when Grieg could no longer walk because of rheumatic pains in both feet, he was obliged to rest up for three weeks. Now he takes the train to town twice a day to have a massage and can walk quite decently again. — Spring has come to us at last, it is splendour without compare. When are you thinking of coming to Norway? We expect you here, you know, by the end of July at the latest, Holter will certainly be coming then. Sinding will probably stay in Dröbak or wherever his — destiny may otherwise lead him. — On 11th June we shall be celebrating our silver wedding anniversary here, I think we both would like to be able to escape somewhere e.g. to Fredriksvaern, but we have become slaves of circumstance and will have to stay at Troldhaugen. We shall take our revenge all right later, I hope.—

If you have not too much on, then, do write soon. I should

like to know: who is the one making the demands on you, your capricious muse or an ordinary mortal?

All good wishes from Grieg and from

Yours very sincerely
Nina Grieg.

Autograph letter, signed and dated.

56. NINA GRIEG TO FRITZ DELIUS

Troldhaugen 29th June.
92.

Dear Delius,

Well then, quelque chose plus fort que les montagnes! 'I fear I shall *not* be coming to Norway' is the long and short of it! There is a saying that goes man's sweetest of dishes is that which he wishes, and perhaps it is true: Your sweetest dish at the moment seems to be '3 rooms and a kitchen' —![1] But, — joking apart, we felt *very* sorry that you intend to leave us in the lurch this year, I had looked forward enormously to being able to wander around 'on Vidderne' with you again. Another time is a mischievous thing to say and I am pessimistic enough not to expect much from the future, it is very dangerous for us human beings, who must inexorably drift along with the stream, to put things off till tomorrow. Mais — nous verrons! — I don't wish to be indiscreet, so I won't ask you *why* you are not coming, you can speak if you wish, if you prefer to keep it to yourself — to be 'gentlemanly' about it, I shall certainly not pry into your innermost self.—

Thank you very much for your greetings on our wedding anniversary. It turned out to be a real festival with sunshine from morning to evening, with thousands of happy people, with bonfires on the islands in the Nordåsvand and with masses of boats on the calm water. Up at Troldhaugen as many guests as possible in the house and garden, singing and 'skåls' long into the wonderful brightly shining summer night. Finally a beautiful song by Sinding to the most moving words of Jonas Lie.[2] Bergen presented us with a beautiful Steinway, Christiania with a Werenskjold[3] and a splendid bear skin. Do you still remember the bear skin you fell in love with last year in Haukelia? This one is much more beautiful and bigger, I can stretch out full length on it — goodness, I have to laugh when I think how little is needed, — but I am certain that it is even big enough for you and that says more. Just come and try it yourself. You would not at all recognize our simple living room any more, it is all so fine and splendid here, really far too elegant for us. — I don't yet know what we shall do this summer, whether we shall go to the mountains somewhere together, or whether just Edvard will visit the Saeter-jentene[4] with Fr. Beyer. If by any chance you have changed your plans and come to Norway after all, please write to us at once so that we do not miss each other. In the autumn we are certainly going away, but *where* we have not yet decided. I am glad that we are not going to spend another winter here, life is not long enough that one can afford to be wasteful with it. — Finally, many hearty thanks for the songs. I am very fond of them, the last one especially appeals to me. Only it's a pity for me that they are so *highly* erotic, and it just doesn't work, to transpose Love.[5]

— Now farewell, dear Delius, let us hope that we shall meet up with each other again in life somewhere; I would not like it to end with this, we are too fond of one another for that, aren't we?

— Many, many good wishes from yours very sincerely

Nina Grieg.

The Engdronninge[6] are beginning to blossom again.—

Holter spent a week here, perhaps he will be coming again, I don't know.

Autograph letter, signed and dated.

1 Delius had moved towards the end of 1891 into Paris itself, taking a modest apartment in the rue Ducouëdic, in the Montrouge district.
2 'To Edvard and Nina Grieg on their Silver Wedding' ('Tungsind, o tungsind i tause Fjeld'), published by Hals in July 1892. Grieg wrote of the occasion to Röntgen on 19 June: 'I may say that if I exclude the exhibition in the Crystal Palace at Sydenham, I have never seen so many flowers.'
3 Erik Werenskjold (1855–1938): Norwegian painter and illustrator. His various portraits of Grieg, Ibsen and Bjørnson are well known, as are his illustrations to Asbjørnsen and Moe's *Norske Folkeeventyr*. He also

depicted vividly and realistically Norwegian peasant life and land-scapes.

4 *Farm girls, milkmaids*. In Norwegian in the original letter.

5 In *Delius: A Life in Letters 2*, I assumed that this was more likely a reference to the *Seven Songs from the Norwegian* than to the *Three Shelley Songs* (RT V/12) also published by Augener in 1892. However, Nina's allusion to their being '*highly* erotic' should really have made it obvious that it was the Shelley songs she was writing of, in particular the last of these, 'To the Queen of my Heart'.

6 *Meadowsweet*. In Norwegian in the original letter.

57. EDVARD GRIEG TO FRITZ DELIUS

[Troldhaugen, 29 June 1892]

Dear friend,

I am not at all pleased that you are not coming to us this summer![1] I cannot show you any new music, the only new thing I have available is this cursed gout in my feet, which has been plaguing me since February and has driven off the urge to work. But if you come and bring summer with you, then the gout must go, I am quite sure. Some Norway would do you a lot of good. And you would find here a friendship that will be just as new as it is old! Think the matter over. At any rate, we are staying here for the whole of July and the first half of August.

Many good wishes!

Yours
Edvard Grieg

We must talk further about your songs. There are some very lovely things in them. I feel, however, that in some respects you are treading dangerous ground. But one cannot put these things in writing.

Autograph letter, signed and undated, following immediately on from Letter 56.

1 'This summer I am staying in Bretagne,' Delius wrote on 1 July to another acquaintance, Ola Thommessen, editor and proprietor of the Christiania daily *Verdens Gang*, '& hope next summer to be able to come to Norway again & of course hope to meet you well & healthy.' Delius had left for Brittany around the end of June. It seems that he stayed on the Breton and Norman coasts for the entire summer.

58. NINA GRIEG TO FRITZ DELIUS

Troldhaugen, 27th July 92.

Dear Delius,

Sad, sad, all is dark and sad! How feeble and insignificant one feels when one is forced to let fate have its way. Edvard has been lying ill here for so many weeks now and we cannot find the herb which will cure him. I would like to fly around like the peri in order to seek out the gift which could propitiate the gods, but — I would not, like the peri, succeed.—

The doctors aren't really there to any purpose, it's almost as easy to treat oneself as well, or as badly, as they. He is suffering from enteritis and is able to digest hardly any food, he has grown thin and pale and dreadfully weakened. Fortunately he hardly notices the rheumatism any more, but I really don't know if we should prefer this present condition. Do you not know of a 'snakeskin' which can cure stomach ills? I almost begin to fear that we are to be chained here for the winter, i.e. starve spiritually. What would you prefer: never to see the mountains again or be forced never to leave them? No, we *must* get out and away again, our migratory nature keeps asserting itself, we cannot possibly marry the daughter or the son of the mountain king, can we?

29th

Thus I wrote the day before yesterday. I was utterly disconsolate then and, in addition, selfish enough to burden you with my grief. Please do not be angry with me for doing so, and rejoice with me because things look much brighter today. Hope is not far off thank God, a glimmer of it is just breaking through again.

— Dear Delius, I find it so very difficult to accept the fact that we are not going to be seeing you here this summer, but now I understand that it cannot be otherwise and so must therefore try to let the bird fly. I have to think of you continually though, for the air is saturated with the smell of the Engdronninge and there is a profusion of flowers in field and forest which is quite unique. But the little blue flowers

15 First page of autograph MS score of *Paa Vidderne*

16 Bjørnstjerne Bjørnson, having already helped Grieg to obtain a composer's grant, now supports an application for Sinding. Contemporary caricature

17 At the Birmingham Music Festival, 1888. Grieg's host, Charles Harding (second left) and members of his family are seen with Frants Beyer (left), Grieg (centre) and poet Didrik Grønvold (right). Harding's son, Copeley, would in his turn be appointed to the Birmingham Festival Committee and, in 1907, to the committee of the newly-founded Musical League, his appointment to the latter being approved by the League's Vice-President, Frederick Delius

18 Gudvangen, on the route taken by Grieg, Delius and Sinding on 24 July 1889

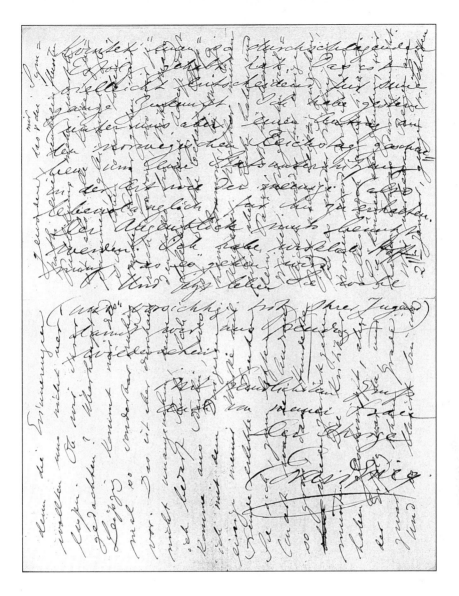

19   Extract from a letter from Grieg to Delius, 4 February 1889

20 Sketches by Delius of exterior and interior of Leirungs Hytte on Lake Gjendin, where he, Grieg and Sinding stayed from 31 July to 8 August 1889

21   Delius, by Edvard Munch, c. 1890

22   Untitled MS sketch by Delius, written while he, Grieg and Sinding
were staying at Leirungs Hytte on Lake Gjendin, early August 1889

23 Page from Delius's orchestration, dated 2 December 1889,
of Grieg's *Norwegian Bridal Procession*

24 Johan Selmer

25 Vilhelm Krag,
by Gudmund Stenersen

26 A Norwegian bridal procession

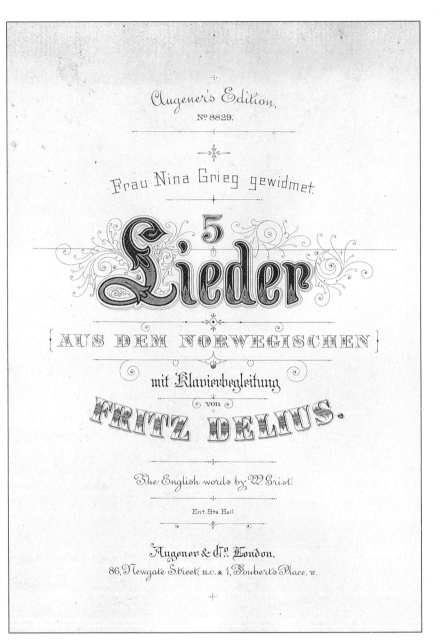

27   Title-page of Delius's *Five Songs from the Norwegian* (with dedication to
Nina Grieg), published by Augener, London 1890

which grow higher up are nowhere to be seen — they were fairytale flowers, you don't find them every day. All the roses have come out in the garden, wonderful — and now, when Edvard gets well again, we shall be able to get out and about in Nature a little and are thinking of setting off in September over the mountains and far away —!!—

Otherwise life glides along quietly and monotonously. In the evenings when I fetch the post at the station I meet Herr Mohn, who politely accompanies me home and tells me all about his family. The rattlesnake[1] is living somewhere in the countryside not far from Christiania. —

And what does it look like where you are living now? Brittany! — Tell me something about it. You have, of course, the great, eternal ocean there, which can, I suppose, make up for the mountains. In reality it is treason to go to the seaside sighing from the heart such lyrical-erotic sighs for the 'Vidder', and yet — to the ears of a Norwegian woman they sound beautiful, she would not wish to have it otherwise. — So, you see, I cannot yet tell you anything definite about our plans, but we shall probably go to Leipzig first, as far as I can judge. We surely must be able to meet each other somewhere, mustn't we? — What are your plans? Impossible for you to come to Leipzig for a little while?

Adieu, dear Delius, all good wishes,

Yours very sincerely
Nina Grieg.

Kind regards from Edvard.

Every morning I sit at the piano down in the hut, where your songs often keep me good company. How is the opera getting on?[2]

Do you read any Norwegian newspapers? What do you say to our sad political circumstances? A situation like this has a frightfully stagnating effect on all progress and all intellectual life[3]

Autograph letter, signed and dated.

1 Evidently a reference to Anna Mohn.
2 Others wanted to know about the progress of Delius's opera: 'How has your libretto turned out?' asked Sinding on 7 July, writing from Drøbak. He again put the question on 18 August. It would seem that he

did not receive a clear reply for some time, but on 17 December he wrote from Berlin: 'Much admire your energy and courage — writing the libretto yourself.'

3   A reference to the political crisis, deepening as the 1890s went on, between Norway and Sweden. Norway wanted its own full foreign service, then still being run by the Ministry of Foreign Affairs in Stockholm. The two countries were to come close to war before Norway finally secured complete independence in 1905, becoming a constitutional monarchy at the same time.

59.   NINA GRIEG TO FRITZ DELIUS

Troldhaugen 1st Sept.
92. —

Dear Delius,

Oh yes, it sounds all very well and you are frightfully persuasive, because you believe in all that. I am prepared to believe that someone who is healthy and who then starts to eat fruit and vegetables, in short becomes a vegetarian, will probably feel quite well, but to offer a sick stomach, which cannot digest anything, fruit as the principal item of its diet, no, dear Delius, you might just as well eat plums as an antidote to cholera. I do not doubt that all I shall get from you now is a scornful smile, but I must run that danger, unable as I am to be one of the faithful. However, that would not matter if Edvard were able to believe in it, but he knows his own nature and knows that it would not allow it. Thank God he is feeling better now, he is beginning to eat again, can take short walks again and — work. In a fortnight's time we would certainly have moved from here, but now this ghastly cholera stands in the way like a 'Böig'.^{1} Que faire? What are you doing? Where are you staying? Are you going to remain in Brittany and is there no cholera there? For heaven's sake, go somewhere where it is healthy, you are free, after all, and can just take yourself off, can't you? We are beginning to talk of going over the other side of the mountains to 'Østlandet'^{2} and to await the course of events somewhere in the countryside, but everything is so much in the air, we just don't know which way to turn. I felt no inclination at all to stay on here at Troldhaugen or in Bergen, I now long to be where life is much more active, it has been quiet around us for so long, but we have never lived through an epidemic, which looms like a spectre there for us. To die — yes, that's the end and we don't need to waste many words over it, but even in death I would rather be an individual, not a number, or a cipher. I should like to talk to you, should like to know how you see it all, perhaps you will smile because of my inability to take a broader view of things, you seem at times to be frightfully calm and balanced. Whatever you do or don't do, don't stay where there is cholera, rather come to Norway. — And now the summer has gone, the summer which didn't even come in the first place, the trees were green, the fields too, all the flowers were there, but we have not had *one single* soft, warm bright summer night, not *once* have we been rocked in the boat by the waves in the twilight of a summer evening. The sun has hardly shown itself at all, it has always been cold and horrid, and for ages now we have had just fog and pouring rain. — And how have things been with you? I ask and you never answer, like a real Englishman. Do you live in a little village, do you go for walks on the seashore, do you look out over the boundless sea??? Forgive me, but I *must* ask, am always curious to know what it looks like elsewhere, especially where those of whom I am fond live. We have seen so little of France, *too* little and I fear that we shall never get to know the country, mainly because we cannot speak the language, and then one feels such an idiot. Will you tell me whether you are working hard and what you are working on or do you want to keep it to yourself? I suppose I hardly need to say that I understand and respect silence. Do tell us soon that all is well with you. At this time one ought not to be without news of one's friends. Carry on writing to Bergen, I hardly dare believe that we shall get away and whatever happens, the letters will of course be sent on.

Ever so many good wishes from

Yours very sincerely
Nina Grieg.

Edvard sends his regards and thanks you for the medicinal herb, of course I do likewise, even if I'm more inclined to believe in a snakeskin or the fur of wild cats.

I see, so you have not kept yourself à jour with our politics.

I really thought that you had your own source of information, — don't be angry with me! — We hear nothing about politics any more, it's all the cholera now.

Why, for heaven's sake, have *you* gone and become a vegetarian?[3] How frightfully boring! You are young and healthy, after all. I hope you will have had more than enough of it by the time we meet again.

Autograph letter, signed and dated.

1   *Bøig: ogre.* In Norwegian in the original letter.
2   *The Eastland,* i.e. the eastern part of southern Norway. In Norwegian in the original letter.
3   Much later in life Delius — long since returned to meat-eating status — was in his turn to poke fun at Percy Grainger for *his* vegetarianism.

60.   NINA GRIEG TO FRITZ DELIUS

Bergen 21st Sept.
92. —

Dear Delius,

Just a few hurried lines before we leave Bergen, — for it really does seem as if this great event will take place, — I say *seem*, for I am by no means certain, Edvard's condition being only just, just tolerable. We intend to leave here the day after tomorrow via Laerdal, Filefjeld. Actually we both wanted very much to go via Haukelid, — I have never travelled by that route, only as far as Haukelid, you know — but it will not be possible unfortunately. When one is ill things must be as little primitive as possible. I am afraid we are both pretty worn out, I have only the one real hope left, that is that a change of air will bring about Edvard's recovery. Thank you very much, dear Delius, for having written back so soon to comfort me. I am indeed very much in need of comforting and what you said about blue skies and sunshine has warmed my heart and filled me with joy, because I have seen it in black and white that there is still sun and blue sky somewhere, here we have forgotten until today what such things look like. At last, after months, today is a beautiful, calm autumn day, clear and cool, with the mountains half-blurred in a veil of mist. How I would love to go to St. Malo — I have just read

Loti's 'Pêcheurs d'Islande', wonderful! — but I hardly dare believe that this can come about, the journey is long, too long for Edvard *now*, if we can manage to get as far as Leipzig, we must of course be glad of that and I suppose for the time being nothing will come of this either. If we manage to arrive safely in Kristiania we shall probably stay there for some time in the hope that the dry air will do Edvard good. Sinding is still there. I had a letter from him yesterday in which he talks of great plans. He also reports chronique scandaleuse from the artist world. Shall I spare you the details? —

So you have had bad luck with your opera, you poor fellow, you once wrote to me of an English poet with whom you were getting on well. What has happened to him? — And what is going to happen to us? — We just do not know where and when we shall meet. How sad! And I had got it so firmly into my head that this winter we should be spending some time so pleasantly together somewhere. What really are your plans for the winter, surely you do not intend to stay in St. Malo? We shall return to the question of our meeting somewhere, shan't we?—

Farewell, dear Delius, and enjoy all the moods of the sun and the sea.

All good wishes from

Yours very sincerely
Nina Grieg.

Edvard sends his best wishes, he has almost lost heart — og jeg synes sa Synd på ham.[1]

Please write to: c/o Brödrene Hals's Musikhandel, Kristiania.

Autograph letter, signed and dated.

1 *And I am so sorry for him.* In Norwegian in the original letter.

61. EDVARD GRIEG TO FRITZ DELIUS

[Christiania, 20 October 1892]

Kjaere Delius!

Der jules[1] (English: It will be Christmassed!) in *Leipzig*! Won't it? It must be so! Well then: here's to seeing you again soon!

Yours
Edv Grieg

Autograph letter, signed and undated, following immediately on from a dated autograph letter of Christian Sinding.

1 In Norwegian in the original letter, Grieg himself supplying a cod translation.

Sinding's letter (quoted below) mentions 'tiresome matters', and this probably relates to his unfortunate but serious split with Holter at this period. Just how the split came about remains unclear, but as a result of it Sinding was to withdraw the original dedication to Holter of his Symphony. 'The painter' is almost certainly Charles Boutet de Monvel; and Mons Lie was Jonas Lie's son.

Thank you very much for the letter and for the news of yourself. God these opera texts! What a rotten business! It's a damned nuisance to be so dependent on others in this sort of thing. To do the text oneself would of course be easiest; it's what I would do too if I were able to discern the slightest talent in myself. Absolutely nothing there. — I shall probably go to Berlin next week, to see if it's possible to get anything done there. I had really intended to give a concert here, but tiresome matters intervened, and I got fed up with it all. It really isn't worth the candle. — Can't you come to Germany too? The Griegs will probably come to Leipzig later; it would be so marvellous if we could all spend another winter together again. — Do give my regards to the Molards and the painter. Have forgotten his name. Do you know Mons Lie's address?

62. NINA GRIEG TO FRITZ DELIUS

Kristiania 26th October 92.

Dear Delius,

Very many thanks for the songs[1] and many more for the dedication! I had almost given up 'little Håkon' for this lifetime, tried as far as possible to resign myself to the fact, which is not at all in my line, — and behold, there he came, accompanied moreover by old friends and bringing new ones with him. He himself is and remains the finest of all, harmonically and melodically taking up all of my heart in his gentle poetic conception. — My head has until now been so full of Sinding — he has written an enormous number of songs by Krag — now I shall lay him aside for a while and listen to your sounds. —

When I wrote to you last time from Bergen I felt rather uncertain, could not bring myself to believe that we could get away, everything was so foggy there. The journey through the countryside too was nowhere near as wonderful as it used to be, that is, the journey in itself was really very pleasant, because the weather was fine, — a miracle for us poor amphibians, who had crawled about in the 'damp and drizzle' for so long — and the late melancholy autumn days so full of sparkle and colours, but we were able to enjoy it very little because all the time Edvard was ailing and finally we had to rest up for a few days on the Randsfjord before daring to come on to Kristiania. He began to get better from the moment we arrived here, thank God. He is almost himself again, and a week on Saturday in the 'Musikforening' he is conducting his pieces from 'Sigurd Jorsalfar'. Soon after that we shall probably be going to Copenhagen, from where we shall certainly not emerge immediately, and then comes Leipzig again. How lovely it would be if we could meet there, do what you can, don't rattle yourself fast in Paris. It is exactly a year now since we were together here, do you remember? Everything looks almost as it did then, just a little more wintry. The last leaves are falling softly, *so* softly and silently, (there is very little 'real' wind here, you know) and on the ground lies a light, white carpet of snow. Today we ought really to have been at Larvik, we had been invited by Nansen to see his ship being launched.[2]

But it was too cold for Edvard, he is not supposed to stand still in the open air for such a long time. We take lunch every day with Holter and Halvorsen in 'Parnas', Sinding lives so far away and is continually very busy. I was at his house yesterday en petit comité,[3] only women, we chatted, drank champagne and smoked cigarettes. He is always saying he'll be off 'next week'. — Well, dear Delius, we shall see each other in Leipzig, shan't we, and have a nice time together again? I should love it if we could. — Edvard sends his best wishes, he is enjoying life again and is not homesick for Troldhaugen.

Write soon, either to Hals or to Vilhelm Hansens Musikhandel, Copenhagen.[4]

Farewell and many good wishes.

Yours very sincerely
Nina Grieg.

Frau Gade[5] and Sinding have just been here, they send you their good wishes, Holter too. I would *not* wish to stay here for long, but am afraid we won't be able to get away until the middle or end of November.

Autograph letter, signed and dated.

1 *Seven Songs from the Norwegian*. 'Little Håkon [*or* Haakon]' is the subject of the 'Cradle Song'.

2 *Fram* ('Forward'), Fridtjof Nansen's polar exploration vessel, was launched on 26 October at the port of Larvik (formerly Laurvig). Nansen sailed to the Arctic from Christiania on 24 June 1893 and was not to set foot on Norwegian soil again until his triumphant return in August 1896.

3 *en petit comité*. In French in the original letter.

4 The Griegs were to move on to Copenhagen in November.

5 Augusta Gade (1858–1936): wife of Fredrik Gade. Sinding had got to know them in Leipzig by 1890, if not earlier. They came to Paris with him when he visited Delius and it was at their home in Drøbak that Sinding often spent his summers. Sinding fell in love with Augusta and they were eventually able to marry in November 1898, following her divorce at the end of October. Daughter of Morten Smith-Petersen, shipowner and member of Parliament, she brought with her the two children from her earlier marriage. Fredrik Gade was trained as a doctor, but during and after his student years he played second violin in

a quartet formed by Iver Holter, the members of which were frequently called in to stiffen the Christiania Musikforening before it became a fully-fledged professional orchestra. He played a number of times under Grieg's baton.

63. NINA GRIEG TO FRITZ DELIUS

Copenhagen 1st Dec. 1892.—

Dear Delius,

Time passes and carries us along with it, our own will has no say in the matter. I would have written earlier, but we have been 'passed on from one place to another', have given concerts, have met a frightful lot of people and — nothing came of it. But I have thought countless times of you and was delighted that you found the libretto, and so nearby at that. A good thing you didn't cross the stream to fetch water, for in all cases it is worth being as little dependent on others as possible. Now at least you can call the tune which suits you, without needing to ask if you may play. Yes, I would really love to know what it is about. Is it a lyrical fairytale, mythological — Endymion — or what?—

I am very sorry indeed that we shall not meet this winter either, when on earth shall we? You see I doubt *very* much if we shall spend next summer at Troldhaugen. So a reunion is up in the air again, and therefore, for those of us who are alive today and dead tomorrow, it hovers rather in the balance.—

I am very happy to be able to tell you that Edvard is much better, he is almost his old self again. As I have already told you, we have given concerts in Kristiania and here in Copenhagen, over there with the participation of Halvorsen (he played the C minor Violin Sonata with Edvard, has made great progess) but here the two of us made music alone for the whole evening, and took part later in a Popular Concert. Fortunately we have now finished and are off on Monday or Tuesday with Holter, who is coming from Norway to pick us up. He is looking forward to enjoying life in Berlin for a while and will return home around Christmas. We go to Leipzig and shall stay there for the time being. How I should love to be off somewhere where the sky is clear and the sun warm!

Farewell, dear Delius, and do be good and tell us how you

are. Many, many good wishes from Edvard and

Yours very sincerely
Nina Grieg.

I suppose you know that Sinding is in Berlin? Well, who knows if he is still there, — anyhow — I just don't understand him.

Our address from now on is: *C.F. Peters, Thalstrasse 10 Leipzig.*

Autograph letter, signed and dated. Envelope addressed: Monsieur Fritz Delius/33 Rue Ducouëdic/Montrouge/*Paris/France*. Copenhagen postmark obscured. Receiving postmark: PARIS 4 DEC 92.

64.   NINA GRIEG TO FRITZ DELIUS

Leipzig 21st Jan.
93. —

Dear Delius,

I have a feeling that it is a long time ago since I wrote to you, but perhaps it is not really so. I should like to know how you are, whether you are hard at work again and whether the opera has made good progress? I hope you spent a pleasant Christmas with your friend Arvesen and that you slipped into the New Year softly and imperceptibly. I hope it will bring you some of the things you wish for, everything — no, there must always be something left over to wish and long for.—

We are middling. Edvard is still not well, he just does not feel his real self. For a time things can go quite well and we just begin to believe it is real, but how long was Adam in Paradise, one fine day things are bad again and we cannot understand why. But he is certainly better than he was in Norway and I am determined not to lose hope. It is our intention to stay in Leipzig until the end of February and then to go somewhere where the air is mild and pure. We are thinking about Merano perhaps, on the Riviera, but shall let things come as they may and shall make no plans. Do you know that Edvard has been made a Doctor at the University of Cambridge? He is to receive this 'new honour' at the beginning of June and so he must go to Cambridge and conduct something there as well. But we shall probably go first to London, where he will perhaps also give some music if he is fit enough to carry it off. So it will be very late before we shall be able to greet our beloved mountains again, but perhaps that is just as well, some time it must be summer again in the north. God knows what it looks like up there now, — snow, stretching to infinity over the Vidder, the great, silent loneliness, swept only by the wild wind that freezes everything to ice. That is probably what it is like now up on Haukelid Fjeld.

Adieu, dear Delius, may you have much joy from life, and think of us now and again.

Many good wishes from Edvard and yours

very sincerely
Nina Grieg.

Sinding was here recently for a couple of days. We dined together in the 'Panorama' again, but I am afraid we had all become blasé, we did not like it any more. Holter and the Musikforening — yes, that didn't *look* good, but it is difficult to judge of course.[1]

We spent Christmas in Berlin, even had a Christmas tree in the 'Hotel Kaiserhof', but it was nothing like the old times here in Leipzig.

Address still:
C.F. Peters, Thalstrasse 10.

Autograph letter, signed and dated.

1   An allusion, it would seem, to the lack of interest that Holter had shown in giving Sinding's Symphony at the Christiania Musikforening concerts.

65.   NINA GRIEG TO FRITZ DELIUS

Menton 8th April 1893.
Hotel de Russie.

Dear Delius,

You see, now I too have become a bad correspondent, have caught it from you, because as you know I used not to be like this. I wonder where you are now, — still in Paris I hope, —

gone with Sinding to Norway? Who can tell which way the hares run, as we say in Norway, not that I find any striking similarity with these little creatures. Do you remember what you wrote to me in your last letter? 'Put it into Grieg's head that you should go to Pau'. That really would have been a nice thing indeed, we arriving in Pau and you safely staying on in Paris. I know my Pappenheimer,[1] you see — quite so reliable you are not. And yet, who knows, perhaps we would have found there the medicinal herb which we have so far sought in vain. As far as his stomach complaint is concerned Grieg is much better, but he has begun to cough here day and night and is so plagued by mucus, so feverish and weak, that I really don't know what to do any more. But people who suffer badly from catarrhal problems and consumption do go to Menton. If it does not get any better I shall be at a loss, but we intend to stay here for the whole month and then perhaps later on to go to Lake Geneva or even to the south coast of England. It is probably written somewhere in the stars what we shall do, but when I look up into the sky, my gaze is lost in the blue. — And here one at least knows for once what blue is, God, how deep a blue both sky and sea are day after day. No, you are certainly right there, people cannot live without the sun, and I believe nearly all of us in winter are to some extent a mixture of south and north. You were here once too, weren't you? So you know how wonderful it is here, how briskly the waves come up from the great sea and break on the beach, how the grey-green olive groves hang down like a veil from the rocks, how the soft air is full of the fragrance of blossoms, absolutely saturated at sunset with the scent of oranges. Unfortunately I have to enjoy all this too much on my own, firstly Grieg is ill, secondly his mind is too full of the Jotunfjelde and all of Norwegian nature. You will understand this, I believe, and I too understand it, but I just cannot close my heart to 'das Land wo die Zitronen blühen'.

— Grieg asks me to send you all his good wishes and to say that he was well and truly annoyed about Dr. A. and your Sonata. He hopes Sinding will have given you a report on the matter.[2] — May all go well with you, dear Delius, with you and your opera (if not opera, what then?) Is it coming along nicely or has it been laid aside for the wicked rattlesnake?

Many good wishes from

Yours very sincerely
Nina Grieg.

How lovely it would be if you could put the idea into Fritz Delius's head to go to Menton for a while and take a look at the sea.

Autograph letter, signed and dated. Envelope addressed: Monsieur Fritz Delius/33 Rue Ducouëdic/Montrouge/*Paris*/*France*. Postmark: M[ENTO]N 8 AVRIL 93. Receiving postmark: PARIS 10 AVRIL 93.

1   From a reference in Schiller's *Death of Wallenstein*: 'Know one's Pappen-heimers, know one's people' (a 'Pappenheimer' being a cuirassier in the regiment of Field Marshal Count von Pappenheim (1594–1632).)
2   Max Abraham had written from Leipzig on 28 February declining to publish Delius's Violin Sonata in B major (RT VIII/3), composed in 1892. Delius had sent it to him earlier in the month. Although he gave other reasons for his refusal, Abraham cited Grieg as saying that the work was full of talent and the Adagio 'wundervoll', but that musicians would find it difficult to play from the manuscript because of the orthography of the musical text (i.e. the pianistic layout being occasion-ally awkward). Sinding's 'report' to Delius, written from Menton on 16 April, expanded on the matter: 'It is very distasteful to Grieg that he has been used and abused in this matter — his words have been quite misconstrued, and it was his wish that the Sonata should be printed. He really was pretty angry with Dr Abraham.' Sinding also affirmed of Abraham: 'He won't have anything to do with uncertainties, the sly old fox. I advise you to wait until the fruits have ripened, with reviews etc, then he'll come to you and will do everything possible to push you.'

Even though another friend of Grieg's, George Augener, had published three groups of Delius's songs in London, Max Abraham was not to be convinced that Delius's work might pay. Delius must have envied Sinding's news from Berlin on 16 February that Abraham had bought his Symphony for 2000 Marks. Sinding had had a rehearsal of the work in Berlin and felt that he had at last got it right: 'The Griegs at least were of this opinion, and dr. Abraham — apparently — was very satisfied, with the result that he offered me as a 'supplementary fee' a trip to the Riviera with himself and the Griegs, and furthermore will print everything I write, and I hardly think he will be niggardly now over the question of fees.' The party had left for the south at the beginning of April.

Another friend of Sinding's, the poet Vilhelm Krag, called on Delius in Paris in the spring, Sinding having told Delius that they would both much enjoy each other's company. 'I hope you met

Vilhelm Krag,' he was to enquire from Christiania on 24 April.

Krag himself was a friend of yet another interesting Norwegian writer, who actually arrived in Paris the same week as he did. This was Knut Hamsun (1859–1952) who, like Delius, had spent a couple of years in America without having made a hoped-for fortune there, and who now had behind him his novels *Hunger*, published in Copenhagen in 1890, and *Mysteries*, which appeared two years later. In 1891, he had caused a scandal at home with an aggressive lecture on Norwegian literature, in the course of which he had attacked the 'Four Great Men' — Ibsen, Bjørnson, Kielland and Lie — an unheard-of action in relation to such national idols. For all his original gifts, Hamsun was sensitive to his lack of social skills: 'It was in pursuit of civilization and refinement that he sailed for France on 13 April 1893, in company with the Danish playwright Sven Lange. French was the language of a cultured man, and Hamsun was going to Paris to learn French, and turn himself into a cultured man' [Robert Ferguson: *Enigma, the Life of Knut Hamsun*. London: Hutchinson, 1987, p.141]. Like Delius, Hamsun moved largely in Scandinavian circles in Paris, and Robert Ferguson considers it 'hardly possible' that the two men did not meet there. They certainly had a fair number of mutual friends and acquaintances, and Hamsun lived close by Delius's haunts in a cheap hotel just to the north of the Luxembourg Gardens. The surest evidence that at this stage they already knew each other is, I feel, to be found in Heseltine's bald statement in his 1923 biography of Delius, that following the composer's visit in 1891 to Bjørnson, 'soon afterwards he met Knut Hamsun and Gunnar Heiberg in Paris' [*Frederick Delius*, p. 37]. Delius could scarcely have told Heseltine of these meetings had they not actually taken place. Among their mutual acquaintances were Verlaine — in Hamsun's words 'an old sot whom I see every day here in the "quartier" ' — and the Danish writer and actor Herman Bang, then down on his luck. 'Things are really bad with Herman Bang. He is both sick and poor', as Hamsun wrote to his friends Bolette and Ole Larsen on 1 October 1893. Bang borrowed money from various quarters, including Delius and Hamsun, but Hamsun was soon to warn Bjørnson off from taking part in any possible concerted effort to help Bang with more money.

At the beginning of 1894, Hamsun began work on his masterly novel, *Pan*. Deep in debt himself, he returned to Norway for the summer and autumn, but came back to Paris in November. He soon met others of Delius's acquaintance, including Paul Gauguin. He began a friendship with his idol Strindberg towards the end of the year. It was to last through the winter, but — like most of Strindberg's friendships — ended in recriminations. Before it did, though, Hamsun — again like Delius — would frequently accompany Strindberg on long walks through the streets of Paris: sometimes Strindberg would talk non-stop, at other times total silence would prevail. Hamsun finally returned to Norway in the summer of 1895.

66. NINA GRIEG TO FRITZ DELIUS

Grefsen Bad[1] 14th June
93.

Dear Delius,

I have just this moment received your lines and am very ashamed that I have not written for so long. Yes, Grieg was very bad both at Menton recently and on the North Italian lakes, at Merano, or rather at Obermais, where we had splendid accommodation at Schloss Labers surrounded by high snow-capped mountains, he got a little better and at the end of April we went northwards. The journey was slow, the nights always spent in hotels and at last we arrived in Leipzig still hoping to visit England. But it was no good. One day things would be a little better, the next they would be worse again, we could not dare risk all the excitement that would go with it and gave England up. Heavens, in the end it is easy enough to get by without a doctoral cap, just as it is without the so-called honour that comes with it. Edvard was enormously glad when we got back to Norway and his doctor in Kristiania thought it would be good for him to go to Tonsåsen. You obviously heard something about this since your letter bore the address. But you know how changeable the weather is here in the North. After some real summer heat we had it cold and damp again and as Tonsåsen is situated in very dark woods and we anticipated snow and cold, the nearby and more friendly Bad Grefsen was to be preferred. Here, thank heavens, things seem really to be progressing, the pine baths, the cold frictions, massage, the lovely fresh air, all seem to do Edvard good, he looks better now and, most important of all, he is now better than he was for the whole of the past year, indeed, since our wedding anniversary last year, when it all began. I do wish he would — how do you say — take himself to bed? for a while here. But he feels impelled to return to the Vestland and in about a fortnight we shall probably be back there again. Then we shall see whether the cure here was not perhaps too short, whether the improvement will last. 'Verhoffentlich' as E. Hartmann put it. —[2]

And how are you? To my great surprise I see you are still in Paris and braving the heat of summer. Well, — one cannot possibly know all that may be going on there, Paris is of course, as we all know, a very dangerous city. I am very pleased indeed that your opera seems to have such good prospects, may you not be disappointed, people are so very, very unreliable. However — you do always say that you know people so very well, don't you? That way you are much more on your guard.

Adieu, dear Delius, don't pay me back in the same coin, rather write soon and tell us how you are and what your plans are. How very glad I am not to have to report that Grieg is 'very ill'.

All good wishes from him and from

Yours very sincerely
Nina Grieg.

There are the most wonderful pine forests here, deep and dark and far, far away from all the world.

We shall probably be returning via Haukelid. I am looking forward to seeing all that high grandeur again.

Autograph letter, signed and dated.

1   A sanatorium on the outskirts of the capital. Sinding had written from Christiania on 11 June: 'Grieg was rather poorly when he got back here; but he is said to be doing better now at Grefsen Spa. Only see him rarely.'

2   *Verhoffentlich* (archaic: *it is to be hoped*); the reference is presumably to the German writer and philosopher Eduard von Hartmann (1834–1906).

Although Nina did not know it, Delius had decided on another summer in Norway — the fourth in alternate years beginning in 1887. Sinding had developed a passion for cycling and had written to him on 10 May: 'This summer I'd like to undertake a longer tour. What are you doing in the summer?' Just over a month later he told Delius that Augusta Gade could take care of his ticket from Antwerp, where he should embark on 22 June, and he proposed that they take inexpensive lodgings together in Drøbak, where Fru Gade would look after them. He would arrange for a piano if Delius needed one.

Of all Delius's Norwegian excusions since 1887, this is the least well documented. There is a letter to Randi Blehr, written from Drøbak on 4 July. Delius had met her sister only the day before: this was Hildur Prahl (1855–1940), like Randi herself, married to a radical politician. 'Where can we meet?' he asked Randi. 'I am staying here in Drøbak for the whole summer. Sinding and I are living together in a nice cottage.' The following day he would go to Christiania for 'a talk with [Ola] Thommessen.' He also mentioned a 'Fräulein Juel', who seems to have been an aspiring singer of some talent. Precisely a month later, he again wrote to Randi Blehr from Drøbak: 'I have written to tell Fräulein Juel that I will come tomorrow Saturday to Kongsvinger and I hope that will suit her. I am sure I will see you there, won't I?'

There do not seem to have been any significant travels, bar the odd trip to Christiania and perhaps some bicycle excursions with Sinding, and no further correspondence with the Griegs during the rest of the year has come to light. Might the Griegs have been piqued that Delius apparently ignored them? He evidently did not make the effort to cross the country again to Bergen. Part of the reason may have been that he was now not too well off: in other words, he could cope with a free trip to Christiania and cheap and easy living at Drøbak, but little more. Here, after all, was a professed composer who simply could not sell his work. Just how relatively frugally he was living in Paris at this period was recorded by a 'society' friend, the composer Isidore de Lara: 'His means were very small, and he cooked his own meals; I have often dined with him in his room on a couple of eggs.'

The Griegs were back at Troldhaugen for July, joined for the holidays by the Röntgen family — something that makes it quite probable that they themselves could not have entertained Delius anyway. Grieg and Julius Röntgen set off together for a tour in the Jotunheim, but before long Grieg once again fell ill and was only too glad to be back at Troldhaugen in August. The usual travels, however, began again in the autumn of 1893. In October they were in Christiania, and in November in Copenhagen. Now it was Nina who fell ill, having to spend six weeks in hospital with a serious kidney complaint. It was during this period that Grieg composed his Krag songs, among others. Towards the end of January, the Griegs left Copenhagen for Leipzig. March saw them in Munich and Geneva, following which they took a holiday in Menton. The next major engagement was to be a concert at the Châtelet Theatre in Paris on 22 April 1894.

Meanwhile Delius was expanding his Paris friendships, at the same time retaining a firm foothold in the circle of William and Ida Molard where many new contacts were regularly made. If his earliest and closest friends in the city had generally been Scandinavians, French artists, musicians and writers were coming increasingly into the picture: Paul Gauguin, Florent Schmitt, Maurice Ravel, Georges-Daniel de Monfreid, Emma Calvé and many more. He began to frequent the crémerie of Madame Charlotte Futterer ('Mère Charlotte') in the rue de la Grande Chaumière, where artists ate cheaply and well. And a glimmer of hope appeared when Isidore de Lara's social contacts proved their worth by earning him a second performance of his 'concert overture' *Paa Vidderne*, given under the title *Sur les Cimes* in Monte Carlo on 25 February 1894. The success was, however, short-lived, and Delius was to have the frustration of waiting another three and a half years for another performance of one of his orchestral works.

At the end of 1893, Delius had sent New Year greetings to the Blehr family. He did not think, he told Randi, that he could come to Norway in the summer of 1894.

67. EDVARD GRIEG TO FRITZ DELIUS

Friday [13 April, 1894]

HOTEL DE SÈZE
16, Rue de Sèze, 16
BOULEVARD DE LA MADELEINE
PARIS

Dear Delius,

How nice that you are here. We arrived here the day before yesterday[1] and since then I have done nothing but revise orchestra parts. I have my first rehearsal tomorrow, but none on Sunday so we must meet then. Do come about 12 o'clock and breakfast with us.

I hope after that I shall have some time to enjoy the 'Holyday'.[2]

Well then! Until Sunday!

Yours
Edvard Grieg

I am not bringing anything new for orchestra. All I have done is to reorchestrate the music to Sigurd Jorsalfar, and the new edition has recently been published by Peters.[3]

Autograph letter written on headed notepaper, signed and undated.

1   Grieg was to conduct the Colonne Orchestra on 22 April in a concert to include the Piano Concerto, played by Raoul Pugno, *Den Bergtekne*, and the song *A Swan* (from op.25), which Grieg had specially orchestrated for the occasion.

2   *Holyday*. In English in the original letter.

3   *Three Orchestral Pieces from 'Sigurd Jorsalfar'*, op.56, published by Peters in 1893 (an arrangement of op.22).

68.   EDVARD GRIEG TO FRITZ DELIUS

Wednesday evening. [18 April 1894]

HOTEL DE SÈZE
16, Rue de Sèze, 16
BOULEVARD DE LA MADELEINE
PARIS

Dear Delius,

I am frightfully run down and must be very careful if I am to do my duty. But I am not so ill as to forget my promise. As you see, we have been lucky enough to manage to get hold of 2 tickets.

Kind regards

Yours
Edvard Grieg

Autograph letter written on headed notepaper, signed and undated.

69. EDVARD GRIEG TO FRITZ DELIUS

Thursday evening [19 April 1894]

HOTEL DE SÈZE
16, Rue de Sèze, 16
BOULEVARD DE LA MADELEINE
PARIS

Dear Delius,

I should really love to see you at the final rehearsal so that afterwards I can hear your opinion on how it came off. Enclosed an admission ticket.

Kind regards
Yours
Edvard Grieg

Start of rehearsal
9.30
Saturday morn.

Autograph letter written on headed notepaper, signed and undated.

70. EDVARD GRIEG TO FRITZ DELIUS

Wednesday morning. [25 April 1894]

Dear Delius,

It's starting at Raffaelli's[1] earlier than originally agreed and I have *promised* to be there *punctually at 4.* It seems likely to be something pretty special — as it's in today's Figaro.
   Looking forward to seeing you!

Yours
Edvard Grieg

Autograph carte-télégramme, signed and undated. Addressed: Monsieur Fritz Delius/Rue Ducouëdic 33./Montrouge/*PARIS.* Postmark: PARIS 25 AVRIL 94.

1 Jean François Raffaelli (1850–1924): French impressionist painter and etcher. 'You must read today's Figaro,' Grieg wrote to Max Abraham on 26 May, 'as there was a big party for us yesterday at the home of Raffaelli, the painter, where the "top people" were present. It

was ridiculous. But it was a colossal success. Figaro reports on that sort of thing, but not on the concert!' In fact, as usual at this period, whenever Grieg performed or was present at concerts of his own works abroad, his success with audiences was assured, as was the case on this occasion. Reviews usually reflected this success, but the very popularity of Grieg's music meant that there would nearly always be one or other carping newspaper criticism following his concerts, and Grieg was ever sensitive to such attacks.

At some stage during this visit to Paris, Grieg paid a call on William Molard, who had invited his friends — including one or two who were studying at the Conservatoire — along to meet the great man. Those present on the occasion are nowhere actually listed, but they must — apart from Molard's family — have included Delius, Léon Moreau and Julien Leclercq, all of whom were frequent visitors anyway to the rue Vercingétorix. And among the friends from the Conservatoire was Maurice Ravel, then aged nineteen, who for his half-yearly examination in January had played the Grieg Concerto. While the company talked music, Ravel stole over to the piano and began to play one of Grieg's dances. Grieg smiled at first, but then grew impatient: the rhythm, he said, should be more marked — it was, after all, a peasant dance: 'You should see the peasants at home with the fiddler stamping time with his foot. Play it again!' And all watched fascinated as Grieg, with surprising agility, skipped across the floor in time with the music.* The occasion was evidently also used to discuss the matter of French translations, for after leaving Paris for London, Grieg was shortly to write to Molard thanking him for the 'masterpiece of translation' of 'Solveig's Song', at the same time regretting that Nina had not been able to come and share 'the fine impression I received of your home.' On 5 June, he wrote from Grefsen Spa thanking Molard for 'the latest translations', suggesting improvements to 'L'espoir' and several other songs, and sending 'hearty greetings to you and your family, Hr Leclerc, Hr Molard [an error for Moreau], Delius.' More suggestions followed on 13 June in connection with other songs, Grieg thanking Molard and Leclercq warmly for their endeavours and again sending greetings to Leclercq, Delius and Moreau. The translations were further discussed in a letter to Molard on 10 July and Grieg ended with greetings to 'all in your friendly little clan.' Molard seems to have had a useful line in taking

* Gilles Gérard-Arlberg: 'Nr 6, rue Vercingétorix'. *Konstrevy* (Stockholm) 2, 1958, p.65.

on occasional translations from the Norwegian. In a letter to Iver Holter, written from Paris on 27 June 1900, Johan Selmer wondered if Molard could perhaps make a reasonable translation in connection with one of his own works. [Original in Oslo University Library]

Mention of Ravel inevitably brings us to Delius's much-quoted definition of modern French music — likely, one feels, to have been made at a rather later gathering of French musicians than on this particular occasion in 1894. To what music was modern French music indebted, was the question asked. The French musicians present proposed that it was to 'Rameau, Couperin, Lully and so on'. Delius's view was that this was nonsense: 'Modern French music is simply Grieg, plus the 3rd act of "Tristan".' And Ravel agreed: 'C'est vrai, cela. Nous sommes toujours injuste envers Grieg.' ('That's true. We are always unjust to Grieg.') [A Delius Companion, p. 127]. We owe this published account to Percy Grainger, but in notes taken by Grainger of a conversation he had with Delius on 19 February 1923, the story is told somewhat differently, Delius being recorded as saying: 'I spoke to Ravel once, he said: nous provenons de Rameau, Couperin etc. I said — Oh nonsense, you don't; you have taken a lot from Grieg — you are influenced enormously by Wagner and especially Grieg. Ravel then admitted that they were very unjust to Grieg.' [Ms in Grainger Museum]

Julien Leclercq was, incidentally, to publish a book on physiognomy some two years after working on the Grieg translations. Grieg and Nina were two of his twenty-five subjects, who included — among others — Ibsen, Rodin, Maeterlinck and Emma Calvé. In his 'character' of Grieg, Leclercq's admiration for the music of his subject emerges very clearly. [cf. La Physionomie: Visages et caractères. Paris: Larousse, 1896[?]]

71.   EDVARD GRIEG TO FRITZ DELIUS

47, Clapham Common
North Side
London S.W.
[12 May 1894]

Dear Delius,

I am ill — just three words. I have written to Molard about the songs. It seems to be a difficult business.

I could have died of laughter at the Doctoral affair the day before yesterday![1] But I didn't laugh, as I was already ill, and the first thing I had to do as a Doctor was — to go to the doctor's. I can neither sit, nor stand, nor walk, nor lie and just don't know how I can carry on. Now I have sent for the doctor, for it cannot go on like this. He must get to the bottom of it. If it had not been for this business, you would have had a jolly letter from Cambridge.

Kind regards

Yours
Edvard Grieg

Autograph letter, signed and undated.

1   On 6 May Grieg had written to Beyer: 'On Thursday (the 10th) I'll play comedy in Cambridge. Costume: blue and white gown, medieval cap. Scene: a festively decorated street. Action: procession through the town.' So Saint-Saëns, whom he had just met in Paris and who already had an honorary Cambridge doctorate, had in all seriousness described the scene to him. Grieg could only see the funny side of the whole affair.

72.   EDVARD GRIEG TO FRITZ DELIUS

London 25/5/94

Dear Delius,

It is inconceivable, but true: that in the matter of the fee for the song translations Dr. Abraham is raising 'difficulties'. He finds the sum asked too high. I have simply written to tell him that he can pay what he likes; I will pay the rest. In other words: I was furious and told him the truth. So now we must wait and see what he does. I hope he has enough of a sense of honour to understand what he should do.

I am more than a little surprised that Hennings[1] has written to you about the opera. If you have any dealings with him: Be careful! Everything in writing. I admit he has always been generous to me. But others complain a great deal.

I am off tomorrow direct to Christiania, *address Gebrüder Hals.*

The success yesterday was very great — called 4 times — and the fellows played well.[2] But the hall was bad.

Many good wishes, to the Molards and Leclerc[3] too.

Yours
Edvard Grieg

When I get to Grefsen near Christania, I shall write to
Levi.[4]

Autograph letter, signed and dated.

1   Henrik Hennings (1848–1923): Danish music publisher and concert
promoter. He was the owner of the Kongelig Musikhandel in Copenhagen. As Delius was only just beginning work on his second opera, *The
Magic Fountain* (RT I/3), the reference here is certainly to *Irmelin*, even if
no conclusive reference to Hennings' promoting a performance of the
work has so far been found. A mutual friend at this period in Paris was
Herman Bang: 'Do drop me a line to tell me how matters stand with
Hennings,' he wrote to Delius around July. This was following a slightly
earlier letter in which Bang told his friend: 'In spite of my illness — for I
have been very ill for several days — I succeeded in writing to Mr.
Hennings and a long letter at that. No doubt he will send me an answer
in a few days.' Grieg's warning in his letter about Hennings proved to
be justified: nothing more was heard of *Irmelin*.

2   At the Philharmonic Society's London concert, Grieg conducted
what was listed as the first performance of his three pieces from *Sigurd
Jorsalfar*.

3   Julien Leclercq (1865–1901): French writer and poet. He was
something of a fixture in the Molard circle and a particularly devoted
follower of Gauguin who, like Delius, did not find much to admire in
him.

4   Hermann Levi (1839–1900): German conductor and general music
director at Munich. Delius had evidently told Grieg of his intention to
go to Munich later in the summer and Grieg must have agreed to
broach the subject of *Irmelin* with Levi.

73.   EDVARD GRIEG TO FRITZ DELIUS

Grefsen Bad
nr. Kristiania
5th June 1894.
(Address: Gebrüder Hals, Kristiania)

Dear Delius,

Following my blast to Dr. Abraham about the matter of the
French translation I received the following reply: 'I intend
neither to get worked up about the matter nor to defend
myself, but will confine myself to the declaration that I agree
to the fee' (35 fr.) 'claimed for the French translation.'

So the matter is settled satisfactorily.

I am looking forward to corresponding with Mr Molard, he has a fine and intelligent nature. — I have just received the brochure. That is certainly a complete contrast to Figaro's deathly silence! Well, I am old enough to know well what I can do and what I — cannot do. I am only too well aware of the latter in particular.

I have peace enough here to write letters. I shall finish the letter to Levi tomorrow.*

Farewell and write soon.

Yours
Edvard Grieg

* Later: The letter to Levi is done and will go off today to Munich, Arcostrasse 2.

Autograph letter, signed and dated.

74. FRITZ DELIUS TO EDVARD GRIEG

33 Rue Ducouëdic
le 15 Juin 94.

Dear Grieg,

I am glad that you are getting on well at Grevsen's Spa.

I am glad too, for Molard & Leclercq, that Dr Abraham has at last agreed to 35 francs: they have taken a hell of a lot of trouble and it cannot be better translated. Molard has a very fine nature: I think highly of him both as a friend and an artist. We have now quite finished one act: now we are working on the second. At the end of this month or at the beginning of July we will, I think, be finished.[1] Many thanks for writing to Levi. I am leaving here on the 25 July. If you write to Dr Abraham, please tell him he could send an advance now to Molard. I think it would be very welcome. He hasn't got much to manage on either.[2]

Write to me again soon & give my greetings to the splendid summer nights & forests and to your dear wife too. Farewell, & have a complete rest

Yours
Fritz Delius

Autograph letter, signed and dated.

1   The clear implication is that it was together with Delius that Molard and Leclercq were working on a translation of numbers from *Peer Gynt*.
2   Early in June, Gauguin, in Pont-Aven, wrote somewhat enigmatically to Molard: 'It is a great pity that the Grieg translation has come to a stop; it means that I shall not have the pleasure of seeing you [here] this summer.'

Delius made his way initially to Bayreuth, where he met Levi and arranged to show him the score of *Irmelin* some time afterwards in Munich. On 11 August, he met Bjørnstjerne and Karoline Bjørnson and one of their daughters on a Munich street, and dined with them the following day. The Bjørnsons had been in the Tyrol since May and invited Delius to come and join them there at Schwaz. Although he was considering doing so, there appears to be no evidence that he ultimately took up the invitation. The summer travels came to an end a week into September, as documented in a letter to Randi Blehr on the 21st of that month: 'I have been back in Paris for a fortnight. I made a trip to Germany: Bayreuth and Munich and also heard a lot of music.' He spoke of the possibility of returning to Norway — and so seeing her again — in 1895.

Meanwhile, after a further period of treatment at Grefsen Spa in June, Grieg returned to Troldhaugen at the end of the month, soon settling down to work on his *Seven Children's Songs*, op.61. At the end of October, the Griegs left for Copenhagen via Christiania and spent the winter in Denmark. Grieg suffered bouts of ill health throughout, culminating in pneumonia in March. Delius appears to have stayed in Paris, working hard on *The Magic Fountain*, which he finished by the middle of 1895 — in other words about the same time as the Griegs returned for their usual summer's stay at Troldhaugen. In the autumn, there were brief visits to Christiania and Copenhagen again before Edvard and Nina arrived in Leipzig to spend the winter there as guests of Max Abraham. In Copenhagen, Grieg fell for the Danish pianist Bella Edwards. During his brief stay there, he was to meet her three times before she prudently declined a fourth meeting. There are curious links here, as Edwards was shortly to team up, as a durable performing duo, with the young British violinist Eva Mudocci. They met Edvard Munch — as well as Delius — in Paris in 1903, and Munch entered into a relationship with Mudocci, making three celebrated lithographs of her. One of them is 'The Recital', where she is depicted together with Bella Edwards.

If Grieg and Munch were not to suffer unduly serious consequences from their affairs, their friend Delius was. A liaison in Paris in 1895 — of which we know no details — resulted in his contracting syphilis, just as his friend Gauguin had done earlier that same year. Treatment was moderately effective, and after a time Delius was able to resume a normal life, but many years later — when he was in his sixties — his health was seriously to decline as a consequence of the disease. Perhaps unsurprisingly in the circumstances, this is the most poorly documented year of Delius's post-Leipzig life. Whether there was any communication with the Griegs, we do not know. Four letters from Sinding form the bulk of what remains extant of the year's correspondence. Writing from Christiania on 25 June, he congratulated Delius on completing *The Magic Fountain* in a tone of almost rueful envy: 'I can't escape from the song and piano piece factory. I recently finished a Violin Sonata — the biggest thing I have been able to do for a long time.'

It would seem that some time later in August 1895, Delius wrote to Sinding in Christiania to ask him what his plans were for the autumn. Sinding replied that he would be off early in September to Berlin. 'You don't seem to be exactly cheerful?' he commented, adding — unaware of how close he was to the truth — 'carefree youth is over, my boy.' One or two allusions in Sinding's letters of this period seem to indicate that Delius hoped that the two of them might make a trip to the Mediterranean together. Sinding had, after all, been one of the most devoted of his friends since their time in Leipzig. What better antidote to the depressing turn of events of the year than to travel to the sun for a while with a trusted companion? Sinding's needs, however, kept him in Berlin. He told Delius on 20 September that old friends from Leipzig were there — Busoni, Hjalmar Borgstrøm and Ottokar Nováček: 'You'll be in good company here.' That was probably enough. A letter from the conductor Felix Mottl, addressed to Delius at a flat in the same house in Berlin where Sinding was living, indicates that Delius was certainly there at the beginning of November. And a note from Sinding on 24 December is evidence that Delius was by then back in Paris, having encouraged Sinding to visit him there again soon. Sinding had written to Anna Brodsky just a little earlier: 'My friend Delius was here for a while. On my advice he sent his Legende for violin to Brodsky. I think it should do very well, especially with orchestra, and well-orchestrated it is too.' [Original letter, dated Berlin, 16 December 1895, in Oslo University Library]

1895 had been a bad year in more than one respect. The family business in Bradford was in trouble and, furthermore, Delius had somehow fallen out with his uncle Theodor. With the quite likely prospect of financial support drying up from both sources, it may be that Delius used his Berlin visit to seek help from his wealthy aunt Albertine Krönig. At some stage he certainly received an allowance from her, and at no other time than now would he have found it more welcome. At all events, it is likely that his stay among old Leipzig friends in Berlin helped him out of a particularly difficult patch of his life. Returning to Paris, he took up the threads again and soon started work on yet another opera, *Koanga* (RT I/4). At the beginning of 1896 his attitude to life and work was again upbeat, his outlook positive and his belief in his music evidently reaffirmed.

75.   EDVARD GRIEG TO FRITZ DELIUS

Leipzig 12/1/96
Hotel Hauffe

Dear Delius,

I hope it is not yet too late to send you best wishes for the New Year. — Perhaps I know more about 'the Magic Fountain' than you do, since Hennings telegraphed me to say that a performance could 'possibly' (what a silly word!) take place in Prague and even as early as February, if the score were to be sent off in good time. As I told Hennings, I strongly advise against sending off a copy of the score which has not first been revised by you. Do believe me. A great deal depends on it.[1]

 I do not doubt that your new idea for an opera is taking shape as you wish it to.[2] At your age one's ideas do indeed become reality, that is precisely the advantage of youth. At my age it is quite different. I do not lack ideas, but my power to organize them is not that of youth. Ever-increasing self-criticism eats away like a poison at each idea until there is nothing left of it. Now, with me you can also add illness to this as the main reason. I really had to laugh at your enthusiasm for Glünecke.[3] I am very ready to believe that you feel healthy and well after its juices, because you were healthy and well before too!

We shall continue to stay here for the time being. But address your letters preferably to Dr. Abraham, Thalstrasse 10, because letters are always sent on to me from there.

Kind regards, from my wife too.

Yours
Edvard Grieg.

Autograph letter, signed and dated.

1   The misplaced belief that Henrik Hennings might hold the key to performances of Delius's operas continued to hold the high ground. Nothing had come of *Irmelin*, but *The Magic Fountain* was now on the agenda. Sinding had written on 24 December 1895: 'Hennings wrote yesterday to tell me that your opera has been accepted in Prague.' He wrote again on 10 January 1896: 'Do you know for sure when your opera will be given in Prague? Hennings wrote to me that it would probably be in February.' Grieg's letter seemed to bear this out, but on 5 February, Sinding was still asking the same unanswered question: 'What is happening about your opera? Am very intrigued. Whatever you do you should get a contract with Hennings. I don't quite trust the man and all his charm.' All talk of Hennings soon subsided, and although later in February Delius told another friend that there was some talk of *The Magic Fountain* being given in Weimar, and he himself was to discuss the situation with Hennings in Copenhagen in June, he was never to see either of his first two operas performed.

2   The new opera was *Koanga*. Delius's English librettist, Charles F. Keary (1848–1917), was living at the time in Bourron, not far from Grez-sur-Loing. He was something of an expert on Scandinavia, having written works on Nordic history and mythology, as well as a book entitled *Norway and the Norwegians* (1892).

3   *Glünecke*: presumably a variety of mulled wine.

If Norway was Delius's first Scandinavian love, both Denmark and Sweden provided him with other friends at different stages of his life. Herman Bang has been mentioned, although the acquaintance was short-lived, but there was also the Danish poet and dramatist Helge Rode, with whom Delius had a particularly cordial relationship, and the industrialist Einar Schou, at whose home in Jutland Delius and his wife were later to be welcome guests. Among his Swedish friends, August Strindberg, with whom at the present time in Paris he frequently kept company, was easily the most celebrated. There was also the sculptor Christian Eriksson, for whom in 1891 he had written a part song to words by Ibsen to be sung at the party held to celebrate Eriksson's move into a new studio in the avenue de Saxe in Paris. And there was another sculptor, Ida Ericson, Molard's wife. Ultimately, the most significant — for Delius — of his Swedish friends, however, was yet a third sculptor, Caroline Benedicks. Her uncle was Oscar Cantzler, one of the Swedish artists in the Scandinavian artists' colony at Grez-sur-Loing which had begun to flourish in the early 1880s, and she had spent her first summer in France at Grez in 1883. Two years later she came to Paris, studying, like Christian Eriksson, with Falguière. In France she met a Canadian painter, William Blair Bruce, and they married in Paris in December 1888. They based themselves at Grez for several years, but in the mid-1890s took a studio at 65 boulevard Arago, a well-known complex of artists' studios, where they frequently entertained. Helene ('Jelka') Rosen, a German artist studying in Paris and painting in the summer at Grez, had met them in the village in 1895 and had subsequently been a guest of theirs from time to time. Delius, too, whom they had got to know in Paris, was another who was welcome at their table. Caroline Benedicks Bruce knew that Jelka loved Grieg's songs, which she sang often: 'You must know a young Englishman, a friend of ours. He also loves Grieg and composes music himself.' Jelka did not, in fact, greatly like Caroline Benedicks and convinced herself that she did not wish to meet the man of whom her hostess spoke so frequently and admiringly. 'But once when I dined there with my mother who was living with me in Paris, he was there too: an aristocratic-looking, rather tall, thin man with curly dark hair with a tinge of auburn and an auburn moustache which he was always twisting upwards [. . .] After dinner Mrs Bruce asked me to sing something — as was then the fashion before there were radios or gramophones. I sang "The Swan" and "Solveig's Song" of Grieg [. . .] Delius seemed to like my singing, for he told me he would come to my studio and bring me a book of his own songs.' The date of this first meeting was 16 January 1896.

Delius subsequently visited Jelka, bringing her first the *Seven Songs* and then the *Five Songs from the Norwegian*. 'Oh, what a glorious revelation these songs were to me! The harmonies, the "Stimmung" were so delightful, more so than anything I had known before in music: the "Cradle Song", "Auf der Reise zur Heimat", "Venevil" and "Twilight Fancies".' Jelka would most probably also have known Grieg's setting of the latter song, published in 1871 as 'The Princess'.

The Griegs were still in Leipzig early in 1896, but for once Grieg himself was beginning to feel out of place there and his longing for Norway, so often felt during the winters of self-imposed exile, resurfaced. Brahms came to Leipzig in mid-January and he and Grieg spent a lot of time together. A few weeks later they 'taverned together' (as Grieg put it) when Grieg visited Vienna for a concert of his own works on 23 March. Their admiration was mutual. Grieg also met Dvořák and Bruckner in Vienna, but his pleasure in this visit to the city was not unadulterated, as he had had to leave Nina in Leipzig where she was treated for what was assumed to be breast cancer. In April, on their way back to Norway, Grieg conducted the Berlin Philharmonic Orchestra in Copenhagen, with Busoni as soloist in the Piano Concerto. In May, he and Nina were back at Troldhaugen.

76. FRITZ DELIUS TO EDVARD GRIEG

c/o a b Brødrene Hals
Christiania
[early June 1896]

My dear Grieg—

I arrived here two days ago — and intend to go up to Valdres in order to work in peace there   Shall we go to Jotunheim together? It would be a very great pleasure for me to make this tour again together with you—

As soon as I arrive in Valdres I will write and tell you my address — I hope you are well. How is Frau Grieg? I heard that she has been ill. — Please let me know — I was terribly sorry to hear about her illness & how glad I was then to hear that it was not after all so dangerous as at first thought.

My temporary address is *c/o a b Brødrene Hals*

Farewell — dear Grieg, I send my kind regards to Frau Grieg & yourself—

Yours
Fritz Delius

Autograph letter, signed and undated.

77. EDVARD GRIEG TO FRITZ DELIUS

Troldhaugen
nr Bergen
18 June 1896

Dear Delius,

Just back from an excursion to Hardanger, I hasten to reply to your letter. Unfortunately I have so many commitments on various sides for the summer holidays that it will not be possible for me to go off to Jotunheim with you. I would find it very difficult to get there at all this time. But if I should, then we will meet there. Will you not, however, be coming somewhere near us? We know there are dangerous young ladies in the neighbourhood, — but no progeny will come of this mere fact!

I am sorry to say that my wife makes only very slow progress. She needs absolute rest, which is very difficult to achieve at Troldhaugen. So I must go away with her too somewhere in July. You will be hearing from me when our plans in this connection have become clear. Perhaps there will then be a chance to get together somewhere.

The operation which my wife had to undergo was enormous. And it turns out afterwards that the learned ones could not even agree anyway whether it was 'cancer' or not. We hope and believe now that it was not the case. At any rate, everything 'vulnerable' in the breast has been removed. So you will understand that it is not a matter of mere trivialities.

The song which you sent[1] was very full of atmosphere and original in its way, — but how very French you have become! Admittedly in the refined sense. And yet, as I believe: Dangerous, there to dream!

Well, 'Sehe Jeder, wie er es treibe,' as Goethe says, and he is quite right!

All good wishes!
Write soon!

Yours
Edvard Grieg

Autograph letter, signed and dated. Envelope addressed: Herr Fritz Delius/Adr.Brödrene Hals/Musikhandel/*Kristiania*.

28   Bjørnstjerne Bjørnson

29   Theodor Kjerulf   30   Andreas Munch, by Jørgen Roed

Warmuths Kgl. Hof-Musikhandel og Concertbureau.

Musikforeningens
2den Concert

Lørdag den 14de November 1891 Kl. 8
i Tivolis Cirkuslokale

under Ledelse af

Hr. Edv. Grieg

og under Medvirkning af

Fru Ellen Gulbranson
Frøken Camilla Wiese
Hr. Thorvald Lammers

samt Korforeningen og et udvalgt Mandskor.

Program.

1. 2den Per Gynt Suite for Orkester. (Første Gang).
   a. Brudrovet (Ingrids Klage).
   b. Daula af Dovregubbens Datter.
   c. Per Gynts Hjemfart.
      (Stormfuld Aften ved Kysten)
   d. Solveigs Sang.
2. Foran Sydens Kloster for Soli, Damekor og Orkester.
   (Solost: *Fru Ellen Gulbranson* og *Frøken Camilla Wiese*.)
3. Norske Folkeviser, behandlede for Baryton-Solo og Kor.
   a. Jeg lagde mig saa sildig.
   b. Springdands. *Hr. Thv. Lammers* og et udvalgt Mandskor.
4. Scener af „Olav Trygvason", udfdndt Drama af Bjørnstjerne
   Bjørnson, for Soli, Kor og Orkester. (Op. 50).

Samtlige Kompositioner af Edv. Grieg.

Harmonium fra Brødrene Hals's Fabrik.

Warmuths Kgl. Hof-Musikhandel og Concertbureau.

Musikforeningens
1ste Concert

Lørdag den 10de Oktober 1891 Kl. 8
i Tivolis Cirkuslokale

under Ledelse af

Hr. Iver Holter

og under Medvirkning af

Hr. Violinist Fred. Frederiksen og
Hr. Barytonsanger Salomon Smith.

Program.

1. Holter, Iver: Suite for stort Orkester efter Musikken til „Gøtz
   v. Berlichingen".
   a. Hyldningsmarsch.
   b. Stilleben, Menuet i gammel Stil.
   c. Scene i Skoven.   Manuskript.
   d. Erotik.   1ste Gang.
   e. Vehmgericht.
   f. Festligt Optog.
2. Raff, Joach.: Concert for Violin med Orkester (1ste Sats).
   Hr. Fredrik Frederiksen.
3. Wagner, Rich.: Wotans Abschied und Feuerzauber for Baryton
   med Orkester (1ste Gang). Hr. Salomon Smith.
4. a. Wagner,-Wilhelmj: Romanze med Orkester.
   b. Popper, David: Elfentanz med Orkester. Hr. Fredrik Frederiksen.
5. a. Sjøgren, Emil: Bergmanden.
   b. Elling, Cath.: Jeg vil ud. Hr. Salomon Smith.
6. Delius, Fritz: „Paa Vidderne". Concertouverture for stort Orkester. (1ste Gang) Manuskript.

   Accompagnatør: Hr. Albert Rietling.

Piano fra Warmuth's Pianolager.

---

31 Programme of Iver Holter's Musikforening concert of 10 October 1891, with first performances of works by Holter and Delius

32 The second Musikforening concert of the season, also in Christiania, sees Grieg conducting the first performance of this *Peer Gynt Suite* no. 2

Musikforeningen

gav Løbag sin søste Konsert for iaar i Cirkuslokalet, hvis akustiske Forhold var undergaat yderligere Forbedringer. Programmet var indholdsvægtigt og interessant. Dirigenten,

Komponist Iver Holter,

I værebe selv Duverturen i sin Suite for stort Orkester, en virkningsfuld Bearbejdelse af hans Musik til „Gøt von Berlichingen". De stemningsrige, sint og varsomt, med udpræget orkestral Formsans udførte Tonebilleder blev fortrinlig hævet ved Bearbejdelsens lydigere og varmere Klangfylde. Stykker som „Stilleben", „Scene i Skoven" og „Erotik" er ikke Hverdagsløst i vor Musikliteratur, for hvilken det er en Vending, at Suiten er løst ud fra det sjelden opførte Drama, der jar afgivet Motiverne. Den modtog efter hver Sats stærkt Bifald. Vi skynder os forbi Reffs Violinkonsert, der bortset fra i Hr. Fr. Frederiksen at præsentere en ny og meget lovende ung Solospiller, nærmest tjene som Programmets Fyldekalk; Hr. Frederiksen fik desuden Anledning til at lade høre en anerkjendelsesværdig Teknik og Smag i en Wagnerparafrase af Wilhelmj og i Poppers lokette „Elefentanz", hvori hans endnu noget spæde, men indsmigrende bløde Strøg bedst kom til sin Ret. Aftenens brillante Storværk var Wagners Walküre-Fragment for stort Orkester med den fremragende svenske Barnton

Solomon Smith som Solist; — det var forslagen, betagende Musik, og den fik en udmærket Udførelse. Hr. Smith forebrog derhos to Sarge, af Sjøgren og Elling. Den fike maatte Hr. Smith efter diverse Fremkaldelser synge om.

Programmet afsluttedes med en interessant Komponist-Debut: „Paa Vidderne", Konsertouverture for stort Orkester af

Fritz Delius.

Den unge Tonedigter — han er blot 28 Aar gammel —, hvis Billede vi idag præsenterer for vore Læsere er af Fødsel Engelskmand; men i Temperament og Uddannelse ved langvarige Ophold i Amerika, Frankrige, Tyskland og Norge er han Kosmopolit. Gjennem Beundring for vor Kunst og vor Natur har han faat vort Land kjært, og han kjender det og dets Kulturliv som fra Udlænbinge. „Paa Vidderne", inspireret af Ibsens Digt, er hans første effentligt opførte Arbejde i større Stil. Det er en fin og indtagende, fantasi- og farverig Komposition, der baade ved sin musikalske Gehalt og sin tildels fortrinlige Form staar langt over, hvad man kan vente af et Begynderarbejde: den vilde vinde ved nogen Koncentration men er, som den foreligger, god, moben og nobel Kunst. Kompositionen slog godt an, og Dirigenten blev fremkaldt.

34   At Aulestad, home of Bjørnstjerne Bjørnson, 8 July 1891.
The foreground group includes Dagny Bjørnson with Delius

35   Edvard Grieg, 1893

36   John Paulsen   37   Henrik Ibsen

38   Hjalmar Johnsen, by Fredrik Kolstø

39 Delius, as portrayed by Christian Krohg
in *Verdens Gang*, 23 October 1897

40 Delius in London, 1899

41 Delius in 1897, by Ida Gerhardi

42 *Sunday Morning in Grez-sur-Loing* (detail), by Christian Krohg

Bjørnson og Grieg paa Villa Troldhaugen

44   Bjørnson and Grieg at Troldhaugen, 15 June 1903.
Picture postcard sent by Grieg to Delius on 23 August 1904

43   Jelka Rosen

Readdressed: Haugen/Söndre Aurdal/Valders. Postmarks: HOP 1[?] VI 96, BERGEN 19-6-1896 and KRISTIANIA 22-6-1896.

1 Probably a proof copy of 'Le ciel est, par-dessus le toit' (RT V/16), to words by Verlaine, published in *L'Aube*, Paris, in July 1896.

Nina's period of recuperation from her illness meant that Delius had to revise his plans. He established a summer base on a farm called Haugen at Søndre Aurdal in the Valdres region, staying there for several weeks in June and July. Knut Hamsun, too, was staying in Valdres. As Robert Ferguson records, 'from the sanatorium at Tonsaasen he [Hamsun] travelled all over the area, visiting old friends like Erik Frydenlund, and the Mjøen family at nearby Gjøvik' [*Enigma*, p. 168]. This gives some credibility to Jelka's recollection — late in life — of what Delius had told her long before: 'On this trip Fred also made a concert tour together with his friend Jebe and with Knut Hamsun. The latter is the well-known Norwegian author. He had quite an imposing appearance and always went about with a grey top-hat and frock coat although the tour took place in all sorts of mountain resorts. Jebe played the violin very well. He had studied in Leipzig and had now been playing in the Colonne Orchestra in Paris for several years. Fred himself of course accompanied Jebe, but also gave a number of solos, I think mostly by Chopin. He always had a rather peculiar smile when mention was made of these performances as he was never a great pianist. Hamsun and Jebe, on the other hand, were apt to get rather drunk. On one occasion Hamsun entered an hotel where they were to perform rather pompously as was his wont. Suddenly he fell down full length on the steps of the veranda where all the guests were assembled, shouting: "Jeg traenger Luft!" (I need air).' What Hamsun otherwise contributed is not, however, specified by Jelka. Did he lecture, recite? We simply do not know.

Delius's correspondence with others, while not mentioning Hamsun or Jebe, helps to fill in the picture of this Norwegian summer: 'I am living on a big farm in Valders, situated on the mountain side of a lovely valley — and working at my opera [. . .] The people here are very simple and very kind — Much better than the norwegian town folk' — this was to Jelka on 15 June. At the end of the month, he was to tell her: 'almost all my time here I spend on my opera.' He also wrote from Haugen to Randi Blehr: 'I am feeling fine here [. . .] I didn't get as far as Ødegaard — Perhaps later I will go to Jotunheimen.' He asked her to pass his regards to Hjalmar Johnsen. On 8 July, he wrote again to Jelka: 'I think I shall leave here about the 20th

or 25th inst & go first to Drontheim [Trondheim] to visit a friend.' Might this friend have been the 'Bruun from Trondheim' who had sent greetings to him via Sinding some three years earlier? The best-known Bruuns in that town were dealers in furs. Their company — one of the largest in Scandinavia — had been founded by Johan Nicolay Bruun (1832–91) in Skien in 1852. Nine years later, he had reestablished the business in Trondheim, where it was now thriving. It may well have been a member of this particular family whom Delius intended to visit.

Delius undertook his tour in the Jotunheim with a guide: 'The feeling is really exquisite up so high & tramping all day — 12 or 14 hours — in that invigorating mountain air & I enjoyed it thoroughly,' he told Jelka on 15 August. The journey continued into the Gudbrandsdal and then the Rondane mountains, 'staying at nights at Saeters in a very primitive style', then on to Foldalen, Østerdalen, Lake Mjøsa, Gjøvik and Odnaes, before arriving back at Søndre Aurdal just before the middle of August. After a further two or three days at Haugen, Delius went off for a few days' stay on a saeter in Hallingdal, probably leaving for Christiania around 20/21 August. There were to be visits to Copenhagen and a number of German cities before he regained Paris shortly before the middle of September.

Delius spent the autumn of 1896 in Paris at work on *Koanga*. He went over to Bradford for Christmas, full of plans for a return to Florida in the new year, 'to settle up that unfortunate grove business', as he put it to a friend. Halfdan Jebe accompanied him to America, as did — in the event — an uninvited friend, Marie-Léonie, Princesse de Cystria. They gave a recital together in Danville, Virginia, and quite probably gave others elsewhere. The princess sang, and Delius and Jebe more than likely returned to the repertoire that had taken them around Valdres for a while the previous summer. But Delius spent most of his time in Jacksonville and on his plantation, Solana Grove, trying to devise methods to make his land pay in the future. While in Florida, he worked on the first version of his one and only Piano Concerto (RT VII/4), a work that is clearly indebted to the Grieg Concerto. By the end of May, Delius was back in Paris again.

For Grieg, the summer and autumn of 1896 proved to be a period of fecundity. The *Symphonic Dances*, op.64, were written for piano, four hands; and the eighth set, op.65, of *Lyric Pieces* was composed, including the magical 'Wedding Day at Troldhaugen'. *Nineteen Norwegian Folk Songs*, op.66, also fall into this period and include 'In Ola Valley, in Ola Lake' (no.14). Grieg's harmonization of this tune was taken up many years later by Delius and incorporated into his orchestral piece *On hearing the first cuckoo in Spring*. There were concerts in Stockholm in October and November, and then two months were spent in Vienna from mid-November. The Griegs then returned to Leipzig for a month, before spending the spring of 1897 in Copenhagen. It was back to Troldhaugen for most of the summer. As usual there had been concerts and concert-giving throughout the winter, and the Griegs were lionized wherever they went.

If the correspondence between Delius and the Griegs had been noticeably sporadic from the summer of 1894 on, the letter that Grieg wrote from Troldhaugen on 18 June 1896 would appear to be the last between them for almost seven years. It may just be that one or two communications have not survived, but the fact that Delius could write, almost apologetically, in June 1903: 'It is such a long time that we have heard nothing from each other' makes it clear enough that, for whatever reason, the mid-1890s had seen them gradually drifting apart. Although nothing is explained in the correspondence, the reasons for this are various and perhaps to a degree self-evident when their respective lives in the meantime are scrutinized.

'I don't see many Norwegians here apart from Munch,' Delius told Randi Blehr in December 1896, writing to her from his Paris apartment. It is this friendship with Edvard Munch that perhaps symbolizes the gap that seemed to be opening up between Grieg and Delius. Although Munch and Delius had become acquainted around 1890, they seem not to have met frequently until the middle of the decade, when Munch came to live for a time in Paris. Their friendship became a solid one and was to survive the vicissitudes of their later lives. Munch was not particularly musical, and there is little evidence that he ever heard very much of Delius's music. Delius, on the other hand, recognized early in Munch a master artist of his time, experimental, radical, pathbreaking. What Munch found in Delius was an immediate sympathy with his art and an extraordinary strength of character: here was a genuine, unvacillating friend on whom he could always rely. It is this rock-like quality that so many of his Scandinavian friends and contemporaries seemed to find and to appreciate in Delius. Munch was much later to write of the 'optimistic good humour which I have so often envied you — He who has this strong inner self is happier than so many others.' Whenever he felt depressed in Paris, it would be to Delius that he could turn. With little money of his own at the time, he knew he could go over to his friend's rooms in the rue Ducouëdic and be well fed and given decent wine.

Just as important, he realized, 'you would cheer me up with your good humour.' Delius also took him along to the Molards', where once again he could find a hospitality that was welcoming and warming. Munch well appreciated the fact that Delius 'always took an interest in the rest of us' and was, as he put it, 'always modest about your own things.'

It had been the same with Sinding a few years earlier: 'I have hardly ever before met a person I could trust so completely,' he had told Delius in April 1888. When Sinding despatched Vilhelm Krag to Paris, it was with the promise that he would find in Delius good company. And as we have already seen, Arve Arvesen had noted that when he was in Paris, Delius had 'always been good at keeping tabs on him.' Then there was Halfdan Jebe, who shared with Delius an anarchic view of the world, together with a love of beautiful women and a passion for wandering. For several years after their trip to America, they continued to erect exotic castles in the air in the form of far-flung world tours that were never to be realized — jointly at least, for Jebe finally loosened the bonds of Europe and only after years of travelling widely settled down in Mexico. He wrote racy letters to his friend: 'I hate you because you know everything better without having tried it. What are you doing now, Superman?'

Of these friends of his earlier years, Delius was to remain closest to those who themselves remained most nearly true to the *vie de Bohème*, notably Munch and Jebe, while gradually growing distant from the more conservative Sinding and Arvesen. Sinding was soon to settle down with Augusta Gade and a ready-made family. His music, so highly regarded by Grieg, yet so squarely in the German tradition and never of a really Norwegian character — that character that had been fashioned by Svendsen, Grieg, Kjerulf and Nordraak and absorbed by various of Sinding's contemporaries — did not appear to awaken any significant appreciation in Delius, and there is no reference to Sinding's compositions anywhere to be found in Delius's letters from the early 1890s on. In this connection, Percy Grainger's description of Sinding may well stand for what is not actually expressed in Delius. Sinding had just appeared in England for the first time, at a Philharmonic Society concert on 13 March 1907, when he had conducted his Violin Concerto, with Johannes Wolff as soloist: 'he is a kind little man, despite (or perhaps because) that he is not a particularly good composer' [Letter from Grainger to Karen Holten, 13 March 1907]. Arve Arvesen was to found a string quartet, to become a teacher and to end his life as principal of the Bergen

Conservatory: not perhaps the lifestyle of Delius's more typical Scandinavian friends. Grieg, too, had become an establishment figure, if only by reason of his inescapable fame. Similarly, Iver Holter, conductor of the Musikforening, and Johan Halvorsen, soon to become conductor of the National Theatre Orchestra, were firmly ensconced in their careers at the centre of Christiania's musical life. After the earlier 1890s, there is no evidence that their paths were ever again to converge with Delius's.

Perhaps Grieg's belief in Sinding's genius says it all: 'Believe me,' he had told Max Abraham back in October 1889, 'he's going to be something really big.' Not only was he convinced that Sinding was the leading Scandinavian composer of the new generation, but he was later to describe him as the best living conductor. Sinding was, after all, regularly getting performances of his own works, not just in Norway and Sweden, but also more widely in Germany; and as he composed, so he was published. Where then was Delius at this point of time — by, say, the end of 1896? By comparison with Sinding almost nowhere. Grieg knew and had shown interest in a few of the apprentice works: *Florida, Paa Vidderne* in its melodrama version at least, probably *Hiawatha*, all dating from the late 1880s. He also knew and liked a number of the songs from the same period. He was aware that Delius had by now written two full-length operas, which remained unstaged, and was working on a third. Now, in 1896, he is found expressing some alarm at one of the Verlaine songs, an echo of his earlier reservations about one or two of Delius's songs.

Apart from the early Augener songs, virtually nothing of Delius's had been published, nor did there even seem to be any prospect of publication on the horizon. If C.F. Peters, in the person of Max Abraham, had been one of the first to turn him down, more were to follow — companies like Wilhelm Hansen, Forberg, Aibl, Breitkopf & Härtel, Brockhaus, Bote & Bock, Kahnt (and no doubt others) — all were to reject him until, out of the blue, the firm of Harmonie, in Berlin, wrote to him in 1906 and offered to take him on. Objectively, it must have seemed to Grieg that the likelihood of Delius succeeding as a composer was fast fading. There was just no evidence to the contrary. Delius cannot have been unaware of Grieg's high regard for Sinding and he must by now have become frustrated at his own inability further to impress his erstwhile mentor. Grieg had simply had no chance to hear the music of Delius's growing maturity, nor even to receive news of any signal success in performance. Even Delius, normally given to expressions of self-confidence, was now finding room for self-doubt. 'I cannot sell a song,' he wrote to Jutta Bell in July 1896. 'It seems ridiculous when one comes to think of it but I cannot make a fiver.'

Then what was Grieg to make of Delius's apparent association with Knut Hamsun? Significantly, Hamsun had little sympathy with those he considered to be of the old guard of Norwegian literature, in particular such friends or collaborators of Grieg as Bjørnson, Lie and Ibsen (even if there was a certain admiration for Bjørnson) and he attacked them openly in lectures, as in his writings. In December 1904, Grieg, incensed by Hamsun's latest attack on Bjørnson, was to write an open letter to *Verdens Gang* in defence of his friend. The old order *was* gradually passing, of course. In the case of Ibsen both Delius and Grieg were certainly aware of the fact. In January 1899, Delius wrote to Jelka after having been to a performance of *Ghosts* in Paris: 'It sounded a bit old-fashioned to my ears — I want much more now — and certain things cease to interest me.' And Grieg, writing to Röntgen after Ibsen's death in 1906, compared the latter's final years to those of the poet Welhaven: 'Both were dead a long time before they actually died. People talked about Ibsen's works, but no more about the man himself. In the national consciousness he had already long since passed on.'

So — Halfdan Jebe, Knut Hamsun and Edvard Munch — these then were the young lions whose company Delius now appeared to seek and enjoy while gradually, if almost unconsciously, distancing himself from Edvard and Nina Grieg and their immediate circle of friends. There seems to be no evidence that Grieg ever met Hamsun or — with his conservative taste in art — that he would even have wished to meet Munch. And what of Gunnar Heiberg, the leading dramatist of the successor generation to Ibsen and Bjørnson, who rejected so much of what Grieg's friend Bjørnson stood for, including patriarchal values and the high moral ground generally, and whose play, *King Midas*, published in 1890, had aimed its barbs at Bjørnson and had set out to attack moral preachings? The story of his latest play *Folkeraadet* ('Parliament') in 1897 is a significant one for Delius, and the events surrounding its production make for an entertaining story.

Shortly before the Christiania Theatre opened its doors on the evening of Monday 1 November 1897, a young man walked into Larsen's the gunsmiths, not far away, and bought for himself a cheap nickel-plated revolver. He had the live cartridges removed on the spot and six blanks substituted. After handing five kroner over the counter he walked out, made his way to the theatre and took up the seat he had reserved for himself in the front row of the stalls. So it was that Albert Tønnesen, a 25 year-old painter and decorator from Flekkefjord, set to procure himself a modest position in the annals of Norwegian theatre history.

The play which was to be given on the capital's principal stage that evening was *Folkeraadet*, which had opened just two weeks earlier and had been playing to packed and excited houses. Gunnar Heiberg, still not 40, and director of the National Theatre in Bergen for four years in the mid-80s, had staged the first-ever performances of *The Wild Duck* and *Rosmersholm* and had discovered and first promoted the career of the young girl who was to become Norway's most celebrated actress — Johanne Dybwad. By the time he started to write *Folkeraadet* in 1896, he had completed such fine plays as *Aunt Ulrikke*, *Artists*, *King Midas*, *The Balcony* and *The Big Prize*, which between them had been performed in Christiania, Bergen, Malmö, Stockholm, Copenhagen and Berlin. But until *Folkeraadet*, the ultimate distinction of having a play given at the Christiania Theatre had eluded him.

Before his spell in Bergen, Heiberg had made something of a name for himself as a theatre critic. And it was with some relief that in September 1896 he had returned to his old vocation in accepting editor Ola Thommessen's offer of the job of drama critic with *Verdens Gang*, one of the leading daily newspapers, as this was to bring to an end a period of some financial difficulty for him. Early in 1897, he was dispatched to France as the paper's Paris correspondent and there he met Delius. The result of the friendship cemented then was the incidental music to *Folkeraadet* (RT I/5), completed just in time for the play's opening on 18 October 1897.

Heiberg's choice of composer was bold, to say the least. His play was a brilliant and often scathing satire on the Norwegian parliamentary system and its politicians. It was furthermore an ironic and peppery comment on the union with Sweden and on Norwegian attitudes to the uneasy state of that union. Delius's brief was to reflect the subject matter of the play in his music, which was largely to consist of an overture and three entr'actes; and he elected to do this — probably at Heiberg's instigation — by taking Norway's national anthem, 'Ja, vi elsker dette Landet', as his point of reference and making extensive use in variation form of the theme.

Delius's credentials for writing the *Folkeraadet* music were impeccable save in one key respect — he was not Norwegian. Almost forseeably, the critics were to seize indignantly on this fact. Christen Collin, Bjørnson's most avid disciple (and Bjørnson had after all written the poem 'Ja, vi elsker'), was to suggest that as it was a question of writing music to poke fun at Norwegian national pride, Delius should have told Heiberg to give the commission to a Norwegian composer: 'Herr Delius's all-too-clever use of one of our most cherished songs is very likely to intensify the prejudices that many Norwegians have against the English.'

By the first night of *Folkeraadet* on 18 October 1897, rumours of a likely sensation had spread. The leading critics were all there. Heiberg's piece was to be played by what was Norway's national theatre company in all but name, with the principal roles taken by Johanne Dybwad, Jens Selmer and Severin Roald. Heiberg himself directed the play, and the Christiania Theatre Orchestra was conducted by Per Winge (who had, incidentally, himself been a student at the Leipzig Conservatory in 1883–84).

On the whole *Folkeraadet* was well-received by that first-night audience; but the music, notably the minor key version of *Ja, vi elsker* employed as a funeral march in the prelude to the last act, caused outrage. Over the following days, a series of lively reviews and impassioned debates filled many pages of the Norwegian daily newspapers. Initially centred on the play itself, the general debate soon turned to the music and to the gratuitous insult that the more diehard critics saw it as presenting to Norwegian national pride. This was indeed a dangerous time apparently to be mocking the national anthem, and the consequences were wide-ranging. Delius was turned out of his hotel and had to seek another where the management was less sensitive; there were demonstrations in the streets as well as inside the theatre; people complained at not being able to make judgments for themselves, as whole stretches of the music were inaudible beneath howls, whistles and counter-applause; and the police were to move into the theatre in force, ejecting and summarily fining offending members of the audience. An inevitable response was that the music rapidly attracted champions, prominent among them being conductor Winge, composer Johan Selmer, critic Sigurd Bødtker and painter Christian Krohg.

The end of the first week's run saw an appropriately dramatic development. A strong and vocal section of the Christiania Students Union — nationalist sentiments among the younger members of the community ran high — called a debate. Delius, alarmed, decided to withdraw his music. With this action the critics' teeth were drawn, and the Union debate itself took an unexpected turn, with the students contritely voting (by 158 to 78) to ask Delius to return his music to the theatre — an action which met with Ibsen's approval. Four days after apparently having been heard for the last time, the incidental music to *Folkeraadet* was again played in the capital.

Almost inevitably, anarchy returned to the theatre. The standard police fine imposed on the most voluble demonstrators seems to have been set at 20 kroner. One particular fine had a cataclysmic effect, extracted as it was from our friend Albert Tønnesen's brother. Whatever outraged national feeling Albert himself may have been subject to, there seems little doubt that his action on the night of 1 November was to a degree motivated by a desire to exact a full fraternal revenge. At the point where Delius's funeral march was in full flow to its counterpoint of whistles, he stood up and levelled his revolver at the conductor. He fired his blanks three or four times in quick succession and then, for good measure, threw the weapon at Winge. There was pandemonium in the house and the offender was removed, to whistling and applause, by the ever-present police. It was some time before the last act got under way. Again the newspapers had a field day, describing the previous evening's events in considerable detail, with not a few of them approving of the action. 'Herostratus-Tønnesen from Flekkefjord', as one of Christiania's journals dubbed him, was fined 200 kroner, but apparently elected to undergo the martyrdom of prison, rather than to pay up.

Folkeraadet continued in repertory until 27 November 1897. But as a *succès de scandale* its days were over when Delius, aware that his musician colleagues in the theatre orchestra were almost at the end of their tether, withdrew the music definitively. It was played for the last time on the evening of Wednesday 3 November, the day Delius left the Norwegian capital for Copenhagen.

Christian Krohg had wryly (and sympathetically) suggested to Delius, immediately after the première, that he might well at just that moment be 'the most unpopular man in Norway' — and Delius had ruefully been obliged to agree.

It might well have been thought that here was Grieg's chance at last actually to hear his friend's latest orchestral music in public performance, but this was not to be, for by pure coincidence, while Delius's music was to be heard almost night after night in the Norwegian capital, Grieg was preparing for his busiest tour yet in Britain. Leaving Norway in the middle of November 1897, he gave ten concerts within the space of a month and furthermore had an audience at Windsor of Queen Victoria early in December. Grieg found that she knew much of his music well and, moreover, liked it.

'The Queen is *sweet*, if one can say this about an elderly lady. She knew almost the entire programme, *enjoyed* Nina's singing in Norwegian, and asked for more,' he told a friend on 6 December. To Röntgen he wrote four days later: 'It was *very* nice. She is so charming and interested, quite astonishingly so for an old lady.' The contrast with the younger composer's extraordinary reception in Christiania at the time is marked: while Grieg is received by the monarch at Windsor Castle, Delius is turned out of his hotel for attacking the Norwegian national anthem. Friends such as the Beyers would almost certainly have kept the later reports of the *Folkeraadet* fiasco to show to Grieg on his return and Grieg can scarcely have been impressed by press comments on the 'mockery', as they had expressed it, of 'Ja, vi elsker dette Landet', viewed, as his funeral march was by many, as a fierce and unfriendly parody of Rikard Nordraak's noble tune. Grieg held Nordraak, of course, in almost sacred memory, and if the one way that Delius could find to bring his music to public attention was by being seen to prostitute Nordraak's work, this would have left a bitter taste with Grieg. Whether Delius wrote to him in 1897 about *Folkeraadet*, we simply do not know. Of the outcome — a pained silence from Grieg — we can be reasonably certain.

Delius's career took yet another erratic step forward in the autumn of 1897, when on 13 November his symphonic poem *Over the hills and far away* (RT VI/11) was performed in Elberfeld, Germany, by Hans Haym, a conductor who was to give pioneering performances of a whole series of his orchestral and choral works in the earlier 1900s. Another landmark came in May 1899, when Delius himself organized an entire concert of his own works in London. This had become possible because of a legacy following the death in 1898 of Theodor Delius. The concert was widely reviewed in the English press, wonderment, praise, bafflement and hostility being present in almost equal measure. No-one knew who Delius was, but it was widely assumed that, although born in England, he had Scandinavian parents. The *Daily Mail*, on 31 May, for instance, told its readers that 'Mr. Fritz Delius — born in England, but in spirit Scandinavian — gave a concert of his own compositions, which was a surprise to most of us. His music has spirit and manliness, imagination also, and honest feeling.' The *Topical Times* of 3 June referred to 'a parentage that established his race kinship with Grieg'; and other newspapers said much the same thing. Musical connections with Grieg were also noted. 'Occasionally,' wrote the *Westminster Gazette*'s correspondent on 31 May, '— as in the opening piece of yesterday's programme, an orchestral fantasia, "Over the Hills and Far Away" — he reminds you of Grieg with a dash of Wagner in his "Charfreitagszauber" vein.' This same work, wrote the *Morning Post* of 3 June, 'at once settled the question as to its author's capabilities. The music of this is highly poetic and imaginative, Northern in character, here and there denoting the influence of Grieg. It is admirably scored, and the working out evinces considerable originality.' *The Times* of 31 May, cautiously conservative, thought the whole concert 'a somewhat depressing affair', the gloom 'scarcely relieved by the pastoral fantasia in Grieg's manner.'

Delius's impresario, Norman Concorde, had ensured that the papers were aware of the composer's fame — or notoriety — in Norway as a result of the *Folkeraadet* affair. 'We had', wrote *The Star* on 1 June, 'two movements from an orchestral suite composed for a drama called "The Council of the People", in which the Norwegian national air is used. It is treated with some of the grotesque bizarre effects over which M. Delius has apparently unlimited control, and this roused quite a patriotic fervour in Norway [. . .] We take our National Anthem less seriously.' The *Daily News* referred to the now-celebrated incident when 'some ultra-patriot [. . .] levelled a pistol at the conductor, forgetful perhaps of the protest of the American manager, "Don't shoot the pianist, he is doing his best".' The tongue-in-cheek tone continued: 'In this country we are not so hot-headed, and even the attempt of the opera chorus to sing "God Save the Queen" never results in a display of "shooting irons". The mistake of the Norwegian critics was all the more extraordinary, inasmuch as Mr. Delius, although, we believe, born in Yorkshire, is of Scandinavian parentage.'

The *Daily News* appears to have been the only newspaper to note that the orchestra was 'led by Mr. Halfdan Jebe, who, we believe, came over for the purpose.'

In spite of all the press interest, the true breakthrough that Delius was hoping for in his native land was not to occur for another eight years, ironically enough only shortly after Grieg's death.

During these years of temporary disengagement between the friends, Grieg and Nina continued the usual pattern of spending their summers at Troldhaugen and the rest of the year travelling and concert-giving. Grieg himself organized the first Bergen Festival in 1898, an event which proved a runaway critical success, crowned by the presence of Röntgen and his Concertgebouw Orchestra. The remarkable song-cycle *Haugtussa* (op.67) was published that year.

There were also two final books of *Lyric Pieces*, op.68 and op.71, to come, in 1899 and 1901. And Grieg composed in 1902–3 the extraordinary series of *Slåtter*, op.72, arrangements for piano of traditional Hardanger fiddle dance tunes that had been initially transcribed for him by Halvorsen.

In one of the curious byways of music, Grieg and Delius were, during this period of separation, reunited, as it were, in the pages of Debussy's music criticism. At the Société Nationale in Paris on 16 March 1901, Vincent d'Indy had conducted a performance of two of Delius's *Danish Songs* with orchestra. In the following issue of *La Revue Blanche* Debussy loftily dismissed them in terms almost identical to those he would use to describe Grieg songs some two years later: 'They are very sweet songs, very pale, music to lull convalescent ladies to sleep in well-to-do neighbourhoods. . . There always seems to be one note that drags over a chord; like a waterlily on a lake whose flower is tired of being watched by the moon, or again . . . like a tiny balloon obscured by the clouds.'*

78. FRITZ DELIUS TO EDVARD GRIEG

Grez sur Loing
Seine & Marne
[mid-June 1903]

Dear Grieg—

I have just heard that you have celebrated your 60th birth-day.[1] It is such a long time that we have heard nothing from each other which is certainly my fault, but my wishes & greetings for this day are none the less heartfelt. I still think with pleasure of the lovely times we have had together & I hope that life will bring us together again — Unfortunately I was not in France during your stay in Paris otherwise I would have greeted you there.[2] As for me I am quite well, I live in the country near Fontainebleau devoted entirely to my work & am slowly making progress. I have just come back from Basel where my Mitternachtslied from Zarathustra for bari-tone solo, men's chorus & orchestra was played at the German Tonkünstlerfest[3] — I even think that I have man-

---

* *La Revue Blanche*, XXIV, no.188, 1 April 1901, p.551. Also published in the same issue was an instalment of Knut Hamsun's novel *Pan*.

aged to get a publisher thereby!! I should be very glad to hear that you and your dear wife are really well — Once again heartiest greetings to you both—

Yours
Fritz Delius

Autograph letter, signed and undated.

1 Grieg had celebrated his birthday — 15 June — at home at Troldhaugen, as well as in Bergen, the festivities lasting for three days. There were concerts, receptions and a banquet at which Bjørnson made the major speech. Halvorsen brought the National Theatre orchestra from Christiania to grace the celebrations.

2 A white lie, apparently, as in March Delius had written to Edvard Munch from Grez: 'I shall be in Paris again in the middle of April.' He was certainly still in Grez two days after Grieg's 19 April concert, this time writing to tell Munch: 'We are coming to Paris for a fortnight at the end of the month.' Grieg's return to conduct in Paris for the first time for several years was a popular musical success, even if the voices of his critics — now both on the musical and the political plane — were unusually loud, mainly because his lengthy absence had been self-imposed after he had decided to speak out boldly at the time of the Dreyfus affair. In case of public over-reaction to his return, there had been an extra-large contingent of police at the Châtelet Theatre (shades of *Folkeraadet* in Christiania), packed as it was with an audience some 3500–4000 strong. 'I had taken 5 drops of opium,' Grieg wrote to Röntgen on 22 April, 'which had a remarkably calming effect on me.'

3 The annual festival of the Allgemeine Deutsche Musikverein was in 1903 held in Basel. Delius's *Mitternachtslied Zarathustras* (RT II/1), later to be incorporated into his *Mass of Life*, had been composed in 1898. Its performance on 12 June was a significant step forward in the process of Delius's growing recognition in the German-speaking countries.

79. EDVARD GRIEG TO FRITZ DELIUS

Troldhaugen nr. Bergen
1/9/03

Dear Delius,

Many thanks for your birthday greetings to the 60-year old! It is true that these thanks come late. But I am afraid that I have only too good an excuse. Since the end of June I have been seriously ill and am not really allowed to write letters yet. The festival (a whole week) with concerts and banquets was beyond my strength. I was allright[1] as long as the affair lasted, but afterwards came the reaction. You would however have loved the festival. The concerts were a tremendous success under Halvorsen with his National Theatre Orchestra. And Björnson's speech was something special.

And now, dear Delius, how are you? I missed you *very* much during my stay in Paris. I am very pleased to learn from your letter that you are in a position to work completely peacefully on your own. I hope you have been cultivating your patience assiduously. For an operatic composer must have 50 times more of it than any other musician. He must, too, be an optimist by nature, or else he will worry himself to death or at least make himself ill. Congratulations on Basel! Do send me the piece when it comes out. What a pity it is from 'Zarathustra'. I have to think of Strauss, and I have no stomach for Strauss! That is to say, I am a great admirer of 'Tod und Verklärung'. But afterwards he just becomes insolent and beauty, I mean inventiveness, fantasy, bears no relationship at all to insolence. But of course, German musicians must always have a German beast on the pedestal, which they can worship. Wagner is dead. They must have something to satisfy their national pride. Better then a substitute than nothing at all. It really is too funny for words.

Now, please write again soon. For there will be no further opportunity on the 70th birthday!

Kindest regards, also from my wife.

Yours
Edvard Grieg

Autograph letter, signed and dated.

1   *allright.* In English in the original letter.

80.   FREDERICK DELIUS TO EDVARD GRIEG

Grez sur Loing
Seine & Marne
28 Sept 1903

Dear Grieg—

It was really a pleasure to me to receive your kind letter & to hear something in more detail about you again — On the

25th[1] I married my friend Jelka Rosen here in Grez. (Civilement of course) have got even further away from God & Jesus. We lived together for 6 years, but we found it really more practical to legalize our relationship — One gets everything cheaper & one receives free & without further ado a certificate of honesty & good manners — If you go to Germany next winter let me know for I have several performances & I should very much like to introduce my wife to you & Frau Grieg — She is a painter & very gifted — & then I should so much like you to hear my music — You only know my very first efforts — Unfortunately I can't send you anything either as I still haven't found a publisher although I must say that I haven't tried very much either & am writing orchestral music exclusively. Every year I have 3 or 4 performances in Germany — Buths[2] in Düsseldorf & Dr Haym[3] in Elberfeld give my latest scores every year — Buths has arranged 'Paris' The song of a great city — a symphonic work of mine for two pianos & Dr Haym has done the same for 'Lebenstanz'. I shall try to send you these arrangements if I get the chance. I don't need to tell you that *my* Mitternachtslied has absolutely no relationship with the Strauss Zarathustra, which I consider a complete failure: Yet I find that 'Till Eulenspiegel' & Heldenleben especially are splendid works. Tod & Verklärung I find not so significant although there is much that is beautiful in it. There is still too much Liszt & *Berlioz* about it — I think he will do his best work in humorous things. His tragedy is 'Dick & Deutsch' [*i.e.* 'Fat & German']. Do write to me about your winter plans so that we can perhaps see each other again this winter & spend a few splendid days together & experience old & new moods — I send you & your dear wife my very best wishes & remain affectionately as ever

Yours
Frederick Delius
(new name!)

Autograph letter, signed and dated.

1 The marriage certificate actually bears the date 23 September.

2 Julius Buths (1851–1920): German conductor, composer and pianist. As music director in Düsseldorf, he had given Delius's *Paris* (RT VI/14) there on 12 February 1903. *Lebenstanz* (RT VI/15), like *Paris* also

dating from 1899, was to follow on 21 January 1904 — its first performance. Later, on 24 October 1904, Buths was to be soloist in Delius's Piano Concerto — another first performance — conducted in Elberfeld by Hans Haym, his successor as music director in that town.

3 Hans Haym (1860–1921): German conductor and composer, and music director in Elberfeld. It was he who had conducted the first performance of any Delius orchestral work in Germany — *Over the hills and far away* — at Elberfeld on 13 November 1897. *Paris* had its first performance under his baton there on 14 December 1901, and other works by Delius were to be brought forward by him over the years.

In 1903, Haym and Buths together played through on two pianos Delius's Piano Concerto. 'We consider', Haym wrote to Delius, 'that you still betray your descent from Grieg quite noticeably in the Concerto, although only in occasional turns of harmony. The main thing is that out of the whole there speaks an original spirit. Everyone must come from somewhere, after all.'

81.   EDVARD GRIEG TO FREDERICK DELIUS

Kristiania 23/10/03
Hotel Westminster.

Dear Delius,

Many years ago I got to know and became very fond of a certain *Fritz* Delius. Whether that will be the same with *Frederick* Delius, I really don't know. Where did 'der alte Fritz' go wrong then? Both my wife and I ask: Are we never again to see the selfsame man? We had got to like him very much.

Well now, my dear friend, we are of course looking forward very much to making the acquaintance of the newly-wed Mr. Frederick. Likewise his esteemed wife. Our heartiest congratulations and best wishes to you both. You know me well enough to realize that preachers viewed as a tribe are anathema to me. A marriage without preachers has something much more idealistic about it than a church marriage. But as you say: It is cheaper! (Very good!) And for the masses, more moral! (Just as good!)

You have now reached the zenith of your life, I mean that point in life when the artist does his best work. I should love to have the opportunity to become acquainted with the present products of your muse. Well, we shall be coming to Germany again one day. Perhaps even next year. Unfortunately my uncertain state of health does not allow me a longer stay in damp and unhealthy Leipzig. You see, I have arrived at that stage in life when I could no longer write 'A Dance of Life'. Rather 'Weariness of Life', also a subject for a symphonic poem!

And with this enough for today. We are staying here for the time being and spending Christmas with the Björnsons at Aulestad. The old man is splendid! Strength and gentleness in one!

Our heartiest greetings, also to your wife!

Yours
Edvard Grieg.

Autograph letter, signed and dated.

82. FREDERICK DELIUS TO EDVARD GRIEG

[Grez, 28 December 1903]

Concert in Düsseldorf 21st January & 27th February in Elberfeld[1] — My opera 'Koanga' is being rehearsed in Elberfeld[2]   Hearty New Year greetings to you & your dear wife —

Fr. Delius
Jelka Delius

Autograph picture postcard: *GREZ. — Vue sur le Loing,* signed and undated. Addressed: *Monsieur Edvard Grieg/Hotel Westminster/ Kristiania/Norvège.* Readdressed: *Aulestad/pr Faaberg.* Postmark: GREZ 28 [12] 03. Receiving postmark: KRISTIANIA 31 XII 03. Also signed by Jelka Delius.

1 Haym had projected a first performance of *Appalachia* (RT II/1) for this date, but in the event was unable to find time enough to prepare it.
2 Fritz Cassirer (1871–1926), opera conductor at Elberfeld, gave the first of three performances of *Koanga* on 30 March. This was the first time that any of Delius's operas had reached the stage.

83. EDVARD GRIEG TO FREDERICK DELIUS

[Troldhaugen] 23/8/04.

2 Norwegian peasants send their most hearty greetings to the Breton ditto!

Yours
Edvard Grieg

Picture postcard: *Bjørnson og Grieg paa Villa Troldhaugen* [Bjørnson and Grieg at Troldhaugen], signed and dated. Addressed: M. Fr. Delius/ Loctudy/Finistère./Bretagne, France. Postmarks: HOP 23 VIII 04, BERGEN 23–8–1904. Receiving postmark: LOCTUDY 28 AOUT 04.

Grieg had returned to Troldhaugen at the end of May after a concert tour in Sweden in the spring. In spite of the nature of this greeting, the postcard photograph in fact shows Grieg and Bjørnson together over a year earlier, at the time of Grieg's 60th birthday celebrations. The Deliuses meanwhile were spending the high summer in Brittany, for a part of the time with Fritz Cassirer and his wife and child. Delius and Cassirer were working through Nietzsche's *Also Sprach Zarathustra* and selecting the texts that Delius would use to create his *Mass of Life* (RT II/4). For the Griegs, a quiet autumn in Christiania was followed by winter and spring in Copenhagen, where Grieg was ill for much of the time. They returned to Troldhaugen early in June 1905, leaving again for Christiania on 20 September. They stayed in the capital for the rest of the year, and Christmas saw Grieg in hospital there. Needless to say, very little composing had been done during the year. But Norway's attainment of full independence from Sweden, finally achieved in 1905, had been a source of profound satisfaction.

If it had been a generally depressing period for Grieg, tragedy had struck Sinding. His first extant letter to Delius for seven years, sent from Christiania on 11 March 1905 in reply to an invitation from Delius to visit Grez, reported a serious deterioration in the fragile health of his stepson Morten. Delius immediately sent a comforting letter, but on 24 April Sinding reported Morten's death. His letter ended: 'I want to get out into the world again, and I would love to pay a call on you as soon as possible.' Poignantly, this is however the last letter from Sinding to Delius that remains to us.

By contrast, the upward curve in Delius's career grows more and more marked. In 1905 *A Mass of Life* was completed, *Appalachia* received a widely-noticed first performance at the German Tonkünst-lerfest in Düsseldorf, and *A Village Romeo and Juliet* (RT I/6) was down on the list for production at the Komische Oper in Berlin. In Berlin early in 1906, the composer at last came to an agreement with a publisher, after Harmonie Verlag had sent an unsolicited letter asking him 'to consider our publishing and distributing your works.' Before long, two major compositions were in the press, *Appalachia* (1902–3) and *Sea Drift* (RT II/3) (1903–4).

Grieg meanwhile had left Christiania in April 1906 on a tour that was to include Copenhagen, Berlin, Leipzig, Prague, Amsterdam, London and Hamburg. May saw him in London for the last time. At Queen's Hall on the 17th he conducted an orchestral concert featuring the Danish pianist Johanne Stockmarr as soloist in his Piano Concerto. Other works played included the *Lyric Suite* and the first *Peer Gynt Suite*. On 24 May a new-found friend, Percy Grainger, turned the pages for him at a chamber concert which included the Cello Sonata, in which Grieg accompanied Hugo Becker. Grainger (1882–1961) had been introduced to Grieg at a dinner party given by the latter's hosts on 15 May, and he was also to be present at the dinner on 28 May marking Grieg's departure.* He sent a brief pen-picture of Grieg to his Danish girlfriend: 'Have you seen Grieg and his wife? Can you think of anything more triumphant than the impression of these 2 small people? They are so completely happy together and both so "loveable" and kind [. . .] I think Grieg conducts excellently with much individuality, and many capital and unusual effects.' [Letter to Karen Holten, London, 18 May 1906]

Grieg was particularly moved by the events in London of 17 May, the first National Day to be celebrated since Norway's full independence had been achieved: 'It was a wonderful feeling to have been allowed to represent Norway through my art on this great day.' The evening was spent at the Norwegian Club in London,and Grieg was tearful when Fridtjof Nansen, now Norwegian Ambassador in London, rose to speak to the 200 guests. There were toasts to Grieg and he himself spoke in honour of all who had for so long campaigned for independence, notably Bjørnson to whom he finally proposed a toast. Nansen's welcome to Grieg was particularly warm, and shortly afterwards Edvard and Nina were his guests at a luncheon to which Percy Grainger was also invited. Further honours were heaped upon

* Grainger had played Grieg's *Ballade*, op.24, when he made his London début at Steinway Hall on 29 October 1901.

Grieg during this last visit to England. He had an audience of King Edward VII and Queen Alexandra, and played before the royal couple. He pointedly stopped playing twice during the recital because the King was talking so loudly to Nansen. On his return to Christiania, he mentioned his boldness to King Haakon, to whom he had been charged by King Edward to deliver greetings. Haakon excused the chattering of his royal counterpart: King Edward was, he said, 'the kind of person who can very well listen to music and carry on a conversation at the same time.' Grieg, clearly irritated, exclaimed that it had been a question of bad manners and that such behaviour was quite unacceptable. The King, surprised at Grieg's reaction, smiled and changed the subject. Grieg was later to express the view that although Haakon was a kindly man, he appeared to have absolutely no feeling for music.

Grieg's last major engagement in England was in Oxford on 29 May, when he was awarded an honorary doctorate by the University. Luckily, he had been well enough to attend. Twenty years later, Jelka Delius recorded that Oxford University 'wanted to make Fred Doct. of Music Honor. causa. but as he is unable to go to Oxford for the Ceremony it cannot be done.' For all Grieg's renewed successes in England, he was troubled, not for the first time, at being considered 'popular': 'My reputation as an artist suffers from it and criticism becomes spiteful,' he wrote to Röntgen on 25 May. 'I can't help it if my music is played in third-class hotels.'

Back in Troldhaugen in June, Grieg heard — presumably from Delius himself — that Delius was in Norway.

84.   EDVARD GRIEG TO FREDERICK DELIUS

Troldhaugen 30/6/06.

Dear friend,

An old man, so exhausted by physical suffering that he is fit for nothing more, bids you heartily welcome to Norway. Are you not coming to the Westland? Do try! It would probably be the only chance for us to see each other again. We recently heard some very nice things about your wife from Felix Moscheles[1] in London. Is she with you? Best wishes to you both from Nina and from

yours
Edvard Grieg

Autograph picture postcard, signed and dated. The view is of the Nordaasvand the lake at Troldhaugen. Addressed: Komponisten Hr. Fritz Delius./Fredriksvaern/(Bedes eftersendt) [Please forward]. Postmarks: HOP 30 VI 06 and BERGEN 30 VI 06.

1   Felix Moscheles (1833–1917): German-born artist, resident in London. A son of Ignaz Moscheles, who had taught Grieg at Leipzig, he was Jelka Delius's uncle. 'Send me Felix's letter if there is anything in it,' Delius wrote to Jelka while touring in Norway. It must evidently have contained news of the meeting with Grieg in London.

Delius was back in Norway for the first time in seven years and — for the first time — with his wife. During this Norwegian holiday, it seems that Jelka was for the most time left to paint at Aasgaardstrand, while Delius went on a long tour that was to take him in turn to Larvik, Skien, Fredriksvaern, Aasgaardstrand, Christiania, Atna, and back again on 25 July to Aasgaardstrand, where they both remained for another month or so before returning to Grez. Delius had hoped to see Edvard Munch at Aasgaardstrand, where the painter had a cottage, but found to his disappointment that his friend was away in Germany.

85.   EDVARD GRIEG TO FREDERICK DELIUS

Troldhaugen
Hop nr. Bergen
21/7/06

Dear Delius,

I am very poorly and cannot meet you anywhere, unfortunately, much as I should like to. I have, it is true, always had frail health. But now, with old age as well, life has become more and more of a burden to me. Through physical suffering I am unable to work, although I feel that I still have it in me. That is what makes existence so unbearable for me. That is of course not the right frame of mind for 'Storfjeldsaeter'.[1] Forgive me. But I did not want to put you off with empty phrases. I really am delighted that you are so active; I still have the good fortune to be able to admire and love other artists and other art and so it would be an event for me to be able to be present at a performance of your opera in Berlin.[2] But whether I shall be allowed to travel to Berlin next winter is very doubtful indeed. It is not entirely out of the question however and Berlin particularly attracts me. In later years I always felt better there than in Leipzig and Copenhagen. It looks from your card as if you are not coming to the Westland. But if you should, I know that you will not pass by my door.

My wife sends her greetings to you and to your wife. Likewise does

Yours
Edvard Grieg

Autograph letter, signed and dated.

1 Storfjeldsaeter was Delius's address near the Atna posting station in the Østerdal region of Norway. He stopped for some time here during his tour.

2 *A Village Romeo and Juliet* was, after a long wait, to be premièred in Berlin in February 1907.

86. FREDERICK DELIUS TO EDVARD GRIEG

Grez sur Loing
Seine & Marne
11/10/1906

Dear friend

I send you today the piano score of 'Sea-drift': it is the work which was performed at the Tonkünstler Fest in Essen this summer. The full score, like that of 'Appalachia' too is still not yet ready. I hope you will soon hear it in Germany, it gets performed from time to time & my music does not sound well on the piano. When are you coming to Berlin? My opera will probably not be performed before December (Christmas perhaps). I have read that you are giving a concert in Berlin on the 12th April & look forward to it & hope, however, that you will come to Berlin much earlier. We stayed in Aasgaard-strand until the end of August & then went from Drammen to Rouen by sea & had a splendid journey; utterly peaceful & only sunshine. Here we still have the most lovely summer, no rain & autumn weather yet set in. We are now harvesting our delicious grapes, apples & pears. The poem of Sea-drift was translated by my wife. I hope this letter finds you reasonably well & cheerful & perhaps working on something new. Give your dear wife my best wishes & here's to seeing you again soon in Berlin to which my wife too looks forward

Yours
Fritz Delius

Autograph letter, signed and dated.

The Griegs had returned to Christiania at the end of September, and it was there that they passed the final winter of Grieg's life. The last composition to be completed was the *Four Psalms* for mixed chorus, op.74. Three of the pieces had been composed at Troldhaugen in the summer; the fourth at the Hotel Westminster, Christiania — home for the winter — in November. Intimations of mortality abounded, and that month Grieg wrote to his old friend John Paulsen: 'It seems to me that all my contemporaries are falling away. Thaulow's death affected me badly. In one year: Ibsen, Kjelland, Thaulow! That's a lot for Norway.' There was still some conducting and accompanying to do, and after engagements in Christiania Grieg left in mid-March for a further foreign tour, to Copenhagen, Munich, Berlin and Kiel, returning to Denmark at the end of April. Here he tried to stem the tide of illness with a course of hydrotherapy, followed by a stay at a sanatorium. On 9 May he wrote ruefully to Henry Hinrichsen, Abraham's successor as his publisher: 'Hugely tempting invitations are coming in from America! Too late, too late!' The Griegs returned to Troldhaugen around the middle of June.

Delius's hope that he and Grieg might meet again in Berlin was not to be fulfilled. What might Grieg have made of his friend's masterpiece, *A Village Romeo and Juliet*, when it was produced there? One suspects that Grieg might at last have been convinced of the genius of his protégé, as others were to become convinced both in Germany and in England in this *annus mirabilis* for Delius. The opera opened on 21 February 1907; Delius then travelled to Basel for the second performance of his *Sea Drift*, another major work, before returning to Paris at the beginning of March. Later in the year, Delius's definitive breakthrough in England was to be assured by performances in London of his Piano Concerto and *Appalachia*, successes of which Grieg was never to learn. Grieg and Delius missed each other, then, in Berlin by something like six weeks, Delius leaving for Basel towards the end of February, and Grieg arriving in the German capital for his concerts there on 12 and 14 April.

Grieg's interest in new music never wavered. He liked what he heard of Sibelius and Debussy, for example, and after a performance of Debussy's *Prélude à l'après-midi d'un faune* in Christiania, he wrote of it to Röntgen on 6 February: 'Extravagant music, but very talented and for me 10 times more sympathetic than the new-German plumpudding.' 'Plumpudding' was also the term he had used (again in English) to Henry Hinrichsen just over a year earlier to describe a Reger quintet. Conversely, he was appalled by Strauss's *Salome* — seen in Berlin in April — describing it as 'a triumph of technique over spirit.' Invited to lunch with the Kaiser, he had met Massenet and Saint-Saëns there: 'But as I could not speak French it was a rather embarrassing situation. I also got to know Richard Strauss.' One presumes that Grieg would diplomatically have turned the conversation with the latter to *Tod und Verklärung*, a work that he did find intensely moving.

While Grieg was in Berlin, Delius was in London. What now began to preoccupy him was the fact that Henry Wood had taken up his Piano Concerto and wished to conduct it in the autumn. This would be the first occasion on which a major work by Delius would be given in London since the St James's Hall concert of 1899. By now, news of his successes on the continent had begun to spread and he was a focus of attention for the younger generation of English composers. Delius was genuinely elated at this evidence of widespread interest in his work at last becoming evident in the land of his birth. Among the many new friends he made was Percy Grainger, who marvelled at *Appalachia*: 'I do think the harmonies & all I can make out of the score just *too* moving & lovely.' He wrote to tell Karen Holten of the similarities he could discern between Delius and himself: 'A certain quality of Englishness, of foreignness, & of American & nigger influence, & a great love of Grieg (which he shares with me also)'.

In November 1906, Grieg had written to invite Grainger to join him at the Leeds Festival in October the following year: 'Could we not so arrange it that I include my Piano Concerto amongst the works that I am to conduct, and thus give myself the great joy of seeing Percy Grainger as the soloist in it?' [Grainger's own translation] 'Next year,' he added, 'you simply must come to Norway!' Grainger had replied, in his fluent Danish: 'Do you mean that I could possibly come to you up in "Troldhaugen" next summer? If you could have me, it would indeed be glorious.' The visit was duly arranged, as was the joint concert date at Leeds.

Returning to Grez from London, Delius soon put a score in the post for Grainger, following it up with a letter: 'I sent you "Appalachia", which *please take with* you to Grieg when you go as he knows nothing of my music & it will put us in touch again as I really like him so much.'* Grainger replied a few days later: 'Of course I shall just love to shew it to Grieg & bear him your messages.' Delius responded nostalgically: 'In the summer I have always a great longing to go to Norway & live among the Mountains. I love the light nights so. Which way will you go? Let me know also when. The feeling of nature I think is what I like so much in Grieg's best things. You have it too & I think we all 3 have something in common. I wont swear that I shant turn up on the steamer when you go to Bergen. If Grieg were only young & well enough to go into the hills we might have a lovely time.' For Delius, Grainger's visit to Grieg and Norway was almost a proxy visit for himself. He found it difficult to get it out of his mind: 'I suppose you will be on the point of starting for Norway,' he wrote on 6 July. 'I do hope you will have fine weather [. . .] Salute the hills from me.'

Grainger arrived at Troldhaugen on 25 July 1907 and stayed until 4 August. His visit acted like a shot in the arm to Grieg and, among other things, they spent some considerable time rehearsing the Concerto together. Like so many others, Grieg was entranced by the warmth and exuberance of Grainger's personality, as well as by his extraordinary musicianship. 'You have become for me,' he wrote from Troldhaugen on 11 August, 'a dear young friend who has enriched the evening of my life.' To Röntgen, who had also visited Troldhaugen while Grainger was there, he wrote on 23 August: 'Grainger was a splendid fellow! *How* he played and *how* dear and kind he was!'

On 4 September, just one month after Grainger's departure, Edvard Grieg died in a Bergen hospital. He and Nina had left Troldhaugen two days earlier on what was to be the first careful leg of the very trip to England that was to have culminated on 12 October in Grieg's conducting his Piano Concerto at Leeds, with Grainger as soloist. Delius, in London in October and November, would surely have been there. As it was, he

---

* It is perhaps ironic that the first score to go to Grieg for so many years should have been *Appalachia*, since Delius's first biographer, Max Chop, writing in German in 1907, while accepting that Delius was influenced by Grieg's harmony and Chopin's form, felt that with *Appalachia* the last traces of Grieg had finally disappeared from Delius's style. ['Frederick Delius'. *Monographien Moderner Musiker*, 2, p.93.]

now learned of Grieg's death from the newspapers. 'I am *very very* sorry,' he wrote immediately to Grainger. 'Have you any particulars. Please write me all you know.' Grainger responded from Jutland on 9 September: 'He was always talking of you, affectionately & admiringly, & told me lots of jolly anecdotes of your trips together in the High Hills. I showed him Appalachia & played him bits & he studied often in the score, & was *keenly interested*. On the very day I got Mrs Grieg's wire telling me of his death I was planning to write you & convey to you Grieg's delight when I proposed to him that I'd ask you to send him a score of Appalachia [. . .] Am playing at the 1st Grieg Memorial concert in Denmark Friday next.'

Delius promptly wrote a letter of condolence to Nina, who replied to him from Troldhaugen.

87.   NINA GRIEG TO FREDERICK DELIUS

Troldhaugen 16–9–07.

Dear Delius,

Thank you for having written to me. I am sure I need not tell you 'how and where the misfortune happened', you will have read it everywhere. You will also know without my needing to tell you that I am sad and lonely. Until the day before his death he still hoped to go to England, to fulfil his obligations. He rallied so marvellously and gathered the rest of his energy just so as to be able to live long enough for this. Only the fact that he had to suffer so indescribably during the last months can reconcile me to the thought of his death. I have to return again and again to this thought in order to overcome my own disgust with life. Well, I won't distress you, I think you will understand.

I intend to return to Troldhaugen each spring, as long as I survive. But next week I am going to stay with some friends in the country in Denmark,[1] and perhaps in the New Year with friends in England. I would like to meet you again, dear Delius, and get to know your wife.

In old friendship

Yours
Nina Grieg.

Autograph letter, signed and dated.

1 See Letter 91, note 2.

88. **NINA GRIEG TO FREDERICK DELIUS**

Fuglsang[1] 28–12–07.

Dear Delius,

I thank you from my heart for your friendly letter and for the friendship shown to me by you and your wife through your invitation. How I should love to come and see you, the Graingers and the Brodskys.[2] In the autumn I really did myself believe that I would go to England, but the nearer the time comes, the more I lose my courage. It certainly will not be before March. Because then Percy Grainger is supposed to be giving a concert in Copenhagen,[3] and if he actually does so, I could perhaps travel back with him when he returns to England. But I just don't know, I cannot make up my mind about anything. Whatever happens, though, I am deeply grateful to you and your wife. —

I am very pleased that you intend to come to the Jotunheim with Percy this summer. So I have some hope of seeing you in Troldhaugen once again. You will find it empty everywhere, but you will be very welcome. Percy will come too. We must agree later about the time, for I expect several guests, and, as you know, cannot put up many at a time at Troldhaugen, — unfortunately! However, we shall manage somehow! —

I suppose you were so long in London because of 'Appalachia'? Percy wrote a lot of nice things to me about it.[4]

Do you think it is over my head? Since Edvard is no more with me I feel, both musically and in other respects, like a ship without a rudder.

Finally just: a happy New Year to you and your dear wife, with deepest thanks for all past kindnesses.

From my heart

Yours
Nina Grieg.

On Thursday I am off again to *Copenhagen, Hotel Bristol.*

Many thanks for the photograph! I do not think it is much
of a likeness.[5]

1 Nina was staying at the home of the Griegs' friends, Viggo de
Neergaard and his wife Bodil. See Letter 91, note 2.
2 The implication is not, as it might seem to be, that all would be
together at the same time, but rather that in visiting England Nina
would be able to see not only the old Leipzig friends like Delius and
Brodsky, who was now living and teaching in Manchester, but also
Grainger and his mother.
3 Grainger had played the Concerto under Svendsen's baton at the
Memorial Concert for Grieg on 19 October in Copenhagen. He had had
a considerable success and had spent some time with Nina there.
Whatever plans may have been laid for March in Copenhagen did not
materialize.
4 Following the Piano Concerto, played by Theodor Szántó and the
Queen's Hall Orchestra under Henry Wood on 22 October, Delius's
long-awaited breakthrough in England had come on 22 November, with
a performance at Queen's Hall of *Appalachia*. The New Symphony
Orchestra and the Sunday League Choir had been conducted by Fritz
Cassirer, and in the audience was Thomas Beecham, later to describe
the event as a red-letter day in English music. This was the first time he
had heard an orchestral work by Delius, a composer he was from then
on to champion for the rest of his life. Grainger wrote to Karen Holten
on the following day: 'There were so many lovely things in Delius's
piece [. . .] It was refreshing for me to hear him talk Norwegian to me.'
5 It is not known which photograph Delius sent.

There were two memorial concerts in London that October. Delius
seems to have attended both. The first, on the 16th, had Johanne
Stockmarr playing the Piano Concerto. At the second, on the 23rd,
Grainger accompanied Ellen Beck in some of Grieg's songs and
Brodsky in the second Violin Sonata, as well as playing a group of
piano solos. Robin Legge, another Leipzig contemporary of Delius
and now a leading music critic in London, was also at both concerts.
He had taken, in a letter to Delius on 30 September, a gentle dig at
Grainger's undoubted brilliance as a publicist for his own concert
appearances: 'Percy Grainger is just back, mourning for his beloved
Grieg, who was doing him a good deal of material good, & would have
done more if he survived.' Nonetheless, Grainger was never hesitant
to acknowledge the debt he owed to his twin mentors. He was to write
in an article published in 1934: 'My compositional career owed as

much to Frederick Delius as my pianistic career did to Edvard Grieg.'
[*A Delius Companion*, p.123]

89.   NINA GRIEG TO FREDERICK DELIUS

Copenhagen 24–3–08.
Hotel Bristol

Dear Delius,

Many thanks for your letter and [offer of] hospitality. I do not
lack the inclination, as far as I can understand myself, but
rather the courage, I am fearful of going out into the wide
world, coward that I have ever been! So I shall not go to
England, and will not, I am afraid, be visiting you and your
dear wife either. How wonderful it sounds: a big garden by the
river, with lots of flowers! At the end of April I shall probably
go to Kristiania for a few weeks, and then back to Troldhaugen again. I shall be delighted to welcome you both there
in July or August. The 'hotel' you refer to must be the *Fosli*, I
suppose. It is situated at the top of the Vöringsfos, not really
on the Vidde, but you can trek from there eastwards right
across the whole Vidde. It is magnificent up there, but we
were not very satisfied with the hotel, I am afraid, and since
then it is supposed to have got even worse. You will certainly
get better accommodation at *Framnaes* on the Tyin.

I have not heard from Percy Grainger for a long time, he is
off, so far as I know, on endless concert tours. Give him my
regards if you meet him in London. I would love to hear
'Appalachia' and see you conducting![1]

Kindest regards to you and your dear wife.

In old friendship

Yours very sincerely
Nina Grieg.

Autograph letter, signed and dated.

1   Delius had been invited to conduct *Appalachia* at Hanley, in Stafford-
shire. The Hallé Orchestra gave the work under his baton there on 2
April 1908. It has to be admitted that, unlike Grieg, Delius was a poor
conductor of his own works. Perhaps fortunately for the reputation of
his music, he took this particular responsibility upon himself only a
handful of times.

It was not with his wife, but with Thomas Beecham that Delius undertook his summer tour of 1908. Delius arrived in Norway first and Beecham joined him towards the end of July. 'In Xnia', he wrote to Jelka, 'I saw no one, it was blazing hot & we were both delighted to get out of it.' They made their way together to the Jotunheim region. 'We had a lovely time up in Norway & splendid weather,' Delius told his friend Balfour Gardiner on 11 September. 'Beecham made an excellent travelling companion & we went over some of the roughest & finest mountainous country in the world.' He himself left for home on 4 September, Beecham having had to leave a week or so earlier. Their travels had not taken them to Bergen.

As with Delius, Beecham's introduction to Grieg's music had come when he was a child, and it had clearly proved an equally revelatory experience. In his sixth year he was taken to his first concert: 'It was a piano recital, and a series of new pieces by Grieg gave the programme a distinction we find none too frequently in events of this kind nowadays. Long after I had been put to bed that evening I lay awake thinking hard about my novel experience, and the music revolved distractingly in my head over and over again.' He finally climbed out of bed, went downstairs and asked his parents: 'Please may I learn the piano?' — a plea that set him squarely on the path towards his musical career. [*A Mingled Chime*, 1944, p.11]

90.   NINA GRIEG TO FREDERICK DELIUS

Kristiania 22–5–09.

Dear Delius,

You made me very happy by sending your picture, and I thank you with all my heart. I does me so much good when Grieg's friends remember me, now that I have reached the stage of living largely with my memories. At first I could not recognize you in the picture until I discovered that your moustache was gone, which makes you look very different. You recall the summer morning on the Haukelidfjeld, so do I![1] The gentians, the blue flower, how clearly I see everything before me. Those were happy days. But on the way home Edvard fell ill, as he so often did, and we had to stay in Odda. But we were thankful to be able to roam about for 5 bright summer days. That time, long gone, still has an aura of glory.—

Should love to know how you and your wife are. Are you really doing so much nowadays? Should love to know! — I am well, have been very busy here this winter teaching young ladies to sing songs which, with gifted pupils, interests me a lot. I think I am keeping a tradition alive there with Edvard's songs.

I am afraid Troldhaugen will stay shut this summer. I am going to the Beyers' until 15 June, then to Denmark (Skagen) until the end of July, to friends in the country in Denmark until the beginning of Sept. I have no plans beyond then, — what indeed can one plan! — forgive me for having chattered so much, dear Delius, otherwise I suppose I would be no ordinary woman. If you should ever have the time and inclination to write me a word and tell me something about yourself and your wife, taking in both art and everyday life, I would be so happy.

With my heartfelt good wishes.

In old, true friendship

Yours sincerely
Nina Grieg.

I can send you greetings from the Halvorsens. He has just done Puc[c]ini's 'Butterfly' in a performance which was, by our standards, excellent.—

You did not come to Troldhaugen last summer, — I expected you so often. —

Autograph letter, signed and dated. Envelope addressed: Monsieur Frederick Delius/Grez sur Loing/Seine & Marne/France. Postmark: KRISTIANIA 22 5 09. Receiving postmark: GREZ 26[?]-5 09.

1   The framed photograph, which can still be seen at Troldhaugen, bears the inscription (in Norwegian): 'Remembering a summer morning on Haukelidfjeld.'

91. NINA GRIEG TO FREDERICK DELIUS

Skagen 8–7–09.

Dear Delius,

Many thanks for your kind letter, very nice of you to think of
me and to write! Indeed, how glad I should be to hear
something of yours, although perhaps something from earlier
times, for 'Zarathustra' will probably lie beyond my musical
and literary (aesthetic) horizon.[1] Since we met you have
clearly 'busied yourself' enormously, and I feel the larger
works are now of more interest to me than songs. I myself do
not sing any more, but willingly try to teach others a little
music, rhythm and recitation. Not method and training and
placing of the voice and whatever all that is called. I have
never known much about that — unfortunately — I suppose I
ought to say. How nice it would be to meet you and your dear
wife somewhere in Denmark. In August I shall be at Fuglsang
on Lolland at the home of the landowner Neergård,[2] where
the Frants Beyers and the Röntgens are going too. — I can
well believe that it was a beautiful performance in London,
the choirs there are wonderful of course. Did you yourself
conduct? Many good wishes to you and your dear wife.

Ever yours
Nina Grieg.

Here at Skagen it is very wild and beautiful!

Autograph letter, signed and dated.

1   The first full performance of *A Mass of Life* had been given at
Queen's Hall by Beecham on 7 June.
2   Viggo de Neergaard (1837–1915) married in 1885 Bodil Hartmann
(1864–1959), daughter of the composer Emil Hartmann and grand-
daughter of J.P.E. Hartmann, the composer whose works are said to
have influenced Grieg's earlier style. Musicians were always welcome at
their beautiful home, *Fuglsang*, where there was a splendid music room.
Viggo de Neergaard had been a friend of Grieg's since youth. Grieg and
Carl Nielsen always enjoyed their visits to the estate, and Nina
continued to visit Bodil after both their husbands had died. Bodil was
eventually to turn over both of her inherited estates to social and
philanthropic purposes.

45　Bjørnstjerne Bjørnson, Nina Grieg, Karoline Bjørnson and Edvard Grieg

46　The river Loing at Grez. Picture postcard from Frederick and
Jelka Delius to Edvard Grieg, 28 December 1903

48   Dr Grieg at Oxford, 29 May 1906

PROGRAMME

SONATA in A minor, Op. 36, for Violoncello and Pianoforte   *Grieg*
    (*a*) Allegro agitato.
    (*b*) Andante molto tranquillo.
    (*c*) Allegro marcato.
      Professor HUGO BECKER and THE COMPOSER.

SONGS, accompanied by the Composer
    (*a*) Det Syng (Garborg) ⎤
    (*b*) Möte (Garborg)   ⎟   *Grieg*
    (*c*) Ragna (Drachmann)   ⎟
    (*d*) Ragnhild (Drachmann) ⎦
      Sung in Norwegian and Danish
      Mlle. EMMA HOLMSTRAND.

PIANOFORTE SOLOS—
    (*a*) Gangar (from "Slåtter," Op. 72) ⎤
    (*b*) Popular Air   } from "Impressions," ⎟
    (*c*) The Mountaineer's Song } Op. 73   ⎬   *Grieg*
    (*d*) Wedding-day at Troldhaugen * (from Op. 65) ⎦
      * The Composer's Villa near Bergen
      THE COMPOSER.

SONGS, accompanied by the Composer
    (*a*) Det förste Möde (Björnson) ⎤
    (*b*) Et Håb (Paulsen)   ⎟   *Grieg*
    (*c*) Med en Primulavéris (Paulsen) ⎟
    (*d*) Tak för dit Råd (Björnson) ⎦
      Sung in Norwegian
      Mlle. EMMA HOLMSTRAND.

SONATA in C minor, Op. 45, for Violin and Pianoforte   *Grieg*
    (*a*) Allegro appassionato.
    (*b*) Alla romanza.
    (*c*) Allegro animato.
      M. JOHANNES WOLFF and THE COMPOSER.

47   Programme of Grieg's last concert in England, at Queen's Hall, 24 May 1906

49   View over the Nordaasvand from Troldhaugen.
Picture postcard from Grieg to Delius, 30 June 1906

50   Adolf Brodsky and his family visiting the Griegs at Troldhaugen in 1906.
Nina stands in the doorway with two maids, and her sister Tony sits at bottom left

51 Edvard Grieg, Percy Grainger, Nina Grieg and Julius Röntgen,
Troldhaugen, 25 July 1907

52 Postcard from Nina Grieg to Delius, 4 January 1920

53   Percy Grainger and Nina Grieg

54   Handbill for Grieg recital at Brighton, 9 October 1912, with Nina Grieg as accompanist

55 The Øverli farm at Lesjaskog, Gudbrandsdalen, in the 1920s. Delius's cottage to the right

56 Gudbrandsdalen, seen from the Øverli farm at Lesjaskog

57   Delius and Jelka on the veranda of 'Høifagerli',
their cottage at Lesjaskog

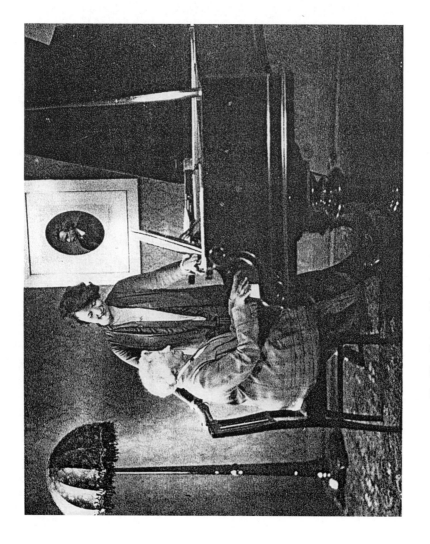

58 Nina Grieg and her niece Annie Halvorsen in 1929

92. NINA GRIEG TO FREDERICK DELIUS

Kristiania 27–4–11.

Dear Delius,

I was so delighted to get another sign of life from you. I am here on my way to Troldhaugen, where I shall stay the whole summer and where you and your wife will be heartily welcome. So I hope and look forward to the pleasure of seeing you again.

Your old friend
Nina Grieg.

Your home looks lovely.

Autograph postcard, signed and dated. Addressed: Monsieur Frederik Delius/Grez sur Loing/France. Postmark: KRISTIANIA 27.4.11. Receiving postmark: GREZ 1 -5 11.

93. FREDERICK DELIUS TO NINA GRIEG

Grez sur Loing
(S & M)
12 May 1911

Dear Frau Grieg—

Many thanks for your card — I would so much love to come to Troldhaugen again & if you would have us for a few days at the end of July we would be absolutely delighted — if July doesn't suit then perhaps August —

We have had splendid weather here for 6 weeks — You really must come one day & see how beautiful it is at our home—

With kindest regards from us both I am ever your old friend

Fr. Delius

Autograph letter, signed and dated.

94.   NINA GRIEG TO FREDERICK DELIUS

Troldhaugen 18–5–11.

Dear Delius,

Of course you and your wife are very welcome here. But August (beginning of Aug.) suits me better than July, as I still have guests here then. A young Finnish lady singer[1] may still be here when you come, but if you and your dear wife are prepared to put up with the modest conditions in my house and with *one* room, I shall be delighted to see you both and extend you a hearty welcome.

Your *very* old friend
Nina Grieg

I rely on your letting me have details from you before you come.

Autograph letter, signed and dated.

1   See Letter 99.

95.   FREDERICK DELIUS TO NINA GRIEG

[Grez, ?28 May 1911]

We shall come then at the beginning of August from the 7th–12th & look forward to it enormously — On the 16th June there is a whole concert of my works in London[1] & we are going there. The weather has been heavenly for 2 months

Kindest regards

Yours
Fr. Delius

I shall of course write again & let you know when we shall arrive.

Autograph picture postcard: *GREZ-SUR-LOING — Le Pont et les Ruines du Château*, signed and undated. Addressed: Frau Nina Grieg/Troldhaugen/Hop Station/près Bergen/Norvège. Postmark: GREZ 28 [May 1911].

1   Thomas Beecham conducted the Beecham Symphony Orchestra at Queen's Hall. The programme consisted of *Appalachia, Songs of Sunset*

(first performance), *Paris* and *A Dance Rhapsody* no.1. Delius was called to the platform.

96. FREDERICK DELIUS TO NINA GRIEG

Lauvaasen Höifjeld Sanatorium
26 July 1911

Dear Frau Grieg—

We have been up here for a week & find it wonderful — The weather is splendid — My wife is painting Rondane in every possible light — We intend to spend a few more weeks here & pay our visit to you later in August — Perhaps the end of August if it suits you then —

I go for long walks paa Vidderne & find it wonderful — How are you?

Kind regards from us both—

Yours
Frederick Delius

My regards to Frantz Beyer—

Autograph letter, signed and dated.

The date of Delius's departure for Norway is established by a postcard which he sent to Béla Bartók later in July. Delius apologized for having missed Bartók, who had arrived in Paris earlier in the month and who anxiously hoped to be permitted to visit Grez and Delius, whose work and whose personality he had come so much to admire. 'I left on the 14th July with my wife for Norway & am now in the high mountains where it is quite splendid — I hope we shall see each other somewhere this winter — I had waited for you in Grez until the 14th July.' The Lauvaasen health resort, where the Deliuses were now staying, was situated towards the southern end of the Gudbrandsdal region.

97. NINA GRIEG TO FREDERICK DELIUS

Troldhaugen 31–7–11.
Hop.
(*not* Bergen)

Dear Delius,

Please, please, don't come so late, for I won't know how to manage then. Can you not come here at the latest about the middle of August and then after that rather go back to Lauvåsen? You will remember that you advised me that the 7th Aug. would be the day you would arrive, didn't you? Do please make it mid-Aug. at the latest. Please do not be angry, I cannot arrange things in any other way.

You and your dear wife are heartily welcome and please be prepared for simple conditions.

With all good wishes

Yours
Nina Grieg.

Autograph letter, signed and dated. Envelope addressed: Hr. Fredrick Delius/Lauvåsen Höifjelds-Sanatorium/pr./Hundtorp Station/Gudbrandsdalen. Postmark: HOP 31 VII 11.

98. FREDERICK DELIUS TO NINA GRIEG

Golaa Høifjelds-Sanatorium.[1]
[. . .]
Harpefos Station, Gudbrandsdalen.   [early August 1911]

Dear Frau Grieg —

We are frightfully sorry not to be able to come now; the matter stands thus — My friend Thomas Beecham — the London conductor — wants very shortly to visit me here & to discuss with me the performance in the autumn in London of the 'Mass of Life' (a work which takes up a whole evening) I must await him here & we were proposing after that to make a little tour to the Jotunheim — It is of course of the greatest importance! & I am terribly sorry that things have turned out so unfortunately — I shall however be coming through

Copenhagen & through Kristiania this winter & hope I shall at least see you there   As long as I know where you are —

My wife regrets from the bottom of her heart as she had looked forward so much to the visit to you —
Warmest regards —

Yours
Frederick Delius

Autograph letter, signed and undated, written on headed notepaper.

1 The Deliuses would seem to have moved, Golaa being a few kilometres to the north-west of Lauvaasen.

99. NINA GRIEG TO FREDERICK DELIUS

Troldhaugen 7–8–11.

Dear Delius,

I am far more sorry, you can be quite sure and I would almost have a mind to wish Mr. Beecham and your 'Mass of Life' right off over the hills, but — joking aside, I would much rather hear it. Just think, I have had guests with me almost the whole summer, but now I have only a young Finnish lady, a singer, and I could therefore quite easily put you and your wife up unpretentiously, later, end of Aug. my sisters-in-law are coming and then Troldhaugen is unfortunately full up. Should your Jotunheim tour bring you, your wife and your friend to Bergen, I implore you not to pass by my door. Percy Grainger has written of Mr. Beecham that he is a conductor of genius.[1] I have acquainted my young Finnish friend, Frau Saima Neovi, with your songs, and we sing them together, both the earlier ones of Fritz Delius as well as a later one (there are possibly others that I do not know) 'il pleure dans la ville',[2] which is more like Frederick Delius. — I do not understand, if you are coming *through* Copenhagen and *through* Kristiania, where you then intend to go — in the winter?![3] In absolutely no circumstances am I in Norway at this time — unfortunately. Fate is unkind to me. I just cried out without thinking: Auf Wiedersehen!
Please give many good wishes to your wife from me —

I should so much have loved to meet her — and please think kindly of me.

Ever yours
Nina Grieg.

Autograph letter, signed and dated. Envelope addressed: Hr. Frederick Delius/Golå Höifjelds-Sanatorium/Harpefos Station/Gudbrandsdalen. Postmark: HOP 7 VIII 11.

1 It happened, of course, that Grainger was right, but Nina was already familiar with his penchant for hyperbole. After he had written to her of Beecham, among others, earlier in July, she had replied (in English) on the 27th: 'I do not know the Conductors you mention, they must be English. Now I know you are very soon to say "the greatest living", you say so today, perhaps not tomorrow. It is likely the same when you mention Delius as "by far the greatest living genius at the moment".'
2 'Il pleure dans mon coeur' (RT V/16), the first of the two settings published in 1896 of poems by Paul Verlaine.
3 In the event, Delius visited neither Copenhagen nor Christiania the following winter.

Any plans that Beecham may have had to come to Norway were shelved, with Delius receiving a telegram from him on 4 August asking him and Jelka to come to England as early in the month as possible. There is no evidence that they did so, and it seems that they returned to Grez some time in September, possibly having stopped with friends in Denmark on their way back. Beecham was apologetic: 'I was so disappointed at not being able to come to Norway,' he wrote on 19 September, 'but I have had the most harassing business affairs to attend to all the Summer.'

At the turn of the year, Delius wrote to ask Grainger where Nina was living at the moment. In the event, the postal address was a familiar one: c/o Wilhelm Hansen, Copenhagen, and Grainger told Delius: 'We saw a lot of her & her sister (Tony Hagerup) in the fall when we were in Norway & had jolly times.' Nina and Tony — a constant companion — together with the Beyers attended Grainger's concert of 16 September in Bergen. An interesting echo of Nina's interest in and advice on Delius's romantic affairs came when she talked long and deeply with Grainger, on the day of the concert, on the subject of his relationship with Karen Holten.

100. FREDERICK DELIUS TO NINA GRIEG

[Grez, 31 May 1912]

Dear Frau Grieg—

You gave me very great pleasure with your Spring greeting & the beautiful picture. I often think of Grieg & of all the lovely times we spent together — I loved [him] very much. I hope we shall meet in London — My 'Mass of Life' will be performed there in December[1] — You really must hear something of mine at last—

Kindest regards & in old friendship

Yours
Frederick Delius

My wife sends her kind regards—
Where will [you] be staying in London?

Autograph letter card, signed and undated. Addressed: Frau Nina Grieg/Troldhaugen/Hop Station/pr Bergen/Norvège. Postmark: GREZ 31 5 12. The postage stamp has been cut away, with the result that two words of Delius's text are lost.

1   Beecham's next performance of the *Mass* did not, in the event, take place until 10 March 1913.

June 1912 saw Delius planning yet another tour in Norway. He wrote on the 23rd to a new friend, Philip Heseltine: 'At the end of next month I intend going to Norway for a 3 weeks walking tour in the mountains — Doesn't it tempt you? I love Norway & the Norwegian peasants.' Little more than a month later, however, he was to report to Heseltine: 'I had such a lot of work to do — correcting proofs etc — that I decided not to go to Norway this summer.' Someone who did, and at Delius's own suggestion, was Béla Bartók, who made a four weeks' tour through the country and bought himself a Hardanger fiddle to take home. [*cf.* Hella Brock: *Edvard Grieg*. Leipzig: Reclam Verlag, 1990, pp.308–9]

101. NINA GRIEG TO FREDERICK DELIUS

Troldhaugen 5–9–12.

Dear Delius,

Just a few words to say that I am going to England on the 1st Oct., first I accompany the songs in some Grieg concerts, end Oct. go to the Brodskys in Bowdon, 30th concert in London, where I stay until 8th Nov. or a little longer. Please do not think that I am giving the concerts, I have nothing at all to do with that. The concerts are being given by two Danish artists, Court Pianist Frl. Johanne Stockmarr[1] and Court Singer Frl. Ellen Beck,[2] I have only allowed myself to be persuaded to accompany them.—[3]

I hope with all my heart that I may be able to meet you and your dear wife and get to hear something of yours.

In any case I will say: auf Wiedersehen and remain ever in old friendship

Yours very sincerely
Nina Grieg.

Address in London: Nottingham Place 12, Mrs. Haywood.

Autograph letter, signed and dated.

1 Johanne Stockmarr (1869–1944): Danish pianist and teacher, well-known as an interpreter of Grieg's Concerto. She played frequently in England.

2 Ellen Beck (1873–1953): Danish soprano and vocal teacher. Like Stockmarr, she studied both in Denmark and in Paris. She sang extensively in the Scandinavian countries, as well as in England and France.

3 Among Nina's appearances in the earlier part of the tour was one as accompanist at The Dome in Brighton on 9 October. The London recital on 30 October was at the Aeolian Hall. Ellen Beck and Saima Neovi gave a song recital at Steinway Hall in London on 9 November, when Nina accompanied four songs of Grieg.

102. NINA GRIEG TO FREDERICK DELIUS

30–10 *1912*.

NINA GRIEG

Dear Delius,

Many thanks! It would have been such a joy to visit you and your dear wife, but unfortunately it will not be possible. 9th Nov. I shall still be busy here, and I have promised to be at the Röntgens in Amsterdam on the 10th in the evening.[1] It was very kind of you to want to have us.

I shall defend my 'Christianity' as well and as long as I can.[2] I cannot live without support, now even less than before.

I was very pleased to hear something by you again. I liked 'Dance Rhapsody' enormously, enormously! I must certainly hear the Concerto more than once.[3]

We brought off the 'Grieg Concert' satisfactorily this afternoon 'a fine Hall'[4] and a wonderful atmosphere. I received masses of flowers.

Kind regards to you both.

Auf Wiedersehen!

Ever yours—
Nina Grieg.

Autograph letter, signed and dated, written on headed notepaper.

1 Percy Grainger was to be on a concert tour in Holland at the time. He met Nina again at least twice.
2 Delius, a lifelong atheist, was always ready to poke fun at the religious beliefs of his friends.
3 Nina had at last got to know some more Delius. She had heard Beecham and the Beecham Symphony Orchestra give the *Dance Rhapsody* no.1 at a National Sunday League concert on 6 October at the London Palladium; the programme had concluded with Grieg's '*March, Sigurd Jorsalfar*'. She had then heard Szántó play Delius's Piano Concerto on 10 October. Delius was present, so they will certainly have met. Her reaction to his Concerto — at least in this letter — is interestingly muted.
4 '*a fine Hall*'. In English in the original letter.

103. NINA GRIEG TO FREDERICK DELIUS

Troldhaugen 27–7–13.

Dear Delius,

If only you had written a few days earlier! But I hope it will work out anyway, I will do my very best and so will await you and your wife on 1st August.
     You are heartily welcome.

Ever yours sincerely
Nina Grieg.

Have only *one* room for you and your wife.

Autograph letter, signed and dated. Envelope addressed: Herrn Fredrick Delius/Finse. Postmark: HOP 28 VII 13.

Delius was on another lengthy walking tour in Norway. He had arrived in Christiania on 8 July 1913, having arranged a meeting on the 9th with Edvard Munch. He then set out for the mountains. On 26 July he sent to his new publisher, Gerhard Tischer, a picture postcard of *Hardangerjökulen*: 'I sit in eternal snows feel marvellously well [. . .] The name I Ola Dalom etc need not appear only Introducing a Norwegian Folksong.' This was a reference to the printing of his recently-completed *On hearing the first cuckoo in Spring* (RT VI/19/i), soon to be premièred at the Leipzig Gewandhaus by Nikisch. It is curious that Delius, having included the melody 'I Ola Dalom' in his piece, then seemed to distance himself almost deliberately from Grieg, who had made his own setting of the folksong some seventeen years earlier. It is just possible that he was troubled at what might have seemed to be an infringement of copyright. At all events, it represents in his music yet another acknowledgement of his love for Norway and his debt to Grieg. In writing of the piece to Grainger a few months later, Delius added: 'Spring always means for me a longing for Norway.'
     After a while he was joined by Jelka, who had written to him from Grez on 24 July: 'I am at Bergen Friday 1. Aug. at noon [. . .] If possible I shd go on to Finsse the same day, unless you come to Bergen and we go and see Mrs Grieg.' In fact, no record has been found of the Deliuses' further travels in Norway during the month of August, although they were evidently planning to go as far north as

Lofoten. Philip Heseltine was to note that on 14 September he saw Delius in Grez: 'he has just returned, in great form, from a two months' sojourn in the Norwegian mountains, and is working hard at his magnificent Requiem.' Interestingly, the Requiem contains, in its fourth section particularly, some of Delius' most magical passages of 'mountain' music — a recurrent theme in his work.

104. NINA GRIEG TO FREDERICK AND JELKA DELIUS

Holmenkollen Sanatorium
Kristiania.
[? end of December 1914]

Dear friends!

How are you? Where are you? Give a sign of life, please! We are always thinking of you, talking of you, wanting to know how you are going on. I try to send this card, perhaps you will never get it, but I will try. We are staying in Norway this winter, will not leave our old dear country, not knowing what is to come. We send you both our heartiest wishes for a happy new year, hoping to see you again on Troldhaugen or anywhere. Keep well and do write a word.

In old friendship

Nina Grieg.

Autograph letter, signed and undated, written in English.

The Deliuses had been in England since mid-November, and were to stay there until early in July 1915. Following the outbreak of war, Grainger had urged them to leave France, and Beecham's proposal that they take his house at Watford, just outside London, had settled the matter. Nina, too, obviously felt safer staying in Norway for the winter and — perhaps for the first time — had sent her New Year's greeting to Delius in English.

105.   NINA GRIEG TO FREDERICK AND JELKA DELIUS

Holmenkollen Sanatorium
nr. Christiania 27–1 *1915*

Dearest friends,

As you write to me in such good Norwegian, dear Fru Delius, I think it best to spare you my bad English, and use my own honest language — I cannot say mother tongue, as my mother was Danish. Good heavens; what haven't you been through! To me it would seem impossible ever to get over such experiences, as if one could never be one's own self again.[1] Indeed, I had never thought I would live to see such horrors, advanced in years as I now am, and it is as if I cannot grasp that Edvard has passed on from it all. It would have been so much easier to endure if he had still been here. You can of course say that I am staying up here in a haven of peace and cannot imagine what war is really like *there* where it is being fought. That may be true, one of humanity's imperfections is that people always must *experience* everything before they really can get it into their heads, but we have the feeling of *here*, too, standing on the brink of an abyss, and if we are to plunge into it, then we want to share in our dear old country's fortunes, good or bad, and that is why we are staying here at home this winter and waiting for what may come. I am still at the stage where I believe that life is *not* without meaning, and that is why I constantly wait for a higher power to come along with its veto. Well, well, dear Delius, I know very well that you smile sympathetically and shrug your shoulders, but people are after all so very different both inwardly and outwardly. I am glad to know that you are in England, and it was really kind of you, dear Fru Delius, to write and tell me about everything you have been through. I wonder if all your lovely things now will remain buried at Grez until the war one day comes to an end. I have heard that life goes on as usual in London, so I can well believe that a lot of English music gets played. The fact that you want to hold an exhibition also shows that the war has not killed people's interest in the arts. Here foreign artists are now beginning to get used to giving concerts again; luckily people are easygoing, and soon fall into the old ways. The Halvorsens are well, he is busy with the theatre and enjoys his work.[2] It seems to be his intention to stage two operas by Schjelderup[3] in the spring, if all goes well. Here at Holmenkollen we really are in the middle of winter, everything is white, forests and fields and all the roads, the weather is fine and the air fresh and pure.

But it doesn't feel like home here, far too many people. I have a little room in another house, all to myself, with a piano thank God.

I suppose we shall stay here till the spring, till we go back to Troldh.

Nice that Beecham plays Grieg.[4]

Fare well, both of you, and do please send me a line now and then.

Tonny sends many good wishes.

Autograph letter, unsigned and dated, written in Norwegian on headed notepaper.

1   Jelka had evidently described to Nina the problems that she and Delius had experienced in September when the Germans had advanced on the Marne. They had joined the general flight from the area in some confusion, but had been able to return to Grez only days later once they had heard — as Delius described it — of 'the great Victory of the allies.'

2   Halvorsen was still musical director at the National Theatre.

3   Gerhard Rosenkrone Schjelderup (1859–1933): Norwegian composer and writer, at one time described as the most eminent music-dramatist produced by Norway. Schjelderup was also Grieg's first Norwegian biographer. At the Paris Conservatoire, Massenet had been one of his teachers. Of his operas, three were performed at the National Theatre: *Vaarnat (Spring Night)*, *En hellig Aften (The Holy Eve)* and *Stormfugl (Stormy Petrel)*. No evidence that he and Delius met has been found, despite the fact that they were contemporaries.

4   Most recently Beecham had conducted Grieg's Piano Concerto at Liverpool on 17 November, with de Greef as soloist. The concert had concluded with the *Homage March* from *Sigurd Jorsalfar*. On the whole, however, Beecham programmed Grieg fairly infrequently, particularly when compared to the enormous amount of concert space he allotted to his twin idols, Mozart and Delius.

In the late spring of 1915, Delius was unwell, and his doctor in London, according to Jelka, 'absolutely advised us to go to Norway [. . .] Norway is Fred's land, and it will make him feel well and it is a country "not at war", which the doctor thinks will be so much better' [Letter to Philip Heseltine, 29 June 1915]. Consequently they sailed, on 6 July, from Newcastle to Bergen. A week later, having established themselves at Sandene on the Nordfjord, Jelka wrote (in English) to

Delius's sister: 'it is specially lovely here this year as there are no foreign tourists, no germans that latterly overran everything here [. . .] one can get *no* English papers and the norwegian ones have very little news. Everybody is pro-British tho'.'

After spending some two months at Sandene, the Deliuses moved to higher ground, at Geilo, Hallingdal, in search of better weather. They enjoyed their time there, which ended with three glittering days of sunshine and snow. 'It was glorious,' Delius told Heseltine. 'Norway is truly a lovely country.' They left for Christiania around the beginning of October, and on the 9th of that month arrived at Juelsminde, in Denmark, where they stayed on the estate of their friends Einar and Elisabeth Schou until the end of October.

Grainger's mother, Rose, had written from New York on 20 August, charging Delius to give her love 'to dear Fru Grieg, the Hals family, & the Halvorsens', but no evidence of any meetings has come to light. The four months in Norway and Denmark were a temporary, but nonetheless complete escape for the Deliuses, and the main aim had been served well, with Delius restored to good health. After a short final stay in London to tie up loose ends, the Deliuses returned to Grez on 20 November, determined to remain at home for however long the war might last.

106. NINA GRIEG TO JELKA DELIUS

Hotel Monopol [Copenhagen]
8–2–16.

Dear Fru Delius,

Thank you for your card. So you ended up in Grez again after all and didn't stay in Norway. Yes, poor Bergen! No, Tyske-bryggen was not burned down, nor the last part of Strand-gaden from Mureporten. But many old houses and properties have gone though.[1] The Bergen people are active and like to help themselves. They turned down France's magnanimous offer. I had Troldhaugen opened up for the victims of the fire, and it's now occupied by Rabe, the music-dealer. If they have to stay there during the summer, I will find somewhere or other to live, the world is a big place. We are in good health, Tonny and I, Carl Nielsen is in Norway. I wonder if Delius knows his new symphony[2] and what he thinks of it? Best wishes to you both. Send a sign of life now and then to your devoted

Nina Grieg.

Tonny sends her regards.[3]

Autograph postcard, signed and dated, written in Norwegian. Addressed: Madame/Jelka Delius/Grez sur Loing/France. Postmark: KJØBENHAVN 18 2.16. Receiving postmarks: PARIS 26.II 1916 and GREZ 27–2 16.

1   Many old parts of central Bergen had been destroyed in January in a disastrous fire. The historic German Quay (Tyskebryggen), with its distinctive wooden warehouses, had fortunately survived.

2   Symphony no.4 ('The Inextinguishable'), composed in 1915–16, was first performed in Copenhagen on 1 February 1916. Although Delius has left no record of any reaction on his part to Nielsen's music, Grieg had been enthusiastic: 'I heard "Maskarade",' he had written from Copenhagen on 23 March 1907 to Julius Röntgen. 'And, what is more, conducted by the composer and excellently in fact! It is very witty, clever and interesting, and I only wished for something that for me was missing: a little more — Music!' Nevertheless he admitted to Röntgen: 'One thing is certain: a young master has created the work.' Grieg had talked a little with Nielsen, but it was with Nina that the friendship had had to continue. In 1911, having just finished his third symphony, Nielsen was invited by her to spend part of the summer at Troldhaugen and actually began work on his Violin Concerto in Grieg's hut.

3   Tonny (or Tony) Hagerup, the Griegs' companion-housekeeper, continued to live with her sister Nina to the end.

107.   NINA GRIEG TO FREDERICK DELIUS

> Hotel Monopol 15–1–18.
> Copenhagen.

Dear friends!

How glad I am having had news from you. We are both well and were in Bergen this autumn to the unveiling of Griegs statue.[1] It was a good one. I intend to go to Troldhaugen this summer if I can get to eat and to burn, perhaps for the last time. We send you both our love and warmest wishes for a happy new year. How nice if we could meet anywhere. For ever yours

Nina Grieg.

This horrid time. I think the best we can do is to hear a lot of music!! I do so here, but Copenhagen is not London you know.

Hope this card will find you still in the old place.

Autograph postcard, signed and dated, written in English. Addressed: Mr. Frederick Delius./Grez sur Loing/Marne et Oise/France. Re-addressed: Seine et Marne. Readdressed: hotel Lutetia/Paris. Postmark: KJØBENHAVN 15.1.18.

1 The statue was by the sculptor Ingebrigt Vik (1867–1927). It was unveiled in Bergen's City Park on 4 September 1917, the tenth anniversary of Grieg's death.

The Deliuses returned to Norway early in August 1919. They established themselves at a saeter at Røn, in the Valdres region, and on the 18th Jelka wrote to a friend: 'At last we are here in Norway the land of Freds constant longing [. . .] we need only climb up [from Fosheim Saeter] for an hour or so and then we see the whole chain of Snowmountains.' After a month in Valdres they moved to Voksenkollen, 'a lovely place above Kristiania with a heavenly view,' as Delius wrote to Heseltine on 17 September. They left Norway on 20 September, but not, it seems, before renewing acquaintance with Edvard Munch.

108.   NINA GRIEG TO FREDERICK DELIUS

Fuglsang   Lolland
4–1–20.—

Thank you, dear Delius. Both of us send to both of you our warmest wishes for a happy new year. Well, where are we going to meet this summer? I *must* go to Norway. We would so enormously love to come and see you sometime. No doubt we shall meet somewhere or other. I'll just say: looking forward to seeing you again!

Your devoted
Nina Grieg.

Best of luck with the opera![1]

Autograph picture postcard: *Rosenborg Slot København*, signed and dated, written in Norwegian. Addressed: Mons. Frederik Delius/Grez sur

Loing/France. Postmark: FLINTINGE 5.1.20. Receiving postmark: GREZ 10–1 20.

1 Beecham was to give *A Village Romeo and Juliet* at Covent Garden in March.

The Deliuses were to make three more visits to Norway, in the summers of 1921, 1922 and 1923. In 1921 they set out from London on 17 June, staying at the Mølmen Hotel at Lesjaskog in the Gudbrands-dal for nearly two months. They arranged to have a small house built for themselves overlooking the valley and in 1922, towards the end of June, they took possession of it, staying until 7 September. However, Delius's health was beginning to fail: his eyesight was weakening and he also used two sticks, for some of the time at least, to help him to walk. The holiday nonetheless left him feeling stronger. On the way home, they met Grainger in Christiania at the start of a lengthy recital tour he was making in Norway. And it seems that they again met Munch. The last visit to Norway saw Frederick and Jelka arrive at Lesjaskog on 29 June 1923. Delius's health was now giving cause for real concern and Grainger came for some three weeks to help him complete the urgently-required incidental music to James Elroy Flecker's play *Hassan*, due to begin its London run in the early autumn. They left in mid-August, taking the familiar sea-route from Christiania to Antwerp. Everything was changing. Even Christiania itself had recently lost its sparkling name and had become, prosaically and on debatable historical grounds, Oslo. And neither Delius nor his wife would see Norway again.

On the other hand, what strong and affectionate memories remained, recorded in part by various references to Grieg and his music that we find in and around the Delius literature of the 1920s and early 1930s and reminding us — if we needed reminding — of the influence the Norwegian composer had once had on his younger English disciple and admirer. While he was still able to, Delius would take pleasure in attending performances of Grieg's music. In Frank-furt in January 1921, he and Jelka heard Eugen d'Albert play the *Ballade*. 'We go quite often to the theatre here', he wrote to an English composer friend, C.W. Orr, on 7 February, 'both opera & Drama — We heard Peer Gynt the other night with Griegs music.' When growing infirmity precluded concert-going, the new and — for Delius — priceless gift of public radio arrived. 'We had a lot of pleasure,' Jelka wrote to tell Grainger in May 1926, after a new set had been installed, 'frequent performances of Grieg — Songs, Piano and orch. Suites.'

With Grainger there was of course common cause. In Frankfurt once again in March 1923, Delius wrote to Grainger, who was also staying in the city: 'Do come again soon and play me a lot more Grieg, some of which I do not even know.' He also wanted Grainger to play him some more Bach, and Grainger later wrote: 'As far as I can remember he never varied in his admiration for Bach, Chopin, Wagner and Grieg' [*A Delius Companion*, p.127]. Both were united in their praise for Grieg's American biographer Henry T. Finck, Delius telling Grainger in 1924: 'a man who can enthuse over a genius like Grieg is much more than a musical critic: He is a music-*Lover*.'

Wilfred Orr seems to have been more fortunate than most others in getting Delius, in later life at least, to discuss — as well as to write to him about — music generally. He, too, reminded us of Delius's pantheon: 'I think the only composers I ever heard him speak of with any enthusiasm were Chopin, Wagner and Grieg, more particularly the last-named' ['Delius versus the rest', *Making Music*, 28, Summer 1955, p.6]. Grieg's music, Delius told Orr, 'at its best is so fresh, poetic and original — in fact, just like Norway' [*A Delius Companion*, p.59]. Rather more provocatively, Orr learned from Delius that 'Grieg had more music in his little finger than Stravinsky has in his whole body' [*A Delius Companion*, p.61] — perhaps an understandable reaction if one calls to mind that what is the controversial music of one generation is likely to be the accepted idiom of the next. Delius — of that generation that had come to musical maturity before the arrival of Stravinsky — had admired *The Firebird*, seen on its first production in Paris, and had struck up a cordial relationship with its composer. But the *Sacre* had lost him to Stravinsky's music for ever, alienated as he was by the barbarism expressed in dissonance and jagged rhythms scarcely hinted at in *Firebird*. Bartók's music had been forsaken for much the same reason — more sadly for Delius in that the younger Bartók had been among the most ardent admirers of the man and his music.

Then there was the Danish composer and conductor Paul von Klenau (1883–1946), who became a champion of Delius in the 1920s, conducting for example two performances of *A Mass of Life* in the same year. He told of how, at a time when it was the custom to speak disparagingly of Grieg, Delius had not the least hesitation in express-ing his admiration for the genius of his friend. 'As a harmonist,' Delius would affirm, 'Grieg is particularly excellent', citing to Klenau passages from some of the songs [*A Delius Companion*, p.34]. Grieg's songs, in fact, he loved dearly, having of course a key to them that few non-Scandinavians possessed: a thorough understanding of Norwegian as a language, along with a wide appreciation of the cultural background from which the songs sprang. In younger days, he would accompany his sister Clare, a talented amateur singer, in Grieg's 'I love but thee', which she would sing in German. 'Of this latter song, which of course I had sung hundreds of times, he gave me an entirely new conception, insisting on my singing it "exactly as Grieg meant it to be sung and as Madame Grieg sang it herself".' [Clare Delius: *Frederick Delius: Memories of my Brother*, p.202]. Much later, in 1932 when the English singer Cecily Arnold visited Delius at home in Grez in order to sing a whole range of his own songs to him, she particularly noticed how 'he was quite uninterested in the songs of any other composer save Grieg, whom he admired very much.' [*A Delius Companion*, p.110]

Delius died at Grez-sur-Loing on 10 June 1934. He had spent virtually the last decade of his life blind and paralyzed, but when a young English musician in 1928 offered to help him write down his music, there was an Indian summer of composition that lasted until 1932. Eric Fenby took down Delius's music by a long and arduous method of dictation, and a number of works that would otherwise never have seen the light of day were completed. Although he remembers little mention of the Griegs while he himself was at Grez, he nonetheless has recalled how Delius would always want to know if 'some rare or seldom-heard piece of Grieg' was scheduled to be broadcast and how Delius would then 'listen-in' to it. [*Delius as I knew him*, p.53]

At the time of her husband's death, Jelka had only just been allowed home from hospital at Fontainebleau after an operation for cancer. Delius's body was temporarily buried at Grez, but he had let it be known that he would prefer his final resting place to be a graveyard somewhere in the south of England. It was therefore decided that, nearly a year later, his remains should be reinterred at Limpsfield, just south of London in the county of Surrey. Eric Fenby made most of the arrangements and travelled with the coffin to England. Jelka, mortally ill, had left Grez earlier. Too ill, finally, to be present at her husband's reburial, she died just two days later, on 28 May 1935, to be interred at his side. Nina, having survived her own husband by over 28 years, also died in 1935 — on 9 December, little more than two weeks after her ninetieth birthday. Arve Arvesen was one of the group of musicians who bore her ashes to their final resting-place. Did her final letter, in which she explained why she could not attend the reinterment of her husband's best-loved English friend, arrive in time? Even had it done so, Jelka, on her deathbed, would have been unable to read it.

109. JELKA DELIUS TO NINA GRIEG

[May 1935]

FREDERICK DELIUS

1862–1934

In accordance with her husband's desire that he should be finally interred in this country, Mrs Delius has arranged for the removal of his remains from Grez-sur-Loing.

The English funeral service will take place in Limpsfield Parish Church, Surrey, at 4 p.m. on Sunday, May 26th.

Printed card, edged in black [unsigned and undated], written in English. The original is in the Delius Trust Archive.

110. NINA GRIEG TO JELKA DELIUS

Hotel 'Kongen af Danmark'
Copenhagen.

Dear Fru Delius,   [May 1935]

As there is no address on the very kind invitation sent to me in connection with the removal of your dear husband's body from France to England, could I ask you to be kind enough to convey to the appropriate person my thanks and my sadness at being unable to participate in this touching ceremony owing to age and sickness.

With many heartfelt good wishes

Yours affectionately
Nina Grieg.

Autograph letter, signed and undated, written in Norwegian.

SHORT BIBLIOGRAPHY

Principal works consulted and suggestions for further reading.

More extensive bibliographical listings for each composer respectively will be found in *Edvard Grieg: The Man and the Artist* (Benestad and Schjelderup-Ebbe) and *Delius: A Life in Letters* (Carley).

Bailie, Eleanor. *Grieg: The Pianist's Repertoire: A graded practical guide.* London: Valhalla Publications, 1993.

Beecham, Thomas. *Frederick Delius.* London: Hutchinson, 1959.

Benestad, Finn, and Schjelderup-Ebbe, Dag. *Edvard Grieg: mennesket og kunstneren.* Oslo: Aschehoug, 1980.

——. *Edvard Grieg: The Man and the Artist* (transl. William H. Halvorsen and Leland B. Sateren). Lincoln and London: University of Nebraska Press, 1988.

Bennett's Handbook for Travellers in Norway. Christiania and London, 1902.

Bergsagel, John. 'Scandinavia: Unity in Diversity'. In *The Late Romantic Era.* Ed. Jim Samson. London: Macmillan (Man & Music series), 1991.

Beyer, Marie (ed.). *Breve fra Edvard Grieg til Frants Beyer 1872–1907.* Kristiania: Steenske Forlag, 1923.

Boyle, Andrew J. 'Delius and Grieg: aspects of apprenticeship'. *Delius Society Journal,* 76, July 1982, pp.5–14.

Buckley, Roger, 'Through Norway in Delius's Footsteps'. *The Delius Society Journal,* 99, Winter 1989, and 100, Spring 1989 (29pp.)

Carley, Lionel. 'An English-American Hardangervidde-man'. In *Frederick Delius og Edvard Munch.* Ed. Eggum and Biørnstad, *qv.* Oslo: Munch-museet, 1979.

——. *Delius: A Life in Letters, I, 1862–1908.* London: Scolar Press, 1983. Cambridge, Mass.: Harvard University Press, 1984.

——. *Delius: A Life in Letters, II, 1908–1934.* London and Brookfield, Vermont: Scolar Press, 1988.

——. (with Robert Threlfall) *Delius: A Life in Pictures.* London: Oxford University Press, 1977. Paperback edition, London: Thames Publishing, 1983.

——. *Delius: The Paris Years.* London: Triad Press, 1975.

Delius, Clare: *Frederick Delius: Memories of My Brother.* London: Ivor Nicholson and Watson, 1935.

Delius Society Newsletter (later *Journal*). London, 1962—.

Delius 1862–1934: A Short Guide to his Life and Works. Brochure. London: The Delius Trust, 1992. (An updating of the Trust's 1984 brochure.)

Downs, Brian W. *Modern Norwegian Literature 1860–1918.* London: Cambridge University Press, 1966.

Eggum, Arne, and Biørnstad, Sissel, eds. *Frederick Delius og Edvard Munch.* Exhibition catalogue. Oslo: Munch-museet, 1979.

Fenby, Eric. *Delius.* London: Faber, 1971.

——. *Delius as I knew him.* London: Bell, 1936. New and revised edition, London: Faber, 1981.

Finck, Henry T. *Grieg and his Music.* London and New York: John Lane, 1909.

Foster, Beryl. *The Songs of Edvard Grieg.* London and Brookfield, Vermont: Scolar Press, 1990.

Grainger, Percy. *The Farthest North of Humanness: Letters of Percy Grainger 1901–14.* Ed. Kay Dreyfus. London and Melbourne: Macmillan, 1985.
Grinde, Nils. *A History of Norwegian Music* (transl. William H. Halvorsen and Leland B. Sateren). Lincoln and London: University of Nebraska Press, 1991.

Handbook for Travellers in Norway. London: John Murray, 1880.
Hauch, Gunnar, ed. *Breve fra Grieg: Et Udvalg.* Copenhagen: Gyldendalske Boghandel, 1922.
Heseltine, Philip (pseudonym Peter Warlock). *Frederick Delius.* London: John Lane, 1923. Reprinted with additions, annotations and comments by Hubert Foss, London: The Bodley Head, 1952.
Horton, John. *Grieg.* London: Dent, 1974; rev. 1979.
Hove, Richard. 'Frederick Delius, 1862–1962, Et hundredeårsminde'. *Nordisk Tidskrift*, 1964, pp.93–104.

Jones, Philip. 'Delius's Leipzig Connections: 1886–1888'. *The Delius Society Journal*, 102, Autumn 1989, pp.3–14.

Kayser, Audun. *Edvard Grieg — In Words and Music.* Bergen: John Grieg, 1992.
Kortsen, Bjarne. *Griegs Brev til Frants Beyer.* Stencil edition. Bergen Off. Bibliotek, 1973.

Lowe, Rachel [Rachel Lowe Dugmore]. *A Catalogue of the Music Archive of the Delius Trust.* London: The Delius Trust/Boosey & Hawkes, 1986. (A reprint, with minor corrections, of the original catalogue of 1974.)
——. 'Delius's First Performance'. *The Musical Times*, 106, no.1465, March 1965, pp.190–2.
——. 'Frederick Delius and Norway'. *Studies in Music*, 6, 1972, pp.27–41. Reprinted in *A Delius Companion*.

Mead, William R. 'A Winter's Tale: Reflections on the Delius Festival (1946)'. *The Norseman* (Oslo), 1947, pp.78–81.

Norges Kunsthistorie (Vols 1–7). Oslo: Gyldendal, 1981.
Norsk Biografisk Leksikon (Vols 1–). Oslo: Aschehoug (various dates).
Norsk Kunstner Leksikon (Vols 1–4). Oslo: Universitetsforlaget, 1982.
Norway: Official Publication for the Paris Exhibition 1900. Various contributors. Kristiania: Aktie-Bogtrykkeriet, 1900.
Norway, Sweden and Denmark [. . .] Handbook for travellers, by Karl Baedeker. Leipzig, London and New York, 1912.

Palmer, Christopher. *Delius: Portrait of a Cosmopolitan.* London: Duckworth, 1976.
Popperwell, Ronald G. *Norway.* London: Benn, 1972.

Redwood, Christopher, ed. *A Delius Companion.* London: John Calder, 1976.
Röntgen, Julius. *Grieg* (Beroemde Musici, Deel XIX). 's-Gravenhage: J. Philip Kruseman, n.d.
Rugstad, Gunnar. *Christian Sinding, 1856–1941: En biografisk og stilistik studie.* Oslo: Cappelen, 1979.

Smith, John Boulton: *Frederick Delius and Edvard Munch: Their Friendship and Their Correspondence.* Rickmansworth: Triad Press, 1983.

Threlfall, Robert: *A Catalogue of the Compositions of Frederick Delius. Sources and References.* London: The Delius Trust, 1977.
——. *Frederick Delius: A Supplementary Catalogue.* London: The Delius Trust/Boosey & Hawkes, 1986.
——. *Delius's Musical Apprenticeship.* London: The Delius Trust (to be published in 1994). This work will deal fully with all the early music Notebooks, including those used in Norway.
Torsteinson, Sigmund. *Troldhaugen: Nina og Edvard Griegs Hjem.* Oslo: Gyldendal Norsk Forlag, 1959.

Zschinsky-Troxler, Elsa v., ed. *Edvard Grieg: Briefe an die Verleger der Edition Peters, 1866–1907.* Leipzig: C.F. Peters, 1932.

Index

223